Attachment
Parenting *Tips*

Raising Toddlers to Teens

Judy Arnall

Library and Archives Canada Cataloguing in Publication

Arnall, Judy, 1960-, author
Attachment parenting tips raising toddlers to teens / Judy Arnall.

Issued in print and electronic formats.
ISBN 978-0-9780509-8-6 (softcover).--ISBN 978-0-9780509-7-9 (PDF)

1. Child rearing. 2. Parenting. 3. Parent and child. 4. Attachment
behavior in children. 5. Developmental psychology. I. Title.

HQ769.A7522017   649'.1   C2017-906744-3
                               C2017- 906745-1

Published by Professional Parenting Canada, Calgary, Alberta, Canada
www.professionalparenting.ca
First Edition 2019

Although the author and publisher have exhaustively researched all sources to
ensure accuracy and completeness of the information contained in this book,
we assume no responsibility for errors, inaccuracies, omissions, or any other
inconsistency herein. Any slights against people or organizations are unintentional.
Readers are strongly encouraged to use their own judgement in their parenting
decisions.

Edited by Leila Bassett

Printed and bound in Canada
ISBN E-Book 97809780509-79

ISBN Print 97809780509-86

Advance Praise for Attachment Parenting Tips Raising Toddlers To Teens

"Nowhere will you find a resource like Judy Arnall's comprehensive *Attachment Parenting Tips.* As an experienced parenting educator, writer, speaker and mother of five children, Judy knows first-hand the everyday challenges and questions parents face every day. There is no 'one-size-fits-all' answer because every child is unique. She has addressed the most common questions with a wonderful variety of kind, gentle and respectful options from which to choose. I know I will be referring to it to help me with my grandchildren!"

-Lysa Parker, MS, Certified Family Life Educator, Cofounder of Attachment Parenting International. Co-author of *Attached at the Heart: Eight Proven Parenting Principles for Raising Connected and Compassionate Children.*

"This reference book should be on every parent's phone or nightstand. It is a treasure chest of respectful tips and practical ideas to use for almost every common parenting challenge."

-Elizabeth Pantley, Author of *The No-Cry Sleep Solution* and *The No-Cry Solution* series

"Once again Judy delivers a book that provides compassionate advice backed by developmental science to support empathetic parenting. This book should be in every caregivers back pocket, as it gives easy to reference specific tips by age and situation. This is the parenting tool we have been waiting for!"

-Brandie Hadfield, President of Attachment Parenting Canada Association and creator of *The DREAM Method for healthy family sleep.*

"A ton of parenting ideas for parents who don't have time to read parenting books."

-Sanna Darby, Mom of three attachment-parented adults.

Table of Contents

Baby Health

Baby Parenting with Partner

Baby Play

Baby Siblings

Baby Sleep

Baby Toileting

Toddlers 1- 2 Years

What Can Toddlers Do?

Toddler Behavior

Toddler Development and Learning

Toddler Discipline

Toddler Feeding

Toddler Health

Toddler Parenting with Partner

Toddler Play

Toddler Siblings

Toddler Sleep

Toddler Toileting

Preschoolers 3- 5 Years

What Can Preschoolers Do?

Preschooler Behavior

Preschooler Development and Learning

Preschooler Discipline

School-Aged Development and Learning

School-Aged Discipline

Teenagers 13- 19 Years

What Can Teenagers Do?

Teen Behavior

Emerging Adults 19- 25 Years

What Can Emerging Adults Do?

General AP Parenting Tips for All Ages

Child Development References

About the Author

Acknowledgements

Welcome to attachment parenthood. It's the hardest job on earth, and the most rewarding too. It's also the only job where there are no set-up instructions, operating manual or professional development. However, there are many right ways to parent and a few not-so-right ways. Most parents make decisions based on instinct, and although they are armed with learned theory, they still have lots of questions on how to handle common everyday problems. Thankfully, parents freely share their tips and encouragement with each other.

I wish to extend many thanks and appreciation to the hundreds of parents contributing to this book from my parenting groups (both in person and online) over 25 years. This book is packed with their useful ideas, tips and solutions that worked for them as well as my own tips in attachment parenting 5 children (3 of which were very spirited!) Each problem includes small tidbits of the latest brain and development information from credible health organization sources on why and when children do what they do. All solutions are respectful to the parent and the child, and they not only solve the presenting problem but preserve the parent-child relationship. No forms of emotional and physical punishment are included, in keeping with the evidence-based recommendations from the Canadian Paediatric Society and the American Academy of Paediatrics.

All tips are based on a model of mutual respect between parent and child. A mutually respectful relationship is one in which the parent and child do not punish each other; and share their time, conversations, feelings, dreams, thoughts, needs, problems and joys with each other. Mutual respect is built on the parenting skills of 1)actively listening and validating feelings, 2)asserting needs with I-statements and 3) collaboratively problem-solving for a win-win solution that meets both parent and child needs at the same time. These are skills outlined in many parenting books and programs. Please consult the books, **Discipline Without Distress** or **Parenting With Patience,** which give more extensive knowledge and application of these 3 skills.

Because the suggestions were gathered from groups, some tips may seem to contradict other's offered in the same section. Since there is no one "right" way to do anything, we want to offer you a variety of respectful suggestions that might fit with your unique situation. Our hope is that this resource book will make your life a bit easier so you can enjoy all that parenting has to offer. It's true - the days are very long but the years really do fly by!

Judy Arnall, BA, CCFE-Certified Canadian Family Life Educator and Mom of five children.

Babies 0-1 Years

The stage of "Will I ever sleep eight solid hours again?"

....

What Can Babies Do?

Infants 0 to 6 Months: Sensory Input-Output Stage

Physical

- Sleeps fifteen to twenty hours in a twenty-four hour period

- Settles into a predictable pattern of eating, sleeping, fussing, and eliminating at three to six months

- Can hold head steady while sitting at four months

- Supports weight of torso with arms while on tummy at three months

- Follows objects and will turn head to look at sounds at two months

- Can transfer objects from hand to mouth at four months

- Teething at five months

- Eats every two hours

- Sits with adult support at six months

Cognitive

- Awareness of sensory input and output; feels cold, so cries

- Doesn't think; just experiences and responds to sensory input

- May become scared of certain faces or sounds

Social and Emotional

- Smiles at two months - engages in "serve and return" interactions

- Begins to develop trust and attachment to at least one adult/caregiver

- Crying peaks at two months but remains the main form of communication

Babies 6 to 12 Months: Attachment Stage

Physical

- Can roll and crawl around seven months

- Supports her own weight when held standing

- Can pull up on tables or chairs to stand at ten months

- Walks around twelve months

- Slithers down stairs backwards at one year

- Sleeps twelve to fourteen hours a night with several daytime naps

- Imitates sounds and babbles

- Eats with hands at one year; uses a spoon at eighteen months

- Can hold and drink out of an open cup

- Has most front and side teeth at one year

- Pincer grasp develops

Cognitive

- Explores environment and items with all five senses (mouth, ears, eyes, touch, and hearing)

- No understanding of danger

- No understanding of limits

- No self-control to not do something

- Points to interests

- Develops object permanence at one year; knows something exists even if it can't be seen

- Realizes that he is a separate person around one year

- May understand common words when accompanied by gestures at one year (bye, Mama, ball, shoes)

- Uses words or gestures to express wants by one year

- Is curious; repeats activities to learn

- Short attention span of a minute; is easily distracted

Social and Emotional

- Feels happy, sad, mad, surprise, disgust, joy, distressed, and scared

- Has no control of expressing emotions

- Builds security and attachment with attentive adults

- Dislikes strangers beginning at eight months

- Experiences separation anxiety when left by loved adult around ten months

- Fears beginning at one year: animals, thunder, vacuums, theatres

Baby Behavior - Crying

"My 2 month-old won't stop crying. What can I do?"

Brain development stage: Even though it doesn't seem so at the time, this crying stage passes very quickly. It's very normal for baby to cry excessively at 2 months and this is the peak which is often called the "crying curve." From 4 to 5 months of age, baby's crying time decreases immensely.

Suggestions:

- Offer food first. Even if you've heard that babies should eat every 1.5 to 2.5 hours, perhaps she is going through a growth spurt and needs to "cluster" feed

3

for several days. She should be feeding 12-14 times per day. You can't overfeed a baby. She will turn her head away from breast or bottle and not suck if she has had enough.

- Check for illness next. As you get to know your baby, you will have intimate knowledge when things are not normal for her. Trust your "gut feeling" if you think she is sick or something is seriously wrong. Call your local baby advice line or take her to the hospital emergency or walk-in clinic.

- Check her diaper. A heavily wet or poopy diaper won't bother some babies, but will irritate others.

- Check for gas. Try carrying baby with your forearm under her tummy and gently rub her back. Or lie her down on your forearm with your inside elbow supporting her head and your hand supporting her pelvis. Gently rub her back with your other hand.

- Check for prickly tags on clothing and hairs or threads wrapped around toes, wrists, fingers or neck. Baby may be in pain from some kind of irritant.

- Check if she is too hot/too cold. Baby should wear the same amount of clothing layers that you do.

- Check if baby needs more sleep. Some babies wake up and seem fussy. Try not to disturb her and encourage her to go back to sleep.

- Motion really calms fussy babies. Walk, dance, sway, or rock her. Go for a walk in the car or stroller.

- White noise from a fan, ticking clock, aquarium, vacuum or dishwasher can help too. Buy a white noise machine that will play white noise or nature sounds, or use a phone app.

- Carry your baby in a sling, wrap or similar carrier. Studies done in cultures where babies are constantly carried, show that babies cry very little. Warmth, touch and motion works magic for babies because they simulate life in the womb.

- Wrap baby in a blanket freshly heated from the dryer. Then rock her in a rocking chair.

- Try playing some music. Humming, or shhhhhing may help calm the baby.

- Sway your baby while standing up or sitting on an exercise ball.

- Put baby in the swing.

- Run the dishwasher, vacuum or washer near your baby's seat.

- Go for a car ride. Keep a pillow in the back seat so when baby is asleep and the car is parked, have a bit of a nap yourself.

- Try a baby massage.

- Hold her using the tummy hold. It applies a bit of pressure on her tummy to help relieve gas.
- Bicycle her legs so that gas can move out.
- Calm your baby with a bath.
- Swaddle baby. Flinging arms and legs can upset some babies. Others like loose clothing that allows movement of arms and legs.
- Babies that are over-stimulated from too much activity can be soothed by a dark, quiet room with gentle rocking and sucking.
- Go for a walk outside.
- If your baby's doctor diagnoses colic, or you have a fussy baby, get support systems in place for you and baby. Know your limits. If you start feeling helpless, frustrated, and angry because baby is still screaming, hand her over to partner, or a friend or relative that can give you a break. Make a list of her likes and dislikes to post on the fridge. If no one is around, make a safe choice and put the baby down in the crib while you take some deep breaths and calm down. It's okay to take a breather, even if baby is screaming.

. . . .

Baby Behavior - Clingy

"My 8 month-old daughter is very clingy to me. She won't accept a bottle or care from other people including her dad. She is still breastfeeding."

Brain development stage: Your baby is securely attached to an adult. That is a good foundation for all future relationships.

Suggestions:

- Have Dad do more things with her when you are away. Kids can see, hear and smell you when they sense you are near, even if they can't see you.
- You can start whole fat regular cow's milk at 9 months and perhaps she will take that in an open cup.
- Empower others to do the bedtime routine and let them forge their relationship with your daughter. Perhaps use a consistent caregiver every time you go out.
- Don't worry that you have to "train" her to accept substitute care for an upcoming trip, return to work, or whatever the reason for the absence. She will adapt when the time comes.
- Indulge her attachment needs. As babies feel more secure, they become independent faster.

Baby Behavior – Separation Anxiety at Daycare

"My 1 year-old will be going to daycare 3 days a week. How do I deal with his separation anxiety when I go back to paid work?"

Brain development stage: Your son is developing an awareness that his loved ones can leave him and he feels frightened. Before the age of 1, children do not know where their bodies end and their parents' bodies begin.

Suggestions:
- You don't have to stop nursing. Just save it for the evenings and mornings.
- Drop him off and leave quickly. Wave and say "Goodbye. Mommy loves you. See you later."
- He will eventually get used to the new routine.
- When you leave, hand him over to the same caregiver each time.
- Leave for short periods of time first, and then build up to longer periods. Get him used to the routine of the daycare.
- Make sure the daycare has your written list of ways to comfort your child.
- Find a daycare you really like.
- Send him with framed (in plastic), or printed up-close photographs of you and your partner. You could even put them on a tablet for him to hold close.

Baby Behavior – Separation Anxiety With Partner

"My 1 year-old daughter seems to get severe separation anxiety when I leave for work if she is left at home with my very caring, loving partner. I leave at about 6:30 am. However, she is fine and goes off to play when she is dropped off at daycare. How do I handle this?"

Brain development stage: The child is attached to both her parents but develops a deeper attachment to one - usually the parent who is with her the most. This attachment alternates between parents at different stages in childhood.

Suggestions:

- Have an activity already started or set up that your partner can steer her to, before you say goodbye and leave. Perhaps set it up the night before.

- Definitely say goodbye to her. Sneaking out makes the next time worse because she doesn't develop trust in rituals and routines.

- Get some Busy Bags for those times you have to leave. (Search online for ideas)

- Partner could take a few minutes to read a book to her while you leave.

- Give her a stuffy or special item that is identical to one that you have. Explain that you will both have this and each of you can give the stuffy a hug to "send to each other" when you need it.

- Put on a short 15 minute movie to distract her as soon as you leave the house.

- Do something together with her while you are getting ready. Perhaps she can have her own set of make-up brushes to use while you do your make-up.

Baby Behavior – Getting Things Done

"My 9 month-old loves being held. How do I get anything done in the house?"

Brain development stage: Your child's temperament may be one in that he needs close contact. Most babies become easier to entertain when they develop their hand to mouth coordination. Sometime around 4 to 6 months, they are happy to hold and taste a variety of toys that will keep them amused. Also, many babies settle into a predictable schedule of their own at this age, where you can count on nap times and playtimes to schedule your tasks.

Suggestions:

- Buy, beg or borrow a good, well-padded carrier. Slings and wraps are great for the newborn, and a high quality backpack with adequate head support for older babies can be a lifesaver for parents. The back carriers can be great for cooking and kitchen work. If money is tight, buy a good quality second hand carrier, rather than a cheap new one. The high quality ones have padding in the right places and are designed to support the adult's neck and back muscles much better. Most allow you two free hands to get things done.

- Trade one or two mornings a week with another new parent to watch both babies at one house. That way, you are available for nursing, but can pay bills, do laundry or organize things hands free, all the while knowing your baby is well cared for.

- Give up a nap when baby is napping. Don't do this too often. You need to sleep when baby sleeps, but once in a while, it helps to uplift the spirit, just to have the feeling of accomplishment for a completed job.
- Send your partner out for a walk to the park, zoo, or class with the baby. They can develop some great bonding time and you can get things accomplished.
- Hire a mother's helper to come over and play with baby while you work close by in another room. A mothers' helper is a pre-teen or teenager willing to accept less than babysitting wages for gaining child care experience while having the security of the parent close by for advice and coaching.
- Consider hiring house cleaners, dry cleaners and professionals to help ease the workload.

Baby Behavior - Refuses Pacifier

"My 1 month-old hates her pacifier."

Brain development stage: Some babies don't like pacifiers and will constantly spit them out.

Suggestions:
- Borrow a few types from friends to see if there is one she would like.
- Gently keep holding it in until she keeps it in. Stop if she cries or protests.
- Let your partner give it to her.
- Hold her upright or in a different position than breastfeeding so she doesn't associate it with food and gets frustrated that food is not coming out.
- Accept that some babies hate them and will never take them. The good news is that you don't have to break the habit later!

Baby Behavior - Refuses Dressing

"My 3 month-old doesn't seem to like getting dressed."

Brain development stage: Some babies don't like clothes and especially getting their arms into holes.

Suggestions:

- Distract her with a favorite toy.
- Talk or sing so she focuses on your face.
- Give her a toothbrush or a toy if she can hold it.
- Change her clothes less often.
- Get clothing that goes around the torso rather than over the head.

Baby Behavior - Pulls Off Hats and Mitts

"My 8 month-old doesn't like to wear outerwear. She pulls off her hats and mittens when she can."

Brain development stage: Some babies don't like coverings

Suggestions:

- Use socks as mitts as they are harder to pull off.
- Use hats with velcro-type straps.
- Keep her in the shade instead of using a hat.
- Put sunscreen directly on her head if she doesn't have much hair.
- Accept that it's just not going to happen.
- If it's clothes that are coming off, dress her in overalls or onesies.

Baby Behavior - Hates Car Seat

"My 3 month-old screams every time she is in her car-seat."

Brain development stage: Some babies really dislike car travel.

Suggestions:

- Get someone else to drive so you can sit in the back seat, so she can see you.
- Hold her hands or stroke her face and say soothing words.
- Only do short, necessary trips. It's a stage.
- Go out when you can leave her at home with a caregiver.
- Turn on the car fan for the white noise to lull her to sleep.
- Play a special song just for car trips.

- Consider walking or transit so you can hold her.
- Hang a mirror, toys or a big laminated photo of you on the back seat so she has something to look at.

Baby Behavior - Refuses Hair Cuts, Nail Trims and Hair Washes

"My 6 month-old screams every time I wash her hair, cut hair, or trim her nails."

Brain development stage: Some babies really dislike personal grooming.

Suggestions:
- Get someone else to do them. She might react differently.
- Do the trimming when she is asleep. Put a towel on her pillow and trim her bangs.
- Distract her with a movie, or singing while cutting.
- Wash her hair less often.
- When you have to wash, do it quickly.
- Accept that it is a stage.

Baby Development and Learning - Hates Tummy Time

"My 3 month-old daughter hates it when I put her on her stomach for tummy time. It is necessary?"

Brain development stage: Children are all different. Some babies love being on their tummies, and some don't. The purpose of tummy time is to exercise babies neck muscles while holding up their head, since they no longer do that naturally now that babies are put on their backs to sleep.

Suggestions:
- Put your baby on your chest while you lie on the couch. Sing or talk to her and she will lift her head to see where you are speaking from.

- If she screams and doesn't like it - don't do it! She will still develop okay. Just be sure that she doesn't lie on one side of the head most of the time or she could develop plagiocephaly (flat head).

Baby Discipline - Screeching and Squealing

"My 1 year-old likes to scream and squeal when happy or sad. None of my other kids did this. Should I stop it?"

Brain development stage: Your child is learning the power, vocal variety, tone and pitch of her voice and experimenting with it.

Suggestions:

- When she does this, respond with a new lower-pitched sound. Repeat this over and over until she adopts it.
- It could be just her personality. Plug your ears or use ear plugs.
- Active listen. Say, "Wow, you're really happy."
- Smile and screech back in mimic.
- Have a few words to respond with.
- It's totally normal and a stage. She will grow out of it. As my 10 year-old son said when we listened to a baby screeching at the mall, "Mom, that baby is practicing to be a singer!"

Baby Discipline - Touches Everything

"My 1 year-old likes to empty drawers, cupboards, cases and anything with items in. Should I slap his hands so he learns the word 'NO'?"

Brain development stage: Your child is learning how things work. He repeats actions over and over again to see if it works the same way as before. This is good for his brain connections.

Suggestions:

- Let him touch everything he can to encourage free play and exploration.
- Put away anything dangerous or unsafe. If it is out of sight, it will be out of mind.
- Supervise constantly.

- When visiting, move items out of his reach. Your hosts should know that this is a normal stage.
- Don't punish him for touching inappropriate things. He has no idea of danger at this age or the sense of what he should and shouldn't do.

....

Baby Feeding - Refuses Spoon

"My 9 month-old daughter won't eat anything off a spoon. I'm worried about getting some iron into her."

Brain development stage: Iron stores run out when babies are around 6 months of age and must be replaced by iron rich foods either in solids or formula. Babies this age learn to accept a spoon and try to self feed. It is a new skill to learn. They also play with food as an exploratory phase of development.

Suggestions:

- Feed her really lumpy stiff cereal with a fork.
- Use a spork (spoon and fork combined).
- Let her gnaw on meat – she will definitely get some nutrients.
- Feed her iron rich cooked foods such as beans, spinach and fish.
- Give her plastic blocks or some washable toy to play with and focus on, all the while you feed her cereal by spoon.
- Make muffins that she can crumble and eat and load them with flax, whole wheat, etc.
- Give her a spoon to hold while you spoon feed her.
- Give her a spoon to "feed" you while you spoon feed her.
- Use tofu and roll it in baby cereal.
- Give her small, frozen beans etc.
- She is entering the "feed herself" stage. She needs soft food that is finely chopped up. It's surprising how much food does get in her mouth, even though the floor and the chair is covered!

....

Baby Feeding – Breastfeeding Distraction

"My 5 month-old son is breastfeeding but pulling off when he is distracted by what is happening in the room. It takes so long and it is frustrating to continue feeding him this way."

Brain development stage: Around 5 months is when babies become very aware of their environment; however at this age, they become much more efficient in breastfeeding as well. About 90% of the milk they suck will take only about the first 5 minutes of feeding time.

Suggestions:

- Feed him in a dark, quiet room, with no distractions.
- Feed him facing the distraction so he can watch while feeding.
- Get an busy-baby necklace for you to wear so he has something to catch his attention while he feeds.
- Avoid dangling earrings.
- He may have better feeds at night when it is less distracting, but don't worry, he will get enough food either in the evening feed or during the day.

Baby Feeding - Refuses Milk

"My 1 year-old is transitioning from formula to milk. How do I get her to accept it?"

Brain development stage: A baby's taste buds are just developing. They are sensitive and strong. Different children react to different, unfamiliar tastes. As children age, they naturally accept a wider variety of food.

Suggestions:

- Keep breastfeeding if you both want to. The benefits continue for both you and her.
- Warm up the milk to the same temperature as the formula.
- Mix the milk in with the breast milk or formula in increasing proportions.
- Try goat's milk instead of cow's milk.
- Put milk in other foods such as cereal.
- Try a little bit of chocolate powder mixed in.

Baby Feeding – Low Milk Supply

"My 3 month-old is suddenly constantly breastfeeding. I feel that my breasts are not quite as full as when she was born, and I am losing my milk. I'm considering supplementing with formula, but I heard that doing that, will be the beginning of the end of breastfeeding."

Brain development stage: Babies go through physical growth spurts at ages 3 weeks, 6 weeks, 3 months, and 6 months. They "cluster feed" for a few days up to a week, which builds up your milk supply by increasing demand. Although your breasts feel less full, they are becoming much more efficient and produce about 32 ounces of breast milk per day.

Suggestions:

- Keep breastfeeding if you both want to. The benefits continue for both you and her.
- For the time she cluster feeds, drink lots of liquids, continue eating an extra 500 calories a day (that's all the extra calories a breastfeeding mom needs) and rest, so your milk production keeps up with baby.
- If your baby is producing 6-8 wet diapers per day and is gaining weight over the month, she is getting enough breast milk.
- Your breasts do not feel the same as the engorgement you felt when baby was born and in the first couple weeks. They are softer, and smaller, but produce much more milk.
- Your baby takes in much more breast milk than you can get from a breast pump. She takes in about 5 times as much as you can see from a pump. Babies are much more stronger suckers and draw out milk better than the best pump on the market.
- Drink more and rest more. Both will increase milk supply.

Baby Feeding – Spit-Up or Vomit?

"My 2 month-old spits up a lot of milk after breastfeeding. I worry that the valuable milk is wasted as I have to start again. Is it spit-up or vomit and how do I tell the difference?"

Brain development stage: A baby's tummy size at birth is the size of a marble. At 10 days to 3 weeks, the size is a giant boulder type marble and at 1 month, a baby's tummy is the size of a small bouncy ball with 3 cm diameter. Her tummy is very small and although expandable, can only hold so much milk. She will automatically spit up the rest. Spit-up is different from vomit because vomit smells and looks like curds and has been digested for a while.

Suggestions:

- Keep breastfeeding if she wants. Let her lead and signal to you when she has had enough by turning her face away.
- Try to keep her upright for about 10 minutes after feeding.
- Routinely try to burp her.

Baby Feeding – Bites During Breastfeeding

"My 5 month-old has bitten me a few times while breastfeeding. How do I make him stop?"

Brain development stage: It's common for babies to bite while they are teething.

Suggestions:

- Say in a sharp tone, "Ouch, No!"
- Break the suction between your breast and his cheek by putting your finger between the two. Keep doing it every time he bites.
- If he bites, bring him in close to the breast so his nose and mouth is covered. He will unclamp to breathe.
- Keep repeating this. Babies soon learn how not to bite while feeding. You don't have to stop breastfeeding as soon as they have teeth.

Baby Feeding - Starting Solids

"My doctor suggested starting my 6 month-old on solids. Any tips?"

Brain development stage: Most health professionals recommend to start around 6 months as they tolerate new foods better without potential allergy symptoms and they are sitting up well enough to see the food coming at them on the spoon. Eating is a learned skill and like many other skills, it takes parent patience and child practice.

Suggestions:

- Common practice is that baby can start solids with any iron-rich single ingredient food.
- Make your own solid food. It's easy and healthy.
- Watch for signs that she is ready. Can she sit up on her own?
- It's most important to wait for 4 days before introducing another new food, in order to allow time to observe a possible allergic reaction.
- Research does not support putting cereal in bottles to keep baby asleep longer. There is no evidence that this works.
- Make sure you are giving her the recommended IU of vitamin D daily.
- The most important food in the first year is breast milk or formula. Solids are meant to teach eating skills and get a bit of iron into them. Don't worry about filling her up.
- Feed solids first and then top up with breast milk or formula.

Baby Feeding - Refuses Bottle

"How can I help my 3 month-old take a bottle? I want some time off!"

Brain development stage: Some babies naturally take to a bottle and others don't. Taking a bottle is a new skill to learn for a breastfed baby. Some children are used to the breast nipple and a bottle feels foreign to them.

Suggestions:

- Have your partner give him a bottle instead of you because baby associates you with breastfeeding.
- Make sure you are out of the room or house so that he can't smell you and associate it with breastfeeding.
- Try some different nipples. Trade with a friend instead of buying all different kinds and finding out that the baby hates them all. Same with pacifiers.

- Give breast milk in the bottle.
- If your baby is older than 4 months, try giving a sippy or open cup instead.
- If your baby doesn't take a bottle, feed and then go out. Keep outings to two hours at the most. You can get more time off when baby is on solids around 6 months.
- Give him juice in a cup at around six months, because many babies will accept juice but not breast milk if the breast milk has always been delivered a certain way (breast).
- Try wearing your partner's shirt when giving a bottle so you smell differently, and your baby can't smell your milk.
- Sit baby up to give him a bottle since cradling him would lead him to associate it with breastfeeding.
- Try a newborn size nipple as the flow goes slower so he won't feel like he is choking with an older baby nipple.

Baby Health - Colic

"My 1 month-old might have colic. He is gassy and cries a lot. His back is arched and he doesn't sleep through the night. What can I do?"

Brain development stage: Researchers still do not know what causes colic. Gassy babies are not colicky and colicky babies are not always gassy. Current research shows that colic is an underdevelopment of the central nervous system that rectifies itself when babies are around three or four months of age. Colic is defined as non-stop crying for 4 hours per day, 4 days per week, and for 4 months, and then it stops suddenly. Colic is not related to baby gas, what you eat or what you feed him.

Suggestions:
- Let out some breast milk before you feed him and then it doesn't gush and choke him causing extra air in his stomach.
- Wear him in a baby carrier or wrap.
- Sit down and rest when he sleeps, and do things while you carry him awake in a carrier.
- Use baby hushing sounds.
- Feed him while on your side; lying down.

- Put him asleep in a laid back high chair.
- Get a swing.
- Get a white noise machine.
- Get some relief from people who will help. Give yourself a break when you need one. Other people are fresh and can support baby.
- Don't worry. There are no lasting effects on him from crying. When crying babies are supported (held and comforted) they do not fair any worse in the long run than babies who do not have colic.

Baby Health - Diaper Rash

"My 6 month-old son has bad diaper rash. What can I do?"

Brain development stage: Babies don't know that their end is sore or even where the end happens to be.

Suggestions:

- Sprinkle cornstarch on his bum.
- Put him on a mat with no diaper and let him air dry. Protect carpets and floors by using a washable cushion underneath him and put a small hand towel over his penis so it catches the urine.
- Provide a barrier cream on the diaper rash.
- Change diapers often, especially ones with stool.

Baby Health - Teething

"My 5 month-old daughter is teething and in a lot of pain."

Brain development stage: Babies can be born with a first tooth or it can come in anytime during the first year. Teething is most common in the fifth month. The tooth is erupting through the gums and baby is in pain a few days or weeks before the tooth appears.

Suggestions:

- Give some Tylenol for pain.

- Give a non-liquid teething object to bite down on. Water filled ones can become contaminated.
- Give a cold, clean washcloth to chew on.
- Avoid frozen objects as they are too cold.

Baby Health - Cradle Cap and Skin Rashes

"My 8 month-old son has bad cradle cap. What can I do?"

Brain development stage: Cradle cap is a scaly skin condition that can be present from birth to teens. Skin rashes come in several forms and can be worrisome.

Suggestions:

- Seek medical attention. Home remedies include rubbing a bit of olive oil into the cradle cap skin and letting it soak in for awhile before using a baby hairbrush to get excess flakes off.
- Your baby may have eczema or another skin rash. See your health professional and follow directions and see if it gets cleared up.

Baby Health - Illness

"Every day, my baby has some kind of condition that I worry about. How do I know the difference between serious illness and minor conditions?"

Brain development stage: Babies are affected by a lot of health issues the first year. It's normal as a new parent to be concerned and have your issues checked out with a medical professional.

Suggestions:

- Serious health conditions are ear infections, coughing, high temperature, vomiting, dehydration, seizures, and not eating or not having 6 wet diapers per day. Seek medical attention immediately.
- Minor health conditions that can respond to home remedies are teething, cradle cap, skin rashes, diaper rash, and colds. Seek medical attention if you are worried, and give lots of extra cuddling, holding and care. Follow prescription directions exactly.

Baby and Parenting Partner – More Time with Partner

"How can I make more time with my partner?"

Brain development stage: Young children do not understand that parents need time for themselves, and as a couple, until about age 6 years, when they become less ego-centric and more aware of other people's needs.

Suggestions:

- Have a bi-weekly date night.
- Establish a few lists of really good babysitters. Babysitters can be costly but so is divorce!
- Have a date night at home after the children are asleep.
- Have a date morning at a store that has a child play-place. It can be a coffee shop, or furniture store and a fast food place with a play area.
- Have another couple over to socialize, play games, and watch movies. Even better if they have a same-age child.
- Put in-laws and parents to work if they want some "Grand-parenting time."
- Put kids on a schedule so you have some time each day that is couple time.
- Have a picnic where the kids could play or go to a Drive-In or Movie-in-the-park.
- Go for a car ride. Kids will fall asleep and you can talk uninterrupted.
- Visit "Datenightyyc.ca" blog for great date ideas with and without kids around.

....

Baby and Parenting Partner – Leaving Baby for the First Time

"How can I make leaving my baby easier?"

Brain development stage: Children under age 6 months don't really understand when they are being left by parents as they don't know the concept of "gone" yet. Around age 10 months, babies begin to notice they are missing their loved one's faces and get upset. The term for their distress is called "separation anxiety."

Suggestions:

Tips for Mom

- Have a trial run with your caregiver. Don't really leave the house, but just sit outside or in another room for awhile.
- Ask someone to babysit that you are super comfortable with, such as another mom, or a relative that you trust.
- Phone home as much as you need to in order to feel secure.
- Say a quick good-bye, hug baby and hand her over, and leave fast.
- Leave a shirt or receiving blanket with baby that smells like you.
- Go to something you can focus on such as a movie or show. Dinner is too unstructured and your thoughts may turn to worry.
- Post a list on the fridge of what helps calm babies' crying, positions she likes, food and bath preferences, sleep routine and individual quirks.
- Make sure your caregiver and you share the same parenting philosophy. Ask questions such as "What would you do if baby cries?" to gauge suitability.
- Don't do it again unless you feel ready.
- Don't worry if you only last half the time you planned. It's natural to feel that way.

Tips for Partner

- Recognize this is huge for her.
- Allow her to do what she needs to do in order to feel comfortable. If she needs to cling to her phone, don't tease her!
- Acknowledge her feelings of guilt, worry and anxiety; she is being pulled two ways between wanting to go out and wanting to stay with baby.
- Let her phone home as much as she needs to.
- Let her talk about the baby as much as she wants to.
- Let her go home if she is overwhelmed. This is still a very natural and healthy attachment at this stage. If her baby is going to university and she still can't bear to go home, then it might be a problem! She will love you all the more for your understanding to her needs.

Baby Play - How Much Play

"How much play does my 6 month-old baby need for brain development?"

Brain development stage: Anything that stimulates a baby's 5 senses counts as play. You may find peeling potatoes boring, but your baby will watch you do it from his carrier and find it the most fascinating thing he has ever seen.

Suggestions:

- The simple answer is, "As much as you wish to." Babies love faces and the best time to interact with those they love is face-to-face contact times such as bath times, diaper changes, and feeding times.

- During those contact times, it helps to sing, talk, tickle, read, make facial expressions and use vocal variety with baby. Don't forget to smile. Babies love facial interaction and they will naturally turn their heads away when they have had enough.

- Try to give baby some "tummy time" for several minute periods each day. It helps baby to develop neck and upper arm muscles and it relieves pressure on the head so that the risk of plagiocephally (flat head) is reduced. Many babies don't like tummy time when they are simply placed on a hard floor, so it can be helpful to put baby on your chest while you are lying down on the sofa. This counts as tummy time. Also, keep in mind that tummy time can be several minutes, several times a day, instead of a twenty-minute marathon every day.

- Baby carriers are a wonderful way for babies to be stimulated and entertained through the day. Baby watching you make dinner from the elevated view of a backpack is fascinating for him and is much more stimulating for his brain development than watching "educational" videos on the tablet.

- In spite of our society's intensive push to give early learning to young children, try to avoid worrying about how much stimulation and playtime he is supposed to be getting. If you enjoy spending time with baby, and interacting with him with your natural enthusiasm, rest assured he is getting enough stimulation!

Baby Siblings - Sibling Involvement

"My new baby has an older toddler brother and preschool-aged sister. How can I foster good relationships?"

Brain development stage: Babies see other people but don't understand any of our social categories such as mother or sister.

Suggestions:

- Encourage older brother and sister to play and entertain the baby, but be sure to supervise them together.
- If the play gets rough, show the siblings how to handle the baby gently, rather than to scold the rough play.
- Give lots of attention to the older siblings and play up how they get to do things the baby can't.
- Avoid forcing interaction if the siblings don't enjoy it.
- Involve the baby in the older children's activities as much as possible.

Baby Sleep - Getting to Sleep

"What are the best ways to get my baby to sleep?"

Brain development stage: Babies need simple comforts to get to sleep, just like adults do.

Suggestions:

Recreate the womb!

1. Shushing, white noise, and music lulls your baby to sleep.
2. Darkness, warmth, and familiar smells help baby feel secure.
3. Routine - keep the same bedtime routine of gum cleaning, pajamas (sleeper), story, snack (breastfeeding or bottle) and singing or rocking before bed.
4. Sleep Associations - have several for flexibility. Rock, nurse, music, pacifier, swaddling, etc.
5. Sucking - baby's hands, your breast or pacifier
6. Movement - car, stroller, on you, rocking and carriers
7. Containment - swaddle but leave his hands visible for baby to suck on.
8. Leave to sleep when drowsy - watch for signs: quieter, eyes glazed over and losing interest in things, rubbing eyes, becoming fussy or crying, yawning, slumping over, looking to suck with nursing or bottle.

Baby Sleep - Easier Co-Sleeping

"How can I get more sleep at night with a baby in my bed?"

Brain development stage: Babies need warmth, skin contact, and regular parent breathing to mimic what they are used to in the womb. They sleep best when their original "sleep association" (the womb) is copied.

Suggestions:

- Try to give yourself more room. Spread more mattresses on the floor so everyone has room to move. Bolt the bookcases and dressers to the wall and make sure the room is safe and child-proofed.
- Find a sleep situation that works for you and your family.
- Try a white noise machine, fan or earplugs that will dull the noises baby makes.
- Don't listen to other's comments about "should" and "bad habits." Do what is safe and works for your family so that everyone is sleeping and no one is crying.
- Change habits when they no longer work for you. Don't worry about the future because babies change so fast. When you need to make changes, children will be older and more able to talk and understand the need for change.
- Avoid comparison with siblings and others. All children are very different.

Baby Sleep - Safer Bed-Sharing

"I want to sleep with my baby. How can I make it safer?"

Brain development stage: Babies love to sleep with regular rhythm (your heartbeat), warmth, and touch - all things your body provides.

Suggestions:

There are basically two ways to have a safer sleep-sharing experience. Some parents try the sidecar approach. They put the crib in the master bedroom with one crib side down. The lowered crib side is moved right next to the bed. This is called co-sleeping. Other parents just get rid of the box spring and put a king size mattress down on the floor so there is no danger of falling. Just as adults are aware of the edges of their beds and seldom fall off, mothers and babies become intuitively aware of each other as they sleep, so rolling over on baby is not common. This is called bed-sharing when baby and parents share the same sleep surface. The following tips can reduce the risks of suffocation, wedging, entrapment and falling:

- Never sleep with your baby while under the influence of drugs, prescription drugs, over the counter drugs, and alcohol, or if your partner is under the influence of the same.

- Never sleep with baby if you are so tired that you are zonked out.
- Never leave baby unattended on an adult bed.
- Keep pillows, comforters, stuffed animals and sheets away from baby. Dress baby in a warm fleece sleeper and you in a warm cotton turtleneck so the upper body doesn't get cold and you don't need blankets or comforters to cover up.
- Pin away or braid your long hair to reduce the risk of entanglement.
- Make sure sheets are fitted under the mattress.
- Some parents put pool noodles under the sheets near the edges to keep baby from rolling off the bed.
- Always put baby on her back to sleep.
- Avoid siblings in the same bed. If siblings do share a bed, you should sleep between siblings and baby.
- If using a bed with legs, make sure the spacing between headboard and footboard is no more than currently allowed for mattress-crib spacing in safety approved cribs.
- If you or your partner smoked during the pregnancy, avoid bed-sharing.
- Mattress must be firm and preferably flat on the floor.
- Never sleep on couches, overstuffed chairs or sofas, waterbeds or hide-a-beds.
- Never cover up baby's face.
- The mattress should not be against a wall or furniture because baby could become entrapped.
- Baby should not sleep between you and your partner due to overheating produced from both bodies. Sleeping between you and the end of mattress on the floor is the safest. In many countries where sleep sharing is common, only mom and baby bed-share; not dad, siblings or pets.
- Avoid strings and ties on everyone's nightclothes.
- Avoid overheating the room and baby.
- Avoid sleeping near window treatment cords that could strangle, or windows that could pose a falling risk.
- Avoid using bed rails for infants under one year.

Baby Sleep - Getting Baby to Sleep on Own

"My 7 month-old son will only fall asleep, and sleep soundly on me. Yet, there are times I need to put him down to get things done. What can I do to get baby to sleep on his own surface?"

Brain development stage: Babies love to sleep with warm movement - you!

Suggestions:

- Put him in his crib while drowsy and use a white noise machine to help keep him out longer. He might associate his crib with sleep time.
- Wait until he is past the twenty minute light sleep stage and goes down into the sound deep sleep stage. Then move him to his own surface.
- Take the time to lay down and rest. The laundry and dishes will always be there.
- Use a swing if he falls asleep in it.
- Try rocking or movement.
- Try to keep baby as warm and swaddled as possible.
- Wear him in a carrier more.
- Get him used to sleeping on your partner so you can use the time that your partner is home, to get household things done.
- Consider co-sleeping. Follow safety recommendations for co-sleeping and bed-sharing.
- Pat him gently on the tummy and say Shhhh... to try and settle him in his crib.

Baby Sleep - Refuses Naps

"My 8 month-old won't nap or sleep at night for more than four hours at a time."

Brain development stage: Sleep patterns are as unique as the baby is. Some babies give up naps earlier and some later. Some have shorter naps and some longer.

Suggestions:

- Get classical or relaxing music on the player.
- He may be an active baby. You might just have to accept it and find ways to get your sleep with support.
- Feed him before he tuckers out.
- Give up naps.
- Use white noise to keep him out longer.

- After 20 minutes, when he wakes out of his "light" sleep, re-create the same sleep associations as when he dozed off before the 20 minutes. When he goes down into his "deep" sleep of the same sleep cycle, make sure he is really out and you should get a good hour of napping time.
- Sleep with him. Take the time to rest yourself.
- He is on his time. Accept it for now.

Baby Sleep – Cry-it-Out or Wait-it-Out?

"My baby is 7 months-old and won't go to sleep on his own. He wakes through the night and I'm considering letting him cry it out to teach him to sleep."

Brain development stage: Some sleep facts arise from learning about babies' brains.

All babies eventually learn to sleep through the night. It just depends at what age – 2 months or 5 years. By age 5, most children are through separation anxiety, teething, and night terrors and although they figure out clever ways to stall bedtime, they usually stay asleep all night.

Babies don't need to be taught to "sleep." Sleep is a natural body process and sleep needs are very individual. By the time they are teenagers, your main problem with children will be waking them up.

Babies don't need to be taught to "self-soothe." Some babies do it by sucking on their hands, but other babies need parent-soothing and no amount of teaching will help them to learn how to regulate their emotions and needs.

Leaving babies to cry it out, can increase the production of the stress hormone, Cortisol, which can damage developing neurons when done too often on a regular basis. Producing excess Cortisol on a regular basis is also called toxic stress, because a caring adult is not around to soothe, carry, cuddle or support a crying baby. If an adult can comfort a crying baby, it turns toxic stress into tolerable stress and does no damage to the brain.

Most children sleep well from ages 5 to 12, and too well from ages 12 to 20!

Babies tend to settle into a predictable sleep pattern from ages 3 to 8 months. When that magical time occurs is a matter of brain development and temperament, two factors that are out of parent's control to change.

If baby forms a bad habit, just change it when the time comes that you really need to. Don't worry about prematurely forming bad habits. Habits are easily changed the older a child is and when he can talk, usually around two years of age. When a sleep arrangement is no longer working for the whole family, change it! It will only take a couple of days.

Suggestions:

- Decide if you have the heart for sleep training. Find out if your partner is on board for whatever you decide.
- Read the pros and cons for both sides then make your decision.
- You will have to sleep train again after travelling, teething, sickness, or stressful events. Are you willing to do it again and again?
- Find a sleep arrangement that works for the whole family so everyone is sleeping and no one is crying.

Baby Sleep - How to Beat Tiredness

"I'm really, really tired today after being up with a sick child. How can I stay awake?"

Brain development stage: The most exhausting stage of parenting is caring for babies and toddlers. When the youngest child is around age 5, parents get much more sleep and pretty well get a solid 8 hours per night.

Suggestions:

- Don't sit down. Keep moving. Attack a project, clean or do a job that requires physical engagement.
- Do something that gives you energy and lifts your spirits.
- Vent to a friend who won't try to fix your "problem," or tell you what you are doing wrong. You need friends who sympathize with you.
- Drink coffee or a caffeinated drink every two hours.
- Get some exercise from a walk or the gym.

- Go to bed at night when baby goes to sleep. It's a short phase.
- Get a change of scenery; fresh air and outdoors helps.
- Go outside and play physical games with the kids – tag, red rover, etc.
- Get angry at something – the adrenalin in your system will keep you going!
- Drink green or mint tea that may wake you up.
- Get a shower, get dressed and put on make-up. Looking good uplifts your spirits.
- Grab some company – meet a friend for lunch or a coffee date and enjoy some laughter.
- Try some yoga with "Parent and Baby classes."
- Call a friend who has offered help in the past and beg for childcare relief so you can nap.

Baby Sleep - Frequent Awakenings

"My 11 month-old son's separation anxiety seems to be worsening. He won't calm himself down at night, and requires me to come into his room and get him back to sleep. Should I wait to respond to him, or should I pick him up right away?"

Brain development stage: Babies do not cry to manipulate parents. They don't have those higher order thinking skills until the school-age years of 5 or 6.

Suggestions:

- Sleep issues are very personal and very different for each and every family. It is key that you think for yourself about what works best for you, your partner, and your son.
- You are able to settle him once you respond to him, so bring him into bed with you.
- Let him camp out on the sofa near you so he feels secure. Don't worry - you are not creating bad habits. He will eventually sleep in his own bed - just not now.
- Trust your initial 'gut' feeling regarding your son. Don't let the influences of others dictate your course of action.

- Put a digital photo frame of you and your partner's up-close face photos on slideshow mode and he will constantly have a mental picture of you both being there.

- Sift through whatever advice you receive, use what feels right, and completely discard the rest.

- All children experience sleep disturbances, and will revert back to old patterns, even if they seem to be efficient sleepers.

- Children all go through moments of insecurity and uncertainty; you are there to provide a safe and secure place for him. Let him know you are always there for him.

- Give him extra affection and attention when he is in an insecure place; envelop him in your loving arms and remind him that he is safe, secure, and loved.

- Remind yourself, too, that You are safe, secure, and loved.

- Be extra gentle and breathe deeply. This too shall pass.

Baby Sleep - Surviving Sleep Regressions

"My 9 month-old son used to be a good sleeper but is now waking more through the night. Is this normal and when will it stop?"

Brain development stage: When children ages 0-6 are on a growth spurt or are on the cusp of a new developmental stage, they experience a regression in eating, sleeping, and calmness. They may sleep less, and eat less and appear more cranky overall for a few days to a week until the new stage kicks in.

Suggestions:

- It's a stage. It will pass and he will catch up in sleep and eating and be in a better mood when he accomplishes his new stage of development.

- Try to keep to regular routines.

- Comfort him and pat him back to sleep. Consider co-sleeping.

- Survive the regression any way you can. Remember that it is temporary and you don't have to do anything to ensure change. Things will get better no matter what you do.

- Get your partner to help out more.

- Nap when you can nap. Postpone the work that needs to be done.

Baby Toileting - Constipation

"My 3 month-old is constipated. She is exclusively breastfed and hasn't had a bowel movement for 4 days. What can I give her to help things along?"

Brain development stage: Breastfed babies can have a bowel movement anywhere from several times a day, to not having a bowel movement up to 11 days! There is a huge variation in stool frequency. She may not be constipated. Constipation is defined as hard, lumpy, stools and a long interval between movements (longer than 11 days).

Suggestions:

- If it goes longer than 11 days, see a medical professional.
- Keep breastfeeding. It will come.
- Be sure to keep an extra shirt for you and clothes/wipes for baby packed in the diaper bag for that inevitable blow-out that will come when baby does produce.
- It is very rare for a breastfed baby to be constipated.
- If baby is older than 6 months and has hard, lumpy stools, give prune juice, extra water, and breastfeed more.

Baby Toileting - Smelly Poop

"My 9 month-old son just started solids and his stool looks green and smells awful."

Brain development stage: Whenever there is a change in a child's diet, the change will show up in color, texture, smell or frequency of stool. When breastfed babies begin solids, their stool does become smelly.

Suggestions:

- Have your partner change the diapers.

Toddlers 1-2 Years

The stage of "I don't know what I want, but I want it NOW!"

....

What Can Toddlers Do?

Brain Development: Sensory-Motor Stage

Physical:

- Energetic and active

- Needs meals or snacks every two hours

- Spills and drops

- Can run and climb

- Can use stairs with help

- Opens doors and can press a doorbell

- Needs help with dressing (underwear, socks and shoes); can use shirts and pants

- Can pick up items or throw toys into a bucket

- Can vacuum, sweep and wipe with a cloth

- Sleeps twelve to fourteen hours with one or two naps

- Can drink out of a sippy or open cup

- Can turn doorknobs and open twist lids at three years

- Can walk down stairs holding a railing at two years

- Feeds self but messy; can use a spoon and perhaps a fork

- Can push a ride-on toy with feet

- Loves to push, pull, fill and empty containers

- Loves physical sensation of materials: goop, play-dough, food, sand, water

- Can scribble on paper with crayons

- Can throw a big ball with both hands

- Takes off clothes at eighteen months

- Runs and climbs at eighteen months

Cognitive:

- Can recognise logos and pictures

- Recognises self and loved ones in photos and mirrors

- No understanding of time.

- Can understand that "No!" is a powerful word, but doesn't understand the meaning of "not doing something"

- No idea of danger

- No understanding of tomorrow or yesterday; lives in the moment

- Understands more words than she can speak

- Can say two-word sentences: "More milk," "All gone," "Me go"

- Says ten to twenty words at eighteen months

- Problem-solves through trial and error; puzzles, shape-sorters

- Doesn't know which objects are breakable and which are not

- Earliest memory from two to three years; remembers moments out of the ordinary

- Can't connect actions with outcomes; doesn't understand consequences

- Labels objects, animals, people, and body parts with names

- Short attention span of a few minutes

- Understands simple directions: "Go get your coat," but may be too engrossed in play to comply

- No understanding of ownership, money, or sharing

- Explores the world through five senses; needs to touch and taste to learn

- Points to most common objects by name at two years

- Adults can understand 25 to 75% of her speech

- Mixes up "him," "me," "them"

- Can make simple choices between two offerings

- Enjoys repetition of movies, books, rhymes, daily routines, and habits

- Very little Executive Function: self-control, planning, focus or working memory.

Social and Emotional

- Feelings are intense: feels empathy, frustration, and pride

- Has a favorite cuddly toy that comforts him

- Affectionate to loved ones; loves to cuddle, kiss, pat, sleep with and enjoys being carried

- Excited to see new things

- Becomes stiff or floppy with body when protesting

- Beginning to play with other children, but mostly plays parallel, (side by side) with others

- Tantrums frequent as feelings are overwhelming

- May be contrary. Says "No!" to exert control

- Wants independence to try things and wants to cling to attachment person to build security

- Hoards possessions and people: "Mine!"

- Feels secure in repetition, routines, and familiarity

- Strongly attaches to comforting adults

- Separation anxiety most intense

- Expresses anger and frustration physically and not with words

- Very aggressive: hitting, pushing, biting, and throwing are normal responses

- No self-control to not touch or do things

- Honest

- Night terrors peak at two years

Toddler Behavior - Soother Obsession and Weaning

"My 15 month-old son is obsessed with his soother; he won't sleep or rest without it. He is also teething at this time. Any tips on weaning him off of it?"

Brain development stage: Children are very oral as toddlers. They explore their world and comfort themselves with their mouths. Children go through periods when they are teething and a soother helps to bite or chew. As well, a soother helps facilitate sucking which can also calm a child.

Suggestions:

- Don't worry about it yet. Some doctors recommend not taking the soother away until age 5 so they can get through the tumultuous toddler years with some oral comfort.

- Put a few soothers in his crib, so that if he can't find a particular one in the middle of the night, he has many other ones to choose from. Those glow-in-the-dark ones are great.

- Look for the reasons why he is needing his soother so much: teething, runny nose, anxiousness and fix those.

- Check his sleeping environment to see if anything else is disturbing his sleep (ambient temperature, black out blinds, soothing colors.)

- Administer a pain medicine for his teething pain.

- Offer him a drink in a special cup instead of the soother.

If you want to wean him off:

- Take him to the store so that he can select a new 'special' toy to replace his soother.
- Manipulate or cut the soother end to reduce the sucking aspect and render it an ineffective soothing mechanism.
- Reduce its use in baby steps. Limit times and places he can have it. Reduce it at naps and bedtimes last.
- Try the "Switch Witch" or "Soother Fairy" and get his consent to trade all his soothers in for a "big child" desired toy that the "Witch or Fairy" leaves overnight. He can put them in a gift box. Tell him that the witch or fairy gives them to babies that need them.
- Have a good-bye ritual. Throw it in the back yard garbage and wave goodbye. Help him through his feelings of grief.
- Stage an accidental loss and don't replace it.
- Start gradual and then go soother free.
- Go cold turkey and do it all at once so it is only one transition time.
- When he talks with the soother in his mouth, say, "I can't hear you." He will have to take it out to speak.

Toddler Behavior - Pestering

"How do I keep my toddler busy while making dinner?"

Brain development stage: Young children do not know how to occupy themselves. Your job as a parent is to give them stimulating, safe items to hold, manipulate and play with.

Suggestions:

- Put her on a chair by the sink. Give her some bubbles, dishes, a shallow sink of dish water and a cloth to "do dishes."
- Let her rip up lettuce leaves or stir mixtures.
- Give her a ball of homemade play-dough to use with play dishes, rolling pins, cookie cutters, and muffin cups.

- Give her some focused time before you start dinner. Perhaps read a book together.
- Keep a special box of toys in the kitchen, that she can access only while you are making dinner.

Toddler Behavior - Dawdling

"How do I hurry up my 2 year-old son?"

Brain development stage: Young children do not know about time. They learn how much time "feels" by age 7.

Suggestions:

- Get him ready by putting on his coat or doing it yourself whatever you need him to do. This is not a discipline issue, but a development issue. You need to help him get ready and out the door. This is not coddling him. He will eventually be doing it himself.
- Warn him of the transitions physically – show him how much is 5 minutes with a space between your hands.
- Just scoop him up and go! Acknowledge his feelings if he is unhappy.
- Build in dawdle time in other parts of the day.
- Get a stoplight timer so he can see the colors; green for warning, yellow for last warning, and red is time to go.
- Accept that toddlers have no clue about time.
- Change your schedule so that you have time to be slower.
- Have bins by the door that is easy to access items (hats, mitts) to go.
- Get organized yourself first and then him.
- Keep warm clothing items in the car.

Toddler Behavior - Homebody

"My 2 year-old doesn't like going out anymore. How can I get him to enjoy going out again? If we stay home all day, he melts down by the afternoon."

Brain development stage: Young children require outdoor play time every day. It's hard to get them out, but once they are there, they find things to do.

Suggestions:

- Bribery works for young children. Use the when/then statement: "When we go out, then we can go to ..." (the park after, or pet store, or something else he likes.)
- Have a home day, but get outside in the yard or a nearby playground.
- Have more parent and child play dates at your house if it is company you need. Make sure the visiting child is younger or older to help lessen fighting over territorial space and toys.
- Carry his mittens, coat, and hat for him if he doesn't want to get dressed. Put him in the car and then get his items on, or just carry them with you.
- Toddlers are notoriously difficult to get out of the house and then back home. It's a stage, but remember that you can always pick them up to go while acknowledging their feelings of unhappiness.
- Give him a choice: "Would you like to walk to the car or have Mom carry you?" (Either way, you are going out to the car.)

Toddler Behavior - Runner

"My son, who is almost 3, bolts every time he gets the opportunity when we are out in public, and I have to leave the baby in his stroller or high chair while I run after him. It's getting worse."

Brain development stage: Children love to run with no real awareness of safety or danger. If there is a wide open space either indoors or outdoors, guaranteed, children will run. If you chase them, they perceive it as a game that is lots of fun. They have little self-control, so punishing them for this behavior is useless. Containing them is a better option.

Suggestions:

- Safety first. Get a leash and don't worry about what it looks like or what other people think.

- Pretend you need help and ask him to hold your hand while walking for your safety.
- Constant supervision is required.
- Carry him if you don't trust him not to run or walk safely.
- Give him a job to do or a toy to hold.
- Shop online.
- Carry him in a backpack.
- Get a big shopping cart where you can contain him and the baby car seat and he can't easily escape out of it, (unless he jumps).
- Have a natural consequence. Warn him before you go to a public place that if he doesn't stay close by you, he will not go the next time. Leave him with your other parenting partner. It won't be forever, just during this stage. It's a phase and he will gain the self-control needed to overcome his urge to look at things, and stay with you.
- Read a book or story about children who run away from caregivers so he might understand the seriousness of it. Most kids just think it is fun as it turns into a chase game for them and a nightmare for you.
- Role play before you leave the house. Go over what could happen if he gets away from you.
- If he runs, give the baby to another mom to watch and run after him.
- Give him a special reward for every two times he stays with you. Don't worry – you won't be doing it forever.

....

Toddler Behavior - Whining

"My toddler whines and cries a lot. How do I get him to stop?"

Brain development stage: Toddlers do not have the verbal ability to express their feelings. They do it in body language and voice tone such as crying and whining. Often, they don't even know they are doing it.

Suggestions:
- Be aware of your expectations.
- Teach him emotion words such as, "upset, sad, angry, frustrated, and impatient."
- Ignore the whining. If he doesn't get a reaction or a reward, he won't keep doing it.

- Say, "I can't understand you. Say it like this...," and then display the tone you want him to have.
- Acknowledge the feeling by finding out what he needs.
- Act immediately when he doesn't whine while asking for things. Give him the desired object right away.

Toddler Behavior - Refuses Hat and Coat

"My 20 month-old boy hates hats, coats and shoes."

Brain development stage: Some children dislike clothing types. Most children only wear about 3 to 5 items constantly, in spite of having rooms and dressers full of clothes.

Suggestions:
- Make it routine to always wear sunglasses and a hat outside.
- Buy several at garage sales and offer him the choice of which to wear.
- Compliment his choice.
- Use hats with velcro straps that he can't undo.
- Let him pick out your hat too!
- If he still refuses, put them in a bag and carry them and offer again that he put them on when you reach your destination.

Toddler Behavior - Refuses Dressing

"My 14 month-old son runs away when I try to dress or diaper change him."

Brain development stage: Toddlers are super-active and don't like to slow down for a minute.

Suggestions:
- Get him to help by pulling out the wipes for you.
- Distract to a toy just available for diaper changes or dressing.
- Pretend the clothes are talking to him "I want to get into Jason's leg!"
- Ask him to choose the spot in the house for dressing.

- Sometimes it is a 2-person job! Get your partner to help.
- Undress him in the bathtub and run a bath, if it is a big blowout.
- Put on a movie and change/dress him while distracted.
- Give him a reward. Can be non-food items such as blowing out a candle.
- Lift him up on the bathroom counter facing the mirror and hold him with your stomach. Pull down his pants around his ankle which will anchor his feet and render him stationary. Let him play with the mirror while you unhook the diaper and clean him standing up. Hold the diaper between you and him while your hands hook the tabs around him.

Toddler Behavior - Refuses Help

"My 2 year-old son is in the land of "I do it!" He refuses all my help to get through daily routines."

Brain development stage: The toddler years are a stage of fierce independence, but they are so limited in their capabilities and need a lot of help, even if they don't want it.

Suggestions:

- Build in enough time to let him do whatever he is trying to do - put on shoes, do up a zipper, etc.
- Offer help but don't rush in.
- Set him up for success - buy easy to use zippers and buttons.
- Have his possessions in easy to reach places.
- Put away items that are difficult for him to use.
- Encourage effort rather than end result.
- Practice patience.
- Wait. Say, "That's okay, take your time," instead of "Hurry up!"
- Do a bit and leave the last bit for him to do.
- Praise his successes.

Toddler Behavior - Gets Frustrated When Parent Doesn't Understand

"My 2 year-old son doesn't talk very well and gets frustrated when I don't understand him."

Brain development stage: Children have a very low frustration tolerance at the toddler age.

Suggestions:

- Say, "I don't understand, but I really want to."
- Learn and teach sign language.
- Give him a hug. It starts from a place of understanding.
- Really give focused attention to try to understand.
- Offer your hand and say, "Show me," so he can lead you to what he is pointing at.

Toddler Behavior - Fears

"My son is beginning to fear dogs, the vacuum and loud motorcycles. How should I react?"

Brain development stage: Fears are common and an outcome of brain development. It's good when children begin to understand danger.

Suggestions:

- Accept and validate his feelings. Say "You are scared of the dog? That's okay. You can stay back here until you are feeling more comfortable."
- Avoid fear triggers. Don't expose the triggers to him anymore than absolutely necessary. You can avoid car washes that may scare him, but not the barking dog next door.
- Children this age are too young to reason. It's a stage they will grow out of.

Toddler Behavior - Hates Waiting

"My 18 month-old girl hates to wait."

Brain development stage: Young children do not understand the social need to wait until they are about age 6. That is why they don't begin mandatory school until then. They don't have the executive function of self-control, and hence, the ability to take turns.

Suggestions:

- Bring along items to occupy her while waiting. Bring a bag of play dough, cello tape, pipe cleaners, bottle of bubbles, etc.
- Play finger games such as "Five Little Dickie Birds", "Wheels on the Bus", "Bingo", or "Rock, Paper, Scissors", to practice self-control.
- Sing songs or read books to her.
- Avoid screens and give her attention to build her literacy skills. Talk to her.

Toddler Behavior - Clinginess

"My 2 year-old son is a wonderful child, but very clingy. How do I get some space between us?"

Brain development stage: Young children crave and need physical contact from their attachment adult each day.

Suggestions:

- Introduce a ritual or activity that only your partner does with him. It could be their "special time."
- Cart him around in a carrier, so he has physical closeness.
- Spend lots of cuddle time in a chair or rocker. If not, get down on the floor and sit close to him.
- Don't push him away. If his security needs are met, he will be less clingy as he grows.
- If you can't get away, be good to yourself throughout the day. Take time for little treats like a cup of tea, or watching a movie that you love. Meet your needs to meet his needs.
- You may have to leave the house to get some free time, or send your son and partner out, as he might not accept your partner with you around.
- This may just be a phase while he is young. Soon, he will prefer the other parent.

Toddler Behavior - Favoured Parent

"My 20 month-old daughter loves my partner and gets upset when I interact with them both. How do I handle her hitting me and telling me to go away when she is with her daddy?"

Brain development stage: Although it is usually a preschooler (ages 3-5) behavior, many toddlers do exhibit a preference for a certain parent. They may get hostile to the "intruding" parent.

Suggestions:

- It's a normal phase where they tend to prefer one parent. It's hard not to feel rejected but keep in mind that it has nothing to do with you or your parenting.
- Forge your own trails. Have a special activity that only you do with your daughter. Make it your special time.
- Say "Ouch! Hitting hurts!" and don't let her hit you. Hold her hands so she can't. Wait until she calms down to release her so she is not hitting you more.
- Focus on her behavior and say "That hurts my feelings." Give her feedback.
- Have a few "outings" or "dates" with the other parent to re-connect.
- You should be the first responder when she is sick, hurt or upset. This builds attachment. Be warm and nurturing.
- Just remember that it doesn't mean that she doesn't love you but may just be exercising her power in a way she knows how. It will pass.
- Dad may be a novelty to her because he is not at home during the day.
- She is almost 2 – in the land of "MINE!" It will pass and she may switch allegiance to you instead of her dad.
- Don't take it personally! It's a stage.

Toddler Behavior - Exuberance with Other Children

"My 20 month-old son loves to hug other children. In his exuberance, he sometimes knocks them over. The other parents glare at me. What can I do?"

Brain development stage: A young toddler can't control his emotions very well. Self-control comes with age and brain maturation, more around age five.

Suggestions:

- Teach him to put his hands out in a hug shape if he wants to hug.
- Leave him be. You can't control other people's reactions and hugging other children is better than hitting them. He still is too young to understand.
- Model asking for a hug by doing it yourself.
- Give other parents a heads up before play dates.
- Get him a T-shirt that says "I'm a hugger," or "I love hugs."
- Teach him to not touch faces where most parents are concerned about germs.
- Don't worry. It's a stage. Worry when they are 16 and hugging the girls!

Toddler Behavior - Wandering

"How do I get my young son to not go outside when he first wakes up in the morning and I am not up yet?"

Brain development stage: Toddlers do not understand why they can't do things. They have no concept of restraint or safety so parents must rely on childproofing the home for safety.

Suggestions:

- Keep trying different deadbolt locks on the door.
- Ask him to wake you up in the morning so you can go outside with him.
- Check to make sure the doors are locked at night.
- Put socks on the knobs so he can't turn them.
- Put a bell at the top of the door.
- Use duct tape to keep fridges and toilets closed.
- Supervise constantly.
- Keep him contained in your bedroom or his when you are asleep.

Toddler Behavior - Refuses Bathtub

"How do I get my young daughter to take a bath? She freaks out every time she sees it."

Brain development stage: Toddlers have many fears. They do not understand how machines work and the noise of the water and drain action can be very scary to them, even with parent explanation.

Suggestions:

- Use an infant bath that is smaller and less intimidating. Make it fun.
- Bath or shower with her.
- Show her a shower and invite her into it. Tell her it is rain.
- Switch it up with different times, toys, parent.
- Put her in a swimsuit and say that you are going swimming in the bathtub, if she loves swimming.
- Show pictures of the bathtubs inner mechanical workings.
- Stand in the tub with the detachable water hose and let her control it. Use a clear shower curtain.
- Show her items that don't go down the drain. Make sure they are bigger than what fits in a paper towel holder.
- Get a drain cover that lets the water go down, but nothing else.
- Fill and drain the tub when she is out of the room.
- Turn out the lights and have a glow stick party in the bath.
- Take a bubble bath with just yourself, and with candles, wine, and music, and let her see you have a great time.
- Give her a bubble bath.
- Get her a lot of fun bath toys like crayons, paints, foam wall stickers, magnets, etc.
- Be sure to constantly supervise her until she is at least eight years old as she can slip under the water and drown.
- She probably doesn't get very dirty in the winter. You could let her go for several days without a bath.
- Take her swimming once a week and get her clean that way.
- Wash her in parts. Do her hair under the tap one day, then her feet the next day.

Toddler Behavior - Won't Get Out of Bathtub

"My son loves the bath. How do I get him out without a tantrum?"

Brain development stage: Toddlers love water and don't understand your time constraints.

Suggestions:

- Discreetly pull the plug so the water disappears.
- Offer a snack or book to entice him out. Pull the plug when he is out of the room.
- Set a timer.
- Give him a fair amount of time to play. Toddlers hate doing anything for only five to fifteen minutes.

Toddler Behavior - Splashes

"My son loves the bath. How do I stop him from splashing too much?"

Brain development stage: Toddlers love the water and don't understand messes.

Suggestions:

- Discreetly pull the plug so the water disappears. Say, "Oh, oh. Water's gone."
- Bathe with him and pull the shower curtain so he doesn't get water on the floor.
- Stay with him and tell him "No!" "Water stays in the tub, not the floor."
- Don't fill the tub so full next time.
- Let him splash all he wants in a paddling pool in the yard.

Toddler Behavior - Hates Sunscreen, Nail Trimming, Haircuts and Hair washes

"How do I get sunscreen on a toddler who detests it? She also hates having her hair cut and nails trimmed."

Brain development stage: Toddlers need to be distracted so you can get through daily routines.

Suggestions:
Sunscreen

- Let her smear sunscreen on your face while you do hers.
- Buy some spray on sunscreen and spray it on your fingers and then run it on her skin. Spray on is faster. Be sure she closes her eyes and holds her breath.
- Wait until she is strapped in her car seat and then do it while distracting her.
- Ask her permission first. Show her what a little dab it is.
- Squeeze some in a bowl and use a paint brush to "paint" it on.
- Put little lotion circles all over her legs and let her rub it in.
- Promise she can towel off the excess.
- Keep her in a big hat, and long sleeves if she absolutely refuses sunscreen.
- Don't let her outside until she puts some on. Make it a routine rule for everyone in the family. No sunscreen - no outside

Nail Trimming

- Trim her nails during nap or bedtime when she is in the deep phase sleep.
- Promise her nail polish if she lets you trim her nails.

Hair Cuts

- Pretend to play "spa" and do facials, manicures and pedicures as well as hair styling.
- Trim nails and hair while she is engrossed in a movie.
- Trim her hair while she is in the bathtub. Let her wear a visor on her forehead so she doesn't see you trim her hair.
- Do hair cuts in the high chair while she is engaged in a toy.
- Put her in a kitchen sink so she can play while you cut.
- Call it hair style and not "cut". She may understand "cuts" as a bad thing.
- Let her see you at the salon when you go. Play up what great fun it is!

Hair Washes

- Acknowledge her feelings. Say, "I know you hate having your hair washed."
- Work fast.
- Let her wear a visor hat, ski goggles or a diving mask so shampoo doesn't get in her eyes.
- Put shampoo in her hand and let her apply and rub. You finish off.

- Hold a dry washcloth over her eyes and tell her to look up. Have a decal on the ceiling she can look at. Or let her keep the diving mask on. Carefully pour a container of water over the back of her head while she is looking up, to rinse without getting soap in her eyes.
- Let her shampoo a doll while you do her hair.
- Consider going swimming more often if she really hates shampoo.

Toddler Behavior - Getting Yourself Showered with a Toddler Loose

"How do I keep a toddler busy while I'm getting dressed and showered?"

Brain development stage: Toddlers need to be distracted so you can get through daily routines.

Suggestions:
- Hang a clear plastic shower curtain so you can watch your toddlers while you shower.
- Bring her into the shower with you or consider showering during her nap time.
- Keep a cupboard in your bathroom or bedroom that can house toys to keep her busy while you get ready. Keep the toys only for bathroom use.

Toddler Behavior - Falls Asleep While Driving

"How do I keep my toddler awake while she is in a backward-facing seat, while we are out driving?"

Brain development stage: Toddlers are often lulled to sleep by the hum of car travel.

Suggestions:
- Try to sing or play a peppy music tune.
- Distract with coloring books or an activity to keep her hands busy.
- Have a bucket beside you with new things to pass to her.
- Give her snacks that take a long time to eat.
- Have a sibling sit back with her to poke her, tickle her and keep her awake.

- Open the windows to get a blast of cold air in there.
- Don't drive during her nap or sleepy times.

Toddler Behavior - Holiday Decorations

"How do we have a holiday tree and a toddler in the same house?"

Brain development stage: Young children do not understand "no touching" and often want to touch shiny, sparkly, pretty things. They may even understand "no", but not have the self-control to resist touching the engaging ornaments.

Suggestions:

- Put your good ornaments on top and the plastic ones on the bottom of the tree.
- Get a small tree and put it on a tabletop.
- Wire or tie the tree to a picture hanger on the wall so it can't topple over.
- Set the tree up in a playpen and put the presents around it.
- Get two trees - one for the kids to touch and "play" with and one that is for adults that have the best ornaments.
- Consider doing without a tree for just a year or two.

Toddler Behavior - Getting Them Out the Door

"How do I get my two year-old out the door with being dressed, hair combed, boots and coat on?"

Brain development stage: Getting a toddler dressed and ready for the day is not her priority. She doesn't think of the things she has to do. It's her parent's agenda, not hers.

Suggestions:

- Go as-is. Pajamas, bed-head hair and stinky breath are okay if you need to be somewhere on time. Lower your expectations of yourself. Other people will understand how hard it is to get out the door with young children if they are parents themselves and will give you some leeway.

- Warn her the night before what is expected in the morning.

- Make it a game. Cut big pictures of a toothbrush, a hair comb or a child using those items, out of magazines and laminate them. Tape them to a ribbon on the wall for a sequential visual reminder of the steps needed to get ready.

- Set the timer on your phone for an animal sound indicating time's up. Then when the timer goes off, remind her, "What do we do when the duck quacks? Yes, we get our boots and coat on!"

- Build anticipation. Say "Tomorrow is playgroup and the teacher bought some new hammers for us! We want to get there on time!"

- Put on a movie to fit the time frame you need (not an hour movie when you only need her distracted for 30 minutes) and feed her, or get her dressed while she is distracted.

- Ask questions to distract her from complaining such as "What toys will be at the place we are going to?" "Who will you play with today?" "What stuffed animal do you want to bring in the car?"

- Put on sunscreen while she is sleeping.

- Dress her at night in her next day clean clothes instead of pajamas.

- Get yourself ready first. When she sees you with your coat on, she might understand better.

- Throw a snack in the car like a granola bar and say "Go get it!" Food is a great motivator.

- Get yourself ready and grab her coat, mitts and things in a bag if she won't put them on before heading out. When she sits in the cold car, ask her again if she would like her warm clothes.

- Get dressed together.

Toddler Behavior - Temper Tantrums

"My 2 year-old daughter has tantrums when she doesn't get her way. In the past, we have sometimes given in. Now, her 3 year-old brother even gives in to placate her when she starts screaming. How do I handle this?"

Brain development stage: Young children under 4 do not have the self-control to contain emotions, stop them, or understand them. Temper tantrums begin at age 10 months, peak at 2.5 years and taper off around 4 years of age. They are a normal way for children to express anger and frustration in body language because they often don't have the words yet to express their feelings. The anger and frustration feelings are overwhelming and often frightful to the child. Handling anger becomes easier for children as their hippocampus, and amygdala in the brain matures and their verbal ability improves, usually during the school-aged years.

Suggestions:

Before the tantrum

- Beware of the events and time of day this is most likely to happen and avoid the triggers.
- Use a distraction. Hold and hug her if she allows it.
- Use alternatives to "No". That way, if you cave in, you don't lose your authority.
- Set up an "anger" corner so you can steer her to it when she is over the top. It can be a corner with stuffed animals, books and soothing items. This is not a punishment or a time-out room. Make it work for her. Don't force her if she won't go.
- Sometimes children have tunnel vision during their anger escalation. Distract to a movie to get her to calm down.

During the tantrum

- Stay calm yourself. Wait patiently until the tantrum is over.
- You are not a terrible parent! Hang in there!
- DO NOT give in to the demand. If you have blurted out the wrong answer, take time to think before saying, "Yes" or "No" next time but stay with your answer this time.
- Don't talk much during the tantrum. Many children are "out of control" and can't process what you are saying. Your words will have more effect when everyone is calm after the tantrum.
- While she tantrums, use assuring words, "That's okay to feel angry." This helps you to feel better!
- Ignore the tantrum at home. Take her to a quiet place or car to wait it out if you are in public. Leave your shopping or the restaurant. You can go back in later and arrange for pack-up or shop later in the day.
- Have something for the child to have and hold before she flips out.
- Be close to her physically. Stay with her while she tantrums but go about your business.
- Let her feel her emotions. Allow her the experience of feeling frustrated.

- Don't be afraid of her anger. If you are afraid, don't let it show! If she is a thrower or room wrecker, make sure everything is out of the way.

- If she destroys something in her anger, let it be. Don't clean it up, but stop her. Contain her so the mess is minimal. (Make a mental note to childproof more thoroughly before next time.) Don't lecture, preach or swear. Don't give her anger any emotional attention. After the tantrum is over, you can get her to clean up her anger messes, with your help, so she learns she is responsible for what she does during her anger.

- Minimize the attention you give to her anger. While she is peaking or escalating, put on a video that might catch her attention. Then focus your attention on something to clean. It's mindless, physical and helps to focus you on something so she can see that you are not giving attention to the tantrum.

- Take her to her room and let her out when she is calm. Stay with her if need be. This works for some children but not others. Some children need to see your calmness in action, to help them calm down.

After the tantrum

- Acknowledge her feelings after the tantrum is over and she has calmed down. Say, "You were really angry that you couldn't have the candy at the checkout."

- After the tantrum is over, you can teach her other ways to express her anger, like deep breathing, stomping her feet, etc.

- When she is calm, ask if you can help her.

- The hardest skill children need to learn is how to control their frustration and anger when someone says "No" to them. It's an important life skill and children get better after the toddler years, around 5 years.

- Read the books, "When Sofie Gets Angry" or "Grappling with the Grumblies" to her in a quiet, calm, non-angry time and talk about her feelings. Discuss an activity to direct her to when she is angry next time. Make an anger plan.

- Don't punish her for the tantrum or anger. Just as we wouldn't punish a child in a wheelchair for their physical limitations, we shouldn't punish a child for their age-appropriate emotional limitations. They will get better at handling their anger as they get more verbal.

- Relax. It does get better! Children eventually learn how to handle their anger. If you look around you at all the adults who manage their anger you will feel assured that children have 13 years to get it right! (Ages 0-12)

Toddler Behavior – Hits Me

"My 17 month-old son hits me when I pick him up for getting out of the car seat. He doesn't want to be picked up."

Brain development stage: Hitting is normal for a young toddler to express annoyance. The behavior must be addressed respectfully and consistently and they eventually learn better ways to express their feelings.

Suggestions:

- Perhaps the child wants more independence. Put him on a leash and let him walk.
- Anticipate that changes are hard for small children.
- Give a head's up of what is coming up. Children engrossed in an activity hate to be plucked out of it. Prep, prep, prep and use your words to explain.
- Hold him with two hands so he can't get free. Or get your arm under his torso and the other arm in between his legs and carry him facing out so he can't wriggle away.
- Use your "NO hitting!" strong language for this. Look upset.
- Get a shopping cart and put him in it right from the car seat. It is easier to keep him contained while whisking him to the store.
- Don't take it personally. His anger is not directed at you. He is frustrated at the situation.

....

Toddler Behavior – Exit Strategies

"How do I get my toddler out of daycare, play places, and parks when he doesn't want to leave?"

Brain development stage: Children can get very engrossed in their activities and don't handle transitions very well. It helps to give them a visual cue as a warning, but even then, they might not want to change activities as they have low impulse control.

Suggestions:

- Get eye contact.
- Give a tangible warning. Show 5 minutes with the space between your hands, or hold up one minute per finger.

- Take a cell phone photo of what they made or were doing so they can see it in the car and have lasting memories on the way home.

- Scoop them up and carry them out to the car kicking and screaming.

- Get them buckled safely in their car seat and you may have to go back to retrieve kicked-off shoes, coats, mitts etc.

- Let them have a tantrum if they need to. They have to deal with their frustration some way and expressing their feelings in body language is usually all they can do.

- Accept that it is hard to go anywhere with toddlers. It's hard to transition them to come and hard to get them to leave.

- Acknowledge their feelings of frustration over leaving. "I know that you are upset that we have to go. I would be too."

- Use the when/then tool. Say, "When we get to the car, then we can have our snack." This is using the next activity as an incentive to leave this one. Don't worry. It will not become a bribery habit that will never be broken. It's just a strategy for young children.

- Say "One (or two) more LAST TIMES!", so they start to understand that the last jump, last slide, etc., is a precursor to leaving. If you say "one last time" or "two last times," be consistent that you mean what you say, and really leave!

Toddler Behavior - Clinginess While Making Dinner

"My 14 month-old daughter has become increasingly 'clingy' the last while and I'm having trouble getting anything done around the house, like cooking dinner. I need some tips or tools to help me function!"

Brain development stage: It's normal for toddlers to go through stages of clinginess depending on how secure they feel that moment or hour.

Suggestions:

- Know that this is a normal stage of development for toddlers, and it WILL pass!

- Become best friends with your slow-cooker pot; this will free up your time at dinner and allow you to relax knowing dinner is taken care of.

- Do any dinner prep work in the morning when your daughter isn't as clingy; store all prep work in the fridge, and bring it out at dinner.

- Try getting her involved in 'helping' you in the kitchen. Give her a very small and focused task that she can work on, using plastic tableware and utensils.
- Try putting her in the backpack and carry her around while doing chores if she will tolerate it.
- Have a kitchen drawer full of toys, that get taken out just for kitchen time.
- Sign up for a community kitchen cooking course. This will provide you with 16 pre-made meals and will free up a great deal of your time.
- Consider an internet grocery delivery service that offers home delivery of fresh organic produce and household products.
- Try and take some time for you to replenish yourself.
- Stop and spend 10 minutes focused time with her and then say you need to make dinner. Provide some toys she can play with at your feet.
- Breathe deeply and be gentle with yourself. It's just a stage.

Toddler Behavior - Separation Anxiety

"My 2 year-old son is experiencing some regression with his separation anxiety. He was doing so well and now it seems we're back at the beginning. The regression coincided with a recent illness."

Brain development stage: Illness or vacations can make children more insecure. They need to fill up on security to feel right. Often, they fill up on security by staying very close physically and emotionally to parents or loved ones.

Suggestions:
- Give your son extra love and affection when he is feeling especially vulnerable and uncertain.
- It is important for you to know that your son is displaying normal behavior for his age.
- Explain beforehand what to expect. Re-assure that you are coming back.
- Leave a personal item of yours with your son, something like a scarf that he can 'look after' while you are away.
- Get two identical stuffed toys and give him one, and you keep one. Say that when he is lonely, he can give his toy a hug and you will feel it. You can do the same. (For older children, you can give jewelry.)

- Give him a cloth bag and let him see you fill it with kisses before you part.

- Print about a dozen big, 10 cm, head shot photos of you and get them laminated. Give one to him each time you leave so he can hold the memory of you in his hand. Don't worry about losing them as you have a few.

- Draw a little heart on his hand so that he has something tangible to look at.

- Put a little paper heart in his lunch/snack bag.

- Give him a job or duty to accomplish before you get back; this allows him to focus on the task at hand rather than the fact that you are away from him for a period of time.

- Say a firm, definite, "Goodbye. See you later," to build trust.

- Start a goodbye ritual such as a poem or song, followed by a kiss. Remember kids find security in rituals. Do it every time you leave.

- Put masking tape to mark on the clock when you will be back.

- Walk away with assurance and don't hover or falter. This will only add to his insecurity.

- Be aware of your own level of anxiety and breathe deeply to calm yourself; know how your son reacts to your feelings as well.

- Know that this is only a phase and it WILL pass.

- Have a short cuddle time before you leave.

- Get the sitter to come a half hour early so she can engage your son in an activity before you leave.

- Acknowledge his feelings. Say, "You are sad that Mommy is leaving you. I know. Mommy is sad too."

- Cut down on separation times while going through this phase. It is only a phase and you will get time to yourself again.

Toddler Development - Day-Home Versus Daycare

"How do I choose a day-home or daycare for my 2 year-old?"

Brain development stage: The most important factor to look for is nurturing adult attention and stability in the environment. A caregiver that a child gets to know, and attaches to is the best. This is a bond that is good for future relationships. Daycares are private or non-profit centres which have many paid staff, many policies, and distinct care rooms that are age-graded. Daycares are regulated by government and are like a mini-school. Day-homes are one caregiver in a private home, usually a mom, with a smaller number of children including her own, with flexible entertainment, outings and policies. Day-homes may or may not be regulated.

Suggestions:

- Day-homes usually cost less, but some may not issue a tax receipt. Day-homes are either legally registered under an umbrella company or legally unregistered. Unregistered day-homes may only be limited to several children including their own.
- Day-homes may have TV, tablets and computers where daycares usually don't.
- Day-homes are less structured and more flexible. They can change the day's plan instantly and go on many more field trips because of the lower ratio of adults to children, and easier transportation.
- Day-homes have more variety in terms of the ages of children in care, which enhance socialization. (They don't have a large room of only 2 year-olds that fight over the same ride-on toys.)
- Ask for the discipline policy/procedures and you will get an idea of the philosophy of care.
- Daycares have strict policies on diaper changing and food preparation safety.
- Day-homes are more flexible on drop-off and pick-up times.
- Day-homes are more flexible with part-time care where daycares will charge full rate for taking up a space.
- Get a receipt for either day-home or daycare for a tax deduction (not just a credit).
- Daycares encourage more interactive activities and have mandatory outdoor time, where day-homes may not.
- Due to the large numbers of children in daycares versus day-homes, the risk of illness is greater.
- Daycares may have higher turnover of staff due to the low pay. This creates a problem in fostering your child's attachment to a caregiver. Caregiver attachment is very good for the emotional development of a child and should be encouraged.
- Daycares are regularly inspected and open all the time for drop in. Day-homes have less rigid inspection by government.

- Unregistered day-homes do not have formal vacation or sick day back-up so families may have to find their own plan.

- There are many flavours of both day-homes and daycares. Visit announced and unannounced to get a feel of the atmosphere and policies of the place. Trust your gut feelings.

Toddler Development - Euthanizing a Pet

"How do I tell my children, ages 2 and 4 years, that we are going to put down (euthanize) our cat due to old age?"

Brain development stage: Children grieve differently than adults. They carry on as normal but may display grief in spurts, or outbursts, while upset about something else. They can't think abstractly until about age 13 and don't understand where the person/animal goes, and why the person/animal doesn't come back, or the finality of death.

Suggestions:

- Use real words such as "died", and "death" so they know it's different from "travel," "sleeping," or "moving on" to another place.

- Give them time, materials and space to say goodbye. Set up a shrine in your home with a picture, fake candle, poems, drawings etc, as a place they can visualize and remember their friend.

- Let them make a paw print out of craft clay purchased from a craft store.

- Take a really nice photo of the child and pet together and blow it up to frame for their wall.

- Have them draw a picture of the pet to say "Goodbye."

- Have a formal goodbye ceremony at the grave site. Play music and say last words.

- Take a long, last video of the pet. Let your child see it as often as possible to grieve. Be aware that toddlers and preschoolers may not understand why the pet is in the phone and not the room.

- Find a big rock and let them paint it and place it where the pet is buried.

- Have the child paint a ceramic urn to hold the ashes.

- Have a special corner of the garden for pet burials where they can go visit and talk to the pet.

- Acknowledge the happy moments. Talk about the pet. Say, "Remember when..."
- Assure the child that the pet is still with you, but in a different way.
- Let yourself cry and model it. When you display emotions, you give your child permission to be sad and display their feelings too. Be open and tell the kids why you are crying.

Toddler Discipline – Doesn't Listen

"How can I get my toddler to listen to me?"

Brain development stage: Young children do not have much self-control. It grows with brain development. A recent study by ZerotoThree.org found that 13% of parents thought that children should have self control and listen to parent's commands by age 3.

According to the Harvard Centre on the Developing Child, executive function begins developing at age 3 and increases dramatically at age 5 or 6. Then, it fine tunes and increases slightly from ages 13 to 25.

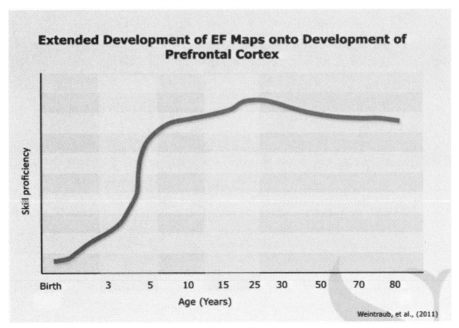

Source: Adapted from The Brain Story, *Palix Foundation, 2017*

61

Executive Function has 4 skills:

1. Self-Control - the ability to take turns, restrain emotions, handle anger, and put aside own needs for others.

2. Focus - the ability to filter out distractions and concentrate.

3. Working Memory - the ability to handle more than one instruction at a time. Holding a thought in the mind while entertaining another thought.

4. Planning and Decision-Making - the ability to recalculate plans when the first plan was canceled. This is the ability to think out consequences and it occurs when the child is age 5 or 6, and not before. Thus, logical consequences as a punishment tool is useless on a baby, toddler or preschooler because they logically can't plan ahead.

The brain development age for curbing a child's wants and putting them aside for parent's wants is somewhere around age 5 or 6. This is why children do not begin mandatory school until this age. This discrepancy between what parents think, and what children can do, creates unrealistic expectations of behavior and unnecessary discipline for children that are simply being children.

Suggestions:

- Give her time and patience.

- Read more on child development. See the list at the beginning of this section on child capabilities for toddlers.

- Use one, two or three word commands: "Bath-time." "Come here." "Sit down." "Get your coat." "Time to eat."

- Say, "I'm the hug machine. I need a hug." She will come to you and you can re-direct her.

- Let it go. You have plenty of years to address it when she can understand your words and talk to you.

- If she doesn't comply, do it for her. This is only a stage and will not last forever.

- Physically help her do what you want her to do, or do it yourself. EG: You could show her how to carry her dishes from the table to the sink, or just do it yourself.

- Don't project that it will always be this way. Your school-ager will be ready and willing to carry her dishes to the sink, even if she refused as a toddler, just because she is in a different stage of development and capability.

Toddler Discipline - Teaching Patience and Manners

"How do I to teach my 14 month-old manners, especially patience?"

Brain development stage: Young children do not have any patience. It grows with time and age. 4 year-olds are getting more patience, and 6 year-olds are even better.

Suggestions:

- Narrate it: "I see you want it now." Explain where things are at.
- Give her the words to use. "You are feeling impatient." Then, distract her by saying, "Lets count to ten."
- Give her what she wants, as soon as you can, if you are able. There will be many other times she has to wait and she will learn patience with time and age.
- Model your manners and she will pick them up. Be sure to say "Please," "Thank-you," and "Excuse me," as well as "I'm sorry."
- Model patience and tell her what you are doing. "Mommy is waiting in line because everyone needs a turn."
- Remember the golden rule of parenting; "They don't have to learn everything today. There are plenty of other opportunities to learn when they are older."
- Sing a song with them. There is a "patience song" on the internet. "Have patience, have patience, don't be in such a hurry..."

Toddler Discipline - Teaching Respect

"How to I teach my toddler respect?"

Brain development stage: Respect is a very abstract concept that most young children don't understand. They understand more concrete examples such as "No hitting."

Suggestions:

- Use the "Golden Rule; Treat others the way you want to be treated."
- Keep talking about respect, and he will eventually get it.
- Model respect.

- Realize it can be a long process to learn respect.
- Treat your child as respectfully as you would your partner, and your child will grow up modelling it to you.

....

Toddler Discipline - Handling Hitting, Biting, Pushing, and Throwing

"How do I handle my toddler and preschooler together when one is a hitter/biter/pusher?"

Brain development stage: Physical expression of anger and frustration is a normal, common stage of toddler and preschooler ages. Parents can teach alternative expressions, but don't expect compliance until the school years when children can handle frustration with more self-control.

Suggestions:

- Apply first aid and comfort to the injured child first. Then you need to address the attacker.
- Find the attacker's need. Do they want the toy, more personal space, attention, a reaction, revenge or choices? Ask them. Tell them how to ask for what they want. Use simple words.
- Make eye contact.
- Say "Ouch! Hitting/biting/pushing hurts!" or "I don't like that!"
- Don't expect sharing until age three.
- Restrain your child in your lap or carry him away to another space to calm down with you.
- Teach your child to "High Five" so he can hit but in a socially acceptable way.
- Rocking your child or rubbing their backs and using a soft, repetitive voice helps your child to calm down also. You are not rewarding the child. You are getting the child to a place of calm so you can apply the teaching.
- Save your loud and sharp "No!" for times like hitting and for safety or emergency situations. Show disapproval in body/facial language and your voice tone.
- Have a lot of similar toys and space to redirect your child to.
- Actively listen: "You're frustrated that he grabbed the toy? You want your toy back?" "We can't hit, but we can ask to have the toy back."
- Teach your child to put up his hand to ward off space invaders.

- Teach I-statements: "I don't like that." "I want the toy." "I'm not done."
- Allow your child his own time to give up a toy. Gently remind him that someone is waiting, but don't force him to give it up. Let him choose when.
- Instead of always saying, "Hurry-up," you could try, "Take the time you need."
- Meeting your child's needs encourages him to think about other's needs.
- Supervise.
- Say "Ouch, that hurt Mommy!" when they bite or hit, and put them down and walk away.
- Teach your child to walk away from annoying situations.
- Say "No! We don't bite. Biting hurts."
- Dramatize your pain and sorrow, so the child knows that you are truly disappointed.
- Give your child something else to bite. "People are not for biting. Here, bite this."
- Remove your child from the situation, but don't banish your child to a room alone. Sit with your child to help him calm down.
- Teach "breathing," "the silent scream," and "stamping feet," when your child is angry.
- Teach "trading," and "taking turns," and "let's make a deal."
- Stay calm yourself.
- Don't grab toys from your child. Model the behavior you want. Ask for the toy and wait for consent. Always ask to use things that belong to your child.
- If a toy is thrown, move them all out of reach. Stop the throwing.
- You could apologize for your child, to the victim, to model what you want to see him do in the future.
- Tell the other child that your child needs space but doesn't have the words to say so yet, so could he please give him some room.
- Shower the victim with attention. Have the victim repeat the rule of "no hitting—hitting hurts" to the attacker. Remove the victim and take them with you to do something else. Be sure to increase the attention to the attacker in peaceful times. Show the attacker more positive ways to get attention.
- Increase one-on-one time with the attacker, later.
- If hitting between two children repeats, find something else for one child to do and separate them.
- Acknowledge the feelings of each sibling or child and repeat it for the other child to hear, so they can start to learn empathy and conflicting points of view.

- If hitting repeats, children may be hungry, bored or tired. Fix the underlying reason.

- Model politeness. Use "Please, thank you, no thanks," with your children.

Excerpted from *Discipline Without Distress: 135 tools for raising caring responsible children without time-out, spanking, punishment, or bribery.*

....

Toddler Discipline - Wants Attention While Feeding New Baby

"When I'm nursing my 2 month-old son, my 2 year-old son starts vying for my attention. He begins to 'act out' such as biting the dog, running around and other misbehavior."

Brain development stage: Having a new baby in the house can provoke jealousy, sadness and anger for an older sibling. These are normal feelings. Young children need a lot of attention and a new baby cuts out attention.

Suggestions:

- Put your older son in overalls. You can easily retrieve your child by picking him up by the overall straps, and you can still continue to nurse your other son.

- Allow your toddler some 'TV time' or 'tablet' time, while you are nursing; make this his special time that he is allowed to watch a favorite show or play a game.

- Have a box of special toys that he has access to only while you nurse. We like to call this box the "Boob Box."

- Buy a doll for your older son, so that he can pretend play and take care of the doll while you tend to your baby.

- Make this special reading time. If you read to him every time you nurse, you will be building his vocabulary and literacy.

- Allow him to do some special crafts, (but nothing messy) or play with toys such as: crayons, blocks, puzzles...only while you are attending to baby.

- Explain what you are doing and make him a part of the experience by asking him to help you out, such as getting a hand cloth for you or fetching other things.

- It's never easy juggling two young children! It does get better!

Toddler Discipline - Bossiness

"My 2.5 year-old is beginning to show bossy traits. She takes toys away from playmates and pushes them when they protest. How do I handle that respectfully?"

Brain development stage: Young children do not share well and can't understand lending or sharing much before age three. They need to grasp the concept of ownership before they understand the true meaning of "sharing" because sometimes sharing means you get it back (like sharing toys on a play date) and sometimes you don't get it back (like sharing a plate of cookies.)

Suggestions:

- Set the kitchen timer to help them take turns.
- Context matters – handle it differently when it is at a friend's house versus a public play place. At a friend's house, you want to spend more time on working it out. At a public place, you can just help your child be more assertive by prompting her to ask for a turn instead of grabbing it.
- Don't grab the toy back – it models aggression. Ask for it back.
- It's a gradual process and they are learning social skills.
- Kids pick up on adult stress. Perhaps don't hover so much in order to make sure they play nicely. See if it works out naturally.
- Unless you see it happen, don't intervene. You don't know what took place. Distract her to another activity.
- It may be a good thing. She is being assertive, but needs to tone it down and learn the adult respectful way of getting what she wants.
- Point out to her that the other child is upset and wants his toy back.
- Put away items beforehand that she doesn't wish to share.
- By age 6, kids get a handle on fairness and really start to police themselves.
- My thoughts are with you – it's a real energy draining experience.
- Kids are ego-centric until about age 6 which means that their world involves around them. It takes a while to learn empathy.
- Help the other child be more assertive by asking him if it really matters to him and showing him how to stand his ground by asking for the toy back.

Toddler Discipline - Aggression

"My 19 month-old daughter is becoming increasingly reactive to other children in the playground. She acts out aggressively, such as shoving and shouting, when other children 'invade' her space."

Brain development stage: Young children have space boundaries that they will protect. They will ward off threats to their special people, toys and space, by hitting and pushing other children. They don't mean to be nasty, but they know of no other way to ask other children to back off.

Suggestions:

- Know that this is a normal stage of development. Understanding this can help take any 'charge' away when you are interacting with your daughter

- When you are disciplining (teaching) your daughter, speak loudly and clearly so that other parents can hear you and know that you are handling the situation. This can help take the judgement away that you feel.

- Go over any family ground rules that you have set up; what is acceptable and not acceptable behavior when dealing with anger issues. Say, "It's ok to hit a pillow but not your sister," or "It's ok to jump on your bed but not mummy's flower garden."

- Set up a safe place for her to express her anger such as a corner full of cushions and cuddly things to throw or yell at.

- Have immediate consequences for her when she takes her aggression out on others; if she hits another child at a park, leave the park and go home. Make sure the consequences solve the problem and are not just meant to punish. Discuss this with her before going to the park, and let her know your expectations and what follow-through there will be if she acts out.

- Be consistent with whatever method of discipline you choose. You may not want to leave the park if you have a friend there, but you have to if you have threatened it. If you don't want to leave, don't threaten it.

- This kind of behavior can feel overwhelming for a parent; know that this will pass. Remember to breathe.

- In your home, put away toys she doesn't want to share with others.

Toddler Discipline - Refuses Car seat

"My 17 month-old son hates his car seat."

Brain development stage: Some children hate their seat and that is normal.

Suggestions:

- Say, "I love you and want you safe. Let's sit in it for awhile."
- Use a car seat every time. No exceptions.
- Move him into the seat and acknowledge his feelings. "I know you are unhappy being here."
- Let him bring a toy with him into the seat.
- Offer a snack. Say, "When we are buckled in, then we can have a snack."

Toddler Discipline - Climbs Furniture

"My 14 month-old son likes to move a chair in order to climb on furniture when I'm feeding the baby."

Brain development stage: Children love to climb and love to explore their environment. They have no knowledge of safety.

Suggestions:

- Childproof. Move everything off the counters so he can't see anything enticing him to climb.
- Supervise constantly.
- Hide the chairs when not in use for meals. Put them up high on the table.
- Put a stick into the drawer handles or buy locks so they don't open by children's hands.
- Anchor big pieces of furniture to the wall - TV's, dressers, bookcases, etc.
- Take him to the park or playground so he can climb there.
- Get up and remove him and say, "No climbing." Repeat over and over. Learn to feed baby upright!

Toddler Discipline - Jumps on the Bed and Sofa

"My 19 month-old daughter loves to jump."

Brain development stage: Young children love to move their bodies, including through climbing and jumping.

Suggestions:

- Give her something to jump on. When we say "No!" we need to distract to something that is a "Yes!" Bouncy balls, mini-trampolines, and old sofa cushions are great to jump on.
- Take her to the park often. She needs to expend energy.
- Accept that a designated bed or sofa will be the jumping one and that you will just eventually have to replace it.

....

Toddler Discipline - Makes Messes and Doesn't Clean Up

"My children make so many messes every day. They pull out toys, and empty my drawers and never put anything away."

Brain development stage: Toddlers are messy in their exploration and don't understand how to clean up. It's normal behavior and a necessary part of their learning. With time and patience, they will learn how to clean up but not until the preschool years. They are capable of learning sorting about age 5 or 6. They can pick up a few items and throw them in a bin though.

Suggestions:

- Only allow them to dismantle one thing at a time. If they pull out a game and then another, stop them and get some help picking up the first game.
- Get them to eat popsicles, watermelon, and messy foods outside. Have a bucket of soapy water and a cloth for clean-up before they come back in.
- Lay out plastic shower curtains under messy activities like painting, play-dough and sand play. Supervise to monitor the mess. Once they start throwing, the play is done and they need you to stop them.

- Give up folding clothes in drawers. They really love to pull out clothes. Someday you will have folded clothes again, but right now, what's the point?
- Have a few drawers they can dismantle such as a plastic container cupboard in the kitchen or a drawer of clothes in your bedroom.
- Jam books (other than board books) into a bookcase so tight that they can't pull them out.
- Provide a lot of interesting, safe toys to play with and rotate them every week so they don't get tired of them. Pack away the current selection and bring out some new ones (not new, but ones that they have not seen for awhile,) so the children don't go rummaging through the cupboards.
- Pack away 90% of the toys so they won't get overwhelmed. When too many toys are out, they play with nothing.
- On days that you are really tired, redirect them to some non-messy play such as big floor toys that are easy to clean-up.
- Make clean-up easy. If toddlers and preschoolers clean up by putting all toys in one bin, that is great. Don't expect sorting.
- Children are more likely to clean up if you work with them. They often won't do it alone by just your command until ages 9-12 years.
- Allow them to combine toys. The creativity builds their brains.
- Have them help you clean up but don't worry yet if they don't. You have plenty of years to teach cleaning. Say, "Let's pick up the blocks," as you are doing it.
- Give up and have a big sort/clean-up once a week or month rather than daily.
- Give up completely. By the time they are teens, all messy play will not occur. And if it does, teens know how to clean up!

....

Toddler Discipline - Draws on Walls

"My son took a permanent marker and drew squiggles on the wall."

Brain development stage: Toddlers are driven to explore with any available tool. They can't discern between okay and not-okay materials because they don't understand the reasoning behind them.

Suggestions:
- Pack away all markers and writing tools and only allow them out when you can constantly supervise.

- Teach, but without the expectation that he will get it. Say "I don't like drawing on the wall. Here, use paper."
- Have him "help" you clean up. Even if he isn't very good at it, he is beginning to learn how to problem-solve.
- Paint one wall with chalkboard paint.
- Put wall paper up and you can strip it off in a few years.
- Get an easel just for him.
- Get him bathtub markers that are easier to clean up. Tell him that only the bathtub walls are open for coloring.

Toddler Discipline - Pesters Parent on Phone

"My 2 year-old daughter hates it when I'm on my phone. She can be occupied and the minute I'm talking to someone, she notices and then pesters me. She is also bad when I'm trying to have a conversation with someone in the store."

Brain development stage: Toddlers don't understand that the voice on the other end is a real person. This is too abstract a concept for them. Your voice alerts them to pay attention to you and they don't understand why they are not getting attention back. It's also very difficult for toddlers to wait. They have more patience in the school-age years.

Suggestions:
Phone

- Take the time to hug, hold and carry her while you are on the phone.
- If you are in the kitchen, get out play-dough or set up some water in the sink that she can play in.
- Have a bucket of special "phone call" toys that you can bring out for important calls.
- Make calls during her naptime.
- Request return calls via email instead. Leave your email address instead of a phone number.
- Get her a junk real phone to pretend with.
- Show her that there is a voice on the other end but don't let her speak. Avoid ever letting her talk to the person as she will want to do it every time for the next

couple weeks. She is too young to understand why she gets to talk to the person one time and not the next time.

In person

- Say, "Mommy needs to talk for five minutes." Show her with your hands what five minutes look like. Remember that she doesn't understand what time "feels" like until age 7.

- Give her a distraction. Pull a flashlight or a toy out of your diaper bag.

Toddler Discipline - Touches Everything

"My son is really hard to take shopping as he touches everything."

Brain development stage: Toddlers are driven to explore with any available tool including hands and mouths

Suggestions:

- Distract to another focus. Give him a snack to concentrate on while shopping.

- Consider not going to "problem" places like museums or toy stores while he is a toddler. Ages 4 and up is a better time for him to understand why he can't touch.

- Child-proof while visiting other people's places or while travelling. Use duct tape to affix socks to table corners, cover outlets, tape the fridge and toilet lid closed.

- Supervise constantly.

- Teach. Say, "Here is how we touch gently." Show him how it's done but supervise.

- Remember children under age 5 only "listen" about 40% of the time.

- Say, "Touch with one finger," every time he wants to touch something whether it is a breakable ornament or pet. He can't do much damage with only one finger and he can't lift the item.

Toddler Discipline - Says "No!"

"My 2 year-old daughter constantly says "No!" when I ask her to do anything. I'm worried that I'm raising a rebellious teenager."

Brain development stage: Learning the "No" word is very important for toddlers. They recognise that it is a power word and try it out on those around them. This is very normal and no indication that you will have a rebellious teenager on your hands! You will want your teenager to say "No!" to bad influences and she needs practice before then. If she say's "No!" to you, take the time to problem-solve what you need her to do.

Suggestions:

- Give her power in the form of choices. Give two choices for her age.
- Limit use of your "No!" to really important things like running in the street, hitting, or safety issues.
- Vary your vocabulary. Say "danger," "hot," "later," or "gentle," to correct her.
- Respect her "No!" on issues related to her body such as tickling, hugs, holding, kisses, etc. Remember, "No!" is a powerful lesson in giving consent. You want other people to respect her "No!"
- Remember that you really do have all the power at her age. Good leaders rarely need to exercise their power. Acknowledge her feelings of powerlessness, by saying, "You really are unhappy about not being able to go to the park today."

Toddler Discipline - Won't Sit Quietly

"My 2 year-old son won't sit quietly at church, or even at his library story time. I'm worried that he will never develop patience."

Brain development stage: Toddlers are driven to explore their surroundings. They can't be expected to sit quietly. As his brain matures, he will develop that ability later. That is why mandatory school doesn't begin until age 6 when he has more self-control to sit and listen. Even then, it is limited. Children learn best when they are active and engaged but a lot of children's programs are not designed by people who know child development. If they can't be still, it's best to leave them at home with a caregiver.

Suggestions:

- Bring engaging toys to interest him for church, restaurants and concerts; where the program is more for you than him.
- If the program is geared to children but doesn't have active engagement (which young children need) in the program, leave.

- If the toys don't work and he is fussy, take him home. Accept that it is normal and your expectations need to conform to his developmental abilities.
- Consider delaying programs for him (such as library story times) until he is older and mature enough to sit still.

Toddler Discipline - Listens to Partner but Not Me

"My 2 year-old child listens moreto his dad than me."

Brain development stage: A dad's louder, deeper voice may sound scarier to a child than a mom's softer voice. As well, children attach to the parent they spend more time with, which is usually, but not always, the mom. Children feel more safe to "be themselves" with the attachment parent.

Suggestions:

- This is a normal phase that many children go through.
- It may be that Dad's voice is deeper and more "authoritative" than yours.
- It may be that you are with the child more of the day and have become a "known quantity" who is a safe person to relax with.
- Don't stress over it. Moms and dads parent differently and it's okay to have those differences. Children listen to each parent differently and they have different dynamics in their relationship which grow and change as they get older. Work on being nurturing, firm and kind and your children will listen and respect you as they get older.

Toddler Discipline - Throws Food

"My 16 month-old toddler likes to throw food and objects."

Brain development stage: Toddlers like to explore the velocity of items in the air. Throwing is natural science exploration. They don't understand how it can harm them, the environment or others.

Suggestions:

- Don't react. Stay calm. He doesn't understand.

- Allow food exploration like squishing it between his fingers but not food throwing. Stop it as soon as it looks like that is going to happen.
- Don't use dishes. Put the food directly on his high chair tray.
- Put a plastic shower curtain under the high chair.
- Feed him first and then put toys on the high chair tray.
- Get a dog in the house to keep the floors food free.
- Keep repeating over and over; "We don't throw food."
- Is the meal time too long? Shorten it. As soon as he is done eating and begins throwing, meal time is over.

Toddler Discipline - Doesn't Listen in Public

"My 2.5 year-old daughter refuses to respond to my "No" in public. She wanders away from me in the stores and won't listen to me. Help!"

Brain development stage: Children under 5 years "listen" or "comply" to parents' directives less than 40 percent of the time.

Suggestions:

- Use your words and give choices such as, "You can either go in the stroller, or you have to hold my hand. You choose."
- Use a leash and attach it to the stroller under the guise of your daughter being responsible to take care of the stroller.
- Have her "help" you guide the shopping cart around the store.
- Have her "help" you cross the street by holding your hand.
- "Train her" to find certain items. She is young, but you can begin to communicate to her that you need her "big girl" help.
- Adjust your schedule, and shop after your daughter is asleep. A nice quiet grocery store can be a meditative experience.
- Give your daughter the card to hand to the cashier, and make it her "Very Important Duty."
- Let her use the small shopping carts at grocery stores. Watch that she doesn't ram them into the ankles of other shoppers.
- Some stores have double carts and truck carts for children that make shopping fun.
- Sit her in the cart with some snacks.

- Give her something to do in the cart, such as coloring, bubbles, or some other toy that is tactile.

....

Toddler Discipline - Throws My Cell Phone

"How can I get my cell phone/tablet back from my toddler when I need it, without her having a fit and throwing it?"

Brain development stage: Children don't understand what is breakable until about age 5. Toddlers don't understand why they can have an object sometimes but not every time.

Suggestions:

- Say "Oops, the batteries ran out. All done!"
- Distraction works. Say "We are going to have a snack now. Let's put down the phone and come."
- Tell her the phone needs a nap. Bring a case to slip it into and call it the "sleeping bag."
- Say "This is the last song/show/game we are watching." Be consistent and take it away after the warning, no matter what the reaction.
- Give closure. Ask your child to say and wave "bye-bye" to the device.
- Make sure it is in a durable case or at least a rubber/silicone encasement.
- Seriously consider never, ever, giving your toddler your phone in the first place. Designate it an adult toy and off limits.
- Get an old smart phone that is not online and let her play the games on it. Ensure she knows that it is her phone and she can never have your phone.

....

Toddler Discipline - Pushes at Daycare

"My 2.5 year-old is pushing other kids at daycare."

Brain development stage: A child may feel crowded and reacts by pushing back.

Suggestions:

- Talk to the daycare staff about pushing. Your son may be seeing a lot of it at daycare and is trying out that behavior.

- Speak to him about empathy.
- Say, "No pushing." Keep repeating.
- Give him other ways to deal with others when they take his toys or invade his space. Teach him how to gather his toys and move, or to put up his hand to ward off space invaders.
- Toddlers are territorial. As a parent, help him protect his toys.
- Don't worry about how it looks (child pushing) to other parents. Other parents watch and judge what you do, not what your child does. Model confidence and kindness and say "Justin, we don't push. Let's move your toys to here." Other parents want to know that you are addressing the situation rather than ignoring your child's behavior.
- Model an apology for the other child, to save the situation and to teach your son how to apologize. Say, "Justin doesn't have the words right now, but we are very sorry for pushing."
- Have a quiet talk at bedtime with your son, when things are calm, about pushing.
- Repetition is the key. He will not be doing this forever, but he needs lots of practice.

Toddler Discipline - Throws When angry

"My toddler throws things when he is angry. What can I teach him to do instead?"

Brain development stage: Young children automatically throw and learn to not throw through self-control development.

Suggestions:
- Say, "No! We don't throw toys!"
- When you say "No", be sure to find a way he can express anger. Say, "Yes, lets stomp our feet!"
- Teach him to put his hand up and "ask" for space.
- Teach him to growl.
- Ask thinking questions - it invites power and choice. "What would you do if everyone threw things when they are mad?"
- Teach him to squeeze stress balls or any type of soft item.

- Give him foam balls, soft baby toys, sponges, or soft stuffed animals to throw at a designated wall that is safe and won't break anything.
- Get him a little sponge bat and a pillow case over the pillow with an "unhappy face" drawn on the pillowcase with fabric marker. That can be his "angry" pillow.
- Teach him to make fists and hit the ground with them.
- Teach him to breathe.
- Teach him to ask for a hug.
- Teach him to kick, or hit a bean bag chair. Call it the "angry chair." Remember that young children are very physical in their anger and begin to use their words more in the school-age years.
- Whatever he can do that calms him down and doesn't hurt anything or anyone should be acceptable ways of handling anger.
- Congratulate and praise him when he shows restraint.

Toddler Feeding – Picky Eating

"My toddler barely eats anything. I am thinking of supplementing with toddler formula to ease my anxiety about him not eating."

Brain development stage: In the first year, your baby tripled his birth weight and ate quite a lot. In the second year, your toddler might gain 5 to 10 pounds because he is very active, and distracted by discovering the world.

Suggestions:

Learn about Ellyn Satter's Feeding Relationship. The parents decide WHAT, WHEN and WHERE the child eats, and the child decides IF and HOW MUCH. The Feeding Relationship involves the division of feeding responsibilities.

The parent's job

What: The parent controls what food is bought, stored, cooked, and served at meal and snack times. Parents control the money and shopping at this age and make most decisions of what to buy and ultimately, what food gets brought into the house.

When: The parent decides when snack and meal times will be. Toddler's tummies are about the size of a ping pong ball, and they need food and drink every two hours. Three meals: breakfast, lunch, and dinner, and three snacks: mid-morning, mid-afternoon, and bedtime per day, is recommended. The parent keeps the food on the table for 20 minutes and then puts the food away until the next scheduled meal or snack.

Where: The parent decides where eating and drinking will take place. Eating at the table should be encouraged to minimize the risk of choking while running, walking, or climbing. It's also a good habit to get into, as non-aware eating can lead to weight issues. When children eat while watching movies, playing video games, or computers, they are not consciously enjoying the food or even paying attention to what they are eating. Although, I have noticed you can easily slip a plate of raw vegetables and dip, under their noses while they are playing video games, and the whole plate is gone in minutes. I don't even think they notice what they just ate!

The child's job

If: The child decides if he will eat, according to his internal hunger cues rather than the clock or schedule. A meal is only a small part of the day's food intake – only 1/6. If your child chooses not to eat, don't worry. He will make up for it at some time later in the day, next day, or in a few days.

How much: The child decides what quantity will satisfy his hunger. This also helps him decide his internal cues.

- If your son doesn't eat, put it away for another 1 hour and 40 minutes until the next snack or meal time. If your child wants food in between those times, say, "Sorry, the kitchen is closed." You may have to endure a tantrum, but that's okay.

- Consult your local health clinic to see what foods, and portions are appropriate for children ages 1-5. These recommendations change all the time when new research is published.

- Serve water in between meals. Don't dilute water with juice. Children need to learn to enjoy the taste of plain water and water between meals protects their teeth against the sugars of milk and juice.

- Serve fruit with fiber instead of juice.

- Serve milk after the meal so they don't fill up with milk.

- Use reverse psychology, "Don't let me catch you eating that broccoli. Don't you dare touch it!"

- Have at least 1 or 2 foods on the table that you know they will enjoy. Fruit, bread and cheese are perennial favorites.

- Serve a healthy dessert, (fruit, yogurt, oatmeal cookies, ice-cream, pudding) on the same plate as the meal. Don't elevate the dessert as being more desirable than the dinner. Don't use dessert as the reward for eating the dinner. It sets up unhealthy attitudes about food value. Children don't start with those preconceptions – we teach them.

More Meal Time Tips

- Food jags are normal, where the child eats nothing but peanut butter and jam sandwiches for three weeks or a longer period of time. That's okay. As long as it's a healthy food, don't worry about their nutritional intake. Researchers found that toddlers eat a variety of foods when they kept a log of their food intake over a one month period.

- It takes 15 tries to accept a new food. Have a one bite routine – try one bite (the no-thank-you bite) and see if your child likes it. If they don't, let them spit it out into a "No thanks" plate. Don't turn the one bite routine into a power struggle. Young children have very sensitive taste buds and they definitely will change. Toddlers like to feel like they are getting something special. Presentation is everything. Vegetables and fruits arranged in a face will appeal to them when a regular tossed salad is ignored.

- Toddlers usually don't eat much at dinner. They are tired and cranky at the end of the day. Track their lunch and breakfast intake.

- Toddlers usually prefer finger type foods.

- Cut a bathmat in half and use it on the highchair seat so they don't slide out.

- To save time, don't use dishes. Put the food right on the tray. Then the plate won't be thrown.

- Stick a popsicle or ice-cream cone into a paper muffin cup to catch drips.

- Give your toddler a spoon for each hand and then you can feed him with a separate spoon. It keeps his hands busy.

- Give a butter spreader knife to help preschoolers cut food.

- Let a toddler practice drinking from an open cup in the bathtub.

- Fill toddler glasses only one third full, and make sure all dishes are plastic.

- Cool hot food by dumping in an ice cube.

- Don't microwave any liquids in a glass or cup with a straw attached. The liquid in the straw heats up hotter than the cup section and can burn your toddler because he drinks it first.

- For fun, serve food on doll or play dishes.

- Think variety: fill an ice cream cone with egg salad, tuna salad, pudding, or yogurt for easy eating.

- Use the football hold to help get the toddler to the sink and use your other hand to splash water on his chin and guide his arms under the sink to wash. Store clean shirts in the kitchen to save running to the bedroom after meal times. Wash food encrusted shirts within a day or two or the food will become moldy.

- Clean highchairs and strollers in the shower. Run water and let the encrusted food soften. Works as well outside in the summer with the hose.

- Dumping, mashing, and throwing food are exploratory behaviors. A little food exploration is part of development. When the food deliberately hits the walls, or the food exploration is testing your patience on a stressful day, it's a signal that mealtime is over. Remove your child from the eating place.

- If your toddler doesn't sit still at mealtime, schedule a burn up activity right before mealtime, and then he will have used up some energy. Before a restaurant visit, go to a playground. In fact, this works well for any event that requires a certain amount of sit still time: weddings, church, movies, concerts. Be thankful for 10 – 15 minutes, as this is all you might get!

- Let him feed himself with non-messy foods like peas and bread pieces while you can still feed him the messy stuff with the spoon.

- Try serving finger foods with dip or sauce. All children love sauces to swirl.

- Serve mini portions of old favorites: pancakes, muffins, meatballs.

- Let your toddler pour his own milk using the dishwasher door as a counter surface. Then you can just close the door after and the mess goes into the dishwasher.

- Serve a tray of carrot sticks, broccoli florets, red pepper, and salad dressing as you are getting dinner ready. Guaranteed it will be gone!

- You can pretend to sprinkle sugar over the cereal and your toddler will not notice the difference. Just wave your spoon over and your toddler will think you put sugar and salt on their food.

- Buy sugary cereal and only put 10 pieces on top of healthy cereal as a garnish.

- Always serve a plate of raw vegetables as a first course. Children will eat raw vegetables over cooked most days.

- When yogurt and applesauce containers have a lid, leave the lid on and push a straw through so they can suck up the contents without mess.

- Keep a jar of pancake batter in the fridge. Then you could add frozen fruit, or cheese to the batter to make all kinds of pancakes that kids love.

- Young children tend to like their food separated. Avoid casseroles if possible.

- Purée vegetables to hide in soups and sauces.
- Avoid classifying food into "good" and "bad" categories. Use "more nutritious" and "less nutritious" so you get your child into the habit of making better food choice decisions.
- Avoid punishing or rewarding your child with food items.
- Treats are occasional foods. They wouldn't be called treats if they were served every day. Designate a treat day such as Fridays. Have an 80/20 rule. 80% healthy food served and 20% treats. Or, only have treats on picnics.
- Avoid bargaining using food. Parents who say, "Eat four more bites of your hamburger and then you can have your toy," are setting themselves up for power struggles. Children learn very quickly that parents want them to eat, and by refusing, they can get attention and control. Give children attention for positive behavior and control in the form of choices. Don't make eating a power struggle. It's better if you don't watch what and how much they eat.
- Preserve the social function of food. A comforting, social, happy atmosphere at meal and snack time and a wide variety of healthy foods is all that's needed for healthy childhood nutrition.

Toddler Feeding - Refuses High Chair

"My 16 month-old son doesn't like to stay in a high chair. He is even worse in restaurants. Yet, when he is out of a high chair, he runs around while eating."

Brain development stage: Some children dislike being restrained.

Suggestions:
- Go out for meals early so service is fast.
- Pre-feed him so that he is not so cranky.
- Try buffets so you can get food right away.
- Let him play with straws or ice-cubes on the high chair tray.
- Bring snacks and small toys from home.
- Let him color with washable markers on the tray and paper.
- Choose seats near the windows so he can see out of them.
- Tag team with your partner so one person eats and one person takes him out to avoid a tantrum.

- Let him sit in a regular chair but use a restraint to keep him upright. Childproof the table.
- Move him to a booster seat early.
- Say, "You must sit while eating or you could choke."
- If he gets up while eating, remove the food.
- Consider having a floor picnic. Supervise, so he doesn't get up.

....

Toddler Feeding - Handling Halloween Candy

"What do I do with all the Halloween candy that I don't want my young child to eat?"

Brain development stage: Young children do not understand why candy might be bad for their teeth, or their weight.

Suggestions:

- Donate or sell to a teenage neighbor who is too old to go house-to-house but loves candy.
- Sell it at $2 per pound at the neighborhood buy and sell site.
- Hide it in a clean broccoli bag and freeze it in order to hand out next year.
- Save it in order to have more candy to decorate a gingerbread house for the holidays.
- Sell it to the dentists.
- Donate it to a local food bank who gives it to their families for holiday stocking stuffers and birthday party treat bags.
- Ask your child to pick out 30 favorites. Then, leave the rest in a bag on the front step for the Sugar Plum Fairy or the Switch Witch to exchange it for a substantial, really desired toy.
- Sock it away in the laundry room for you to enjoy privately!
- Allow her one treat per day.
- Allow her to eat as much as she wants as long as it is after meals only, and hope she get sick of it soon. (This does work. Children do stop eating it!)
- As one of my children said, "Taking children trick or treating, and then taking away the candy is like winning the lottery and having to give all the money back." Problem-solve with your child for a mutual solution that meets both your needs.

- Pack it away (far away in the garage) to give out to trick-or-treaters next year. This works with most hard candy but not chocolate which can get a white tinge.

....

Toddler Feeding - Only Drinks Milk

"How can I encourage my 16 month-old child to eat more healthy foods? She won't eat meat and only likes yogurt, and drinks a huge quantity of milk served in bottles."

Brain development stage: Children eat according to their body's natural needs. They learn whether foods are good or bad by the socialization from other people.

Suggestions:

- Wean her off the bottles and on to a cup. Offer full strength milk in a cup and dilute the milk in the bottle with water, so the cup becomes the better tasting choice.
- Her eating sounds normal. Young children have food jags where they only eat certain foods for a long time.
- You are in control of giving her healthy foods, regular meals and snacks. Offer milk in a cup and water in a bottle.
- Blend soup and grind meat so she is getting a bit of iron and protein.
- Offer small amounts of foods; perhaps in a different presentation.
- Try giving her more beans and vegetarian options such as eggs, cheese, quinoa and nut butters spread thinly on crackers for protein options.
- Serve a guaranteed-to-eat food at every meal or snack; most kids eat bread, cheese or apples.

....

Toddler Feeding - Refuses Sippy Cups

"My 14 month-old will only drink milk from a bottle."

Brain development stage: Toddlers often find comfort in a bottle. The sucking motion soothes them especially during tumulus times. Unless the dentist is concerned, like pacifiers, children can have them until age 5.

Suggestions:

- Bottles for that age are soothing things. Let her have it. No research supports taking it away just because "it looks bad that a toddler is having a bottle."

- Get a special cup just for milk. Put water only in a bottle.

- Don't worry about it and don't turn it into a power struggle. In the long run, it doesn't matter if she drinks from a cup or bottle. When she heads to Kindergarten, she will not be drinking from a bottle due to peer pressure.

- Read her books about giving up the bottle.

- Don't let the bottle leave the house. Say that the bottle is happier when left at home.

- Put a bigger hole in the top of the nipple so it is not easy to suck out of. Then she might prefer a sippy or open cup.

....

Toddler Health - Refuses Teeth Brushing

"How do I get my 14 month-old to brush his teeth?"

Brain development stage: Most toddlers hate tooth-brushing. They don't like foreign objects in their mouths and it feels invasive to them. Parents should assist with tooth-brushing until the child is 8 years old to ensure a good job is done.

Suggestions:

- Have two toothbrushes, one for your son to use and one for you. You could brush his teeth and he could brush yours at the same time.

- Brush teeth the same time and same place, every day, so it becomes routine.

- Use non-fluoride toothpaste, but get a flavor that tastes good.

- Use a washcloth to wipe gums instead of brushing.

- Have a tooth-brushing song while brushing. Sing or play it on your player.

- Have a nightly family tooth-brushing time where everyone does it together.

- Get a sonic toothbrush so that you catch a good rub if you can't get in there for long.

- Brush in an unusual place; the closet, mudroom, or garage.

- Pretend you are catching the sugar-bugs. Say "Hey, we got them!"

- Pretend that you are the dentist and play make-believe dentist.

- Give him a baby "nubbly" thing to gnaw on. This helps with teething and gets some plaque out of the teeth.
- Sit him in front of a mirror so he can explore his mouth with a brush.
- Get a few colored toothbrushes and let him pick which one to use.
- Have your partner distract him with a story.
- Let him play in the sink while you brush.
- Wait until he is rolled in a towel after a bath and can't get his arms out.
- Brush the teeth with no toothpaste while he is asleep. (You can do this for nail clipping, hair trimming and sunscreen as well!)
- While you are brushing his teeth, get him to open his mouth really wide and you can tell him what you see in there (make up things like a fireperson, dog, lion, the moon, a pineapple, snake, etc). The more fun it is, the less power struggle it is.
- Have a competition to see if you or him can brush the fastest.
- Get a timer that sings a song for the length of time it takes to brush.
- Each time you brush, concentrate on doing an extra good job in one quadrant of the mouth. Rotate.

....

Toddler Health - Cold Weather Exercise

"My child won't play outside. Where can we get some exercise?"

Brain development stage: Small children are easier to entice outside. They will definitely like to go if you go with them. However, indoor play places are great for snowy winter days. Children who get regular exercise tend to eat and sleep better.

Suggestions:
- Moms' time-out groups
- Leisure centers have drop-in playrooms
- School playgrounds and parks
- Walk around shopping malls
- Swimming pools
- Science centers
- Libraries now have play centers

- Zoo's have many indoor exhibits
- Church playgroups
- Airport for the day
- Coffee and play places
- Stores that offer play places

Toddler Parenting Partner - Finding Me-Time

"My toddler is very demanding. How can I find some time just for myself?"

Brain development stage: Toddlers need caregivers emotionally, and physically. However, caregivers need time off to feed their soul and feel good about themselves in order to be a better, patient parent.

Suggestions:

- Instead of you going out, send your partner out with the kids for the whole day if possible.
- Have a mothers-helper come in and play with the kids while you get a nagging job done or work on a satisfying hobby, or just rest.
- Use screen time for the kids, and lose the guilt.
- Have quiet time after lunch where children play in their rooms, even if they don't nap anymore. Keep this time as a regular routine.
- Join a babysitting co-op.
- Drop the kids in those store supervised play areas and go have a coffee in the store cafeteria.
- Join a parent's time-out group with cheap babysitting provided.
- Pay a day-home or daycare for just one day a week.
- Have a sitter come the same evening every week so you and your partner can get out with or without each other.
- Go for a walk with the kids in the stroller and listen to music or an e-book.

Toddler Play - No Friends

"I'm worried about my three sons who don't request play dates, or seem to want closer friends. Should I leave things as is?"

Brain development stage: Young children need adults more than they need peers to play with. Peers are not inherently nurturing, but adults are. Peers are okay to have around, but adults should expect just as much fighting as playing, especially until they head into more cooperative play at around age three and up. Until then, toddlers just engage in parallel play, side by side, until they need to swipe their peer's toy.

Suggestions:

- Don't worry about it - make play dates anyways.
- Children have different friendships based on interests.
- Make sure they have the right "making friends" skills. (See Socialization skills under the General Parenting section.)
- "Friend" to them is different than "friend" to us.
- At this age, adults are more important than friends.
- Be aware of temperament - every child has different social needs.
- Healthy people need only one good friend. And that can be a sibling too!

Toddler Play - Activity Overload

"How do I know if I have enrolled my child in too many activities?"

Brain development stage: Overwhelmed children act out because they don't have the words or ability to tell you that they are stressed. Tummy troubles, tantrums, resistance, headaches, are all ways that small children communicate that they might need some down time and especially chill time with a caring adult.

Suggestions:

- Look at his daily activities does he sleep okay, eat well and is generally active and enthusiastic?
- Does he have some time every day to just zone out, play or think?
- Does he look forward to the next activity meeting date?
- Is his behavior getting worse – cranky, tired, not wanting to go?
- Is his mood generally optimistic?
- Does he resist going to the activity more and more?

- If things are sliding to the point where you are getting more resistance from him, you might want to reconsider dropping some activities.

Toddler and Siblings - Introducing a New Baby

"How do I communicate to a toddler that changes are coming when the new baby comes?"

Brain development stage: Toddlers have no clue of the future or past. Their brains are "in the moment." Preparation is good for you but probably lost on them.

Suggestions:

- Have your toddler sit close to you even though your tummy is big.
- Modify who does what child care jobs. Get your toddler used to your partner doing more things.
- Crouch down to her level.
- Say, "Mommy's tired," or "Mommy's tummy hurts," if you can no longer carry her. Blame your lack of energy or time on anything other than the new baby.
- Explain your situation. She can understand much more than you think.
- Keep routines as much as possible.
- Tell her she can't jump on people.
- Kids adjust. Even if you can't pick her up, she can get close to you while you are sitting down.
- When you introduce the baby to your toddler in the hospital, be sure your hands are free to greet your toddler.

Toddler and Siblings - Transitions with a New Baby

"How do I handle the transition from one child in the family to two children?"

Brain development stage: The first baby is the hardest transition. The second and subsequent children present time management challenges, but those are easier to overcome. The first baby is 90% lifestyle adjustment; the second is only 10%.

Suggestions:

- Ask for help! Then ask for more help! Assign specific jobs to specific people.
- Be good to yourself and give yourself treats every day.
- Don't try to separate them too much. Let the older child touch and interact with the younger one.
- Use swings, bouncy chair, carriers when you need your hands free to attend to the older child.
- Never, ever leave the toddler alone with the baby.
- Grocery shop and buy whatever you can online.
- Hire a housecleaner if you can.
- Get out for walks, fresh air and company every day.
- Pay attention to your partner. Give him some time too.
- A new member of the family is always a transition time. Be easy on yourself and everyone else during this adjustment period.

....

Toddler and Siblings - Both Crying at the Same Time

"My 2 year-old daughter has begun tantrums. She cries when I'm holding her 5 month-old baby brother and then he cries when I put him down to comfort her."

Brain development stage: Toddlers feel jealousy but don't know how to express it to you. Their frustration and anger erupt in tantrums because they don't have the self-control yet to contain or explain it.

Suggestions:

- Sometimes put the baby down so your toddler can see that her feelings matter too.
- Spend a day just with her.
- Sit on the couch and color with her, read to her, or just play with her.

- Carry her in a backpack and him in a front carrier at the same time if you can manage it.

- Say, "Wait a minute son; I'm doing something with your sister right now," so she can hear that she doesn't always come last. Of course, try to attend to the baby too without drawing attention to it.

- Sit in the rocking chair with two crying children and have a good cry yourself! It gets better! Someday, when they are both in college helping each other edit essays, and loaning each other funds, you will know that close sibling relationships pay off!

Toddler and Siblings - Fighting

"My 2 year-old son and my 6 year-old daughter have very different styles of play; it escalates into biting and kicking and I am always having to intervene! My son simply adores my daughter, and my daughter is frustrated with always having to share her space. I need some help with this sibling rivalry!"

Brain development stage: All love relationships have conflict. Conflicts begin and end with feelings. Our job as parents is to help children sort out their feelings and resolve the conflicts.

Suggestions:

- Make sure each child is having adequate independent play time. A chance for them to explore their own world their own way.

- Know in your heart that this too shall pass. Sibling rivalry is a normal part of development and is no indicator of how they will treat each other as adults.

- Use distraction techniques. Take one away to do something else.

- Make her the "daycare" lady; encourage your daughter's own natural nurturing tendencies towards her younger brother.

- Give them both a snack even if it is close to dinnertime. Food helps settle down.

- Acknowledge both their feelings. Say, "It sounds like you are both upset. How can I help?"

- Wear ear plugs when the screaming gets to you.

- Change the environment - Say, "Let's go out!"

- Have your daughter use her words when she feels she needs some personal space. Tell her the words to use.

- Give each sibling space to have alone time - sibs can sometimes be overwhelming.

- Get a mini-trampoline or bounce ball to burn off energy if the weather outside is bad.
- Connect with your daughter and let her know you understand what she is going through by acknowledging her feelings. It's not easy having to share parents.
- Spend lots of time alone with her. Hire a sitter if you have to.
- Make sure the younger one is truly upset at the older one. If not, just let it go. They will sort it out when they are older.

Toddler and Siblings - Making More Time for Older Child

"How can I make more time for my toddler and include him in my day while caring for an infant?"

Brain development stage: Toddlers don't understand parents' duties to other children. They need a lot of attention and do not understand sharing yet.

Suggestions:
- It will get easier – keep reassuring yourself.
- Spend focused time with him when baby is napping or nursing. Read a book, do a craft, play a game, or just cuddle and sleep. Even a nap or cuddle is nice.
- Go for a little walk with the toddler around the house.
- Put the baby in a carrier and take both to the park.
- Take only the toddler out shopping when partner is home to care for the baby.
- Be sure to do some of the toddler's bedtime routine. Don't always leave it to your partner - he needs you too.
- Spend less time on social media and more interacting time with your toddler. He needs you right now.

Toddler Sleep - Won't Sleep in the Crib

"My 13 month-old was sick and slept with us in our bed. Now that she is well, she screams when we put her back into her crib. Our bed is small and she is disturbing my partner who needs a good night's sleep. She also won't nap unless I am there, but I need to get things done."

Brain development stage: A very young toddler doesn't know that when you are out of sight, you are still there. They think you are gone and experience separation anxiety.

Suggestions:

- She might still be sick. Be sure she is 100% better.
- Get a double bed now and try putting her in her bed and stay with her. At least you can sleep with her in that one.
- You could put a futon on the floor in your room and sleep with her there until she is used to sleeping alone.
- If you have clothes with your scent on them, try putting her to bed with those.
- Put your partner on the crib side, so she might just see him and be less likely to wake you.
- Put the crib sidecar to the bed so you can move her over when she is asleep.
- For naps, get her to nap on the couch so she can see you. Make the house boring.
- Get a backpack and let her nap on you while you get things done.
- Do sitting things like surf the internet on your tablet, do email while she is napping on you, so you can get some quiet activities done. Watch You-tube with earphones on.

Toddler Sleep - Wakes too Early From Naps

"How do I keep my 21 month-old asleep longer at naptime?"

Brain development stage: A toddler's sleep pattern may be disrupted due to teething, excitement about exploring, and separation anxiety. Thus, he wakes up sooner. A child's sleep cycle is about 20 minutes light sleep, followed by 1 hour deep sleep and another 30 minutes of dreaming, REM (Rapid Eye Movement) sleep.

Suggestions:

- Lay down with him at naptime. Cuddled children usually sleep longer.
- Go for a drive and if he falls asleep in his car seat, grab a pillow from the back seat, and nap with him in the car.

- Call it "quiet time" instead of "nap time" and give him toys to keep busy. He will nap if he is tired.

- Get your partner to take him out so you can nap.

- Wear him in a carrier so you can get things done. Put him down when he has finished that first 20 minute light sleep, has awoken, and gone back down into the deep sleep portion of the sleep cycle.

- Move the clocks an hour a head and tell him it's naptime.

- Put a movie on to quiet down the house and see if he falls asleep. Usually when children are horizontal and quiet, they fall asleep.

- Run a fan or white noise to keep him out longer.

- Get him to associate sleep with a particular music track or a movie and play the same thing every time you expect him to sleep.

Toddler Sleep - Won't Nap

"My 2 year-old refuses to nap, but still needs one. How do I encourage this?"

Brain development stage: Toddlers vary in their sleep needs. Some toddlers drop all naps around age 18 months and other's need a midday nap until age 6. If a child is cranky, they probably still need a nap.

Suggestions:

- Lay down with her, be still and see if she nods off.

- Make a nap nest. Use a box, corner or small children's tent and set up pillows, blankets, stuffed animals and books.

- Have a routine with same time and place every day. Call it quiet or downtime.

- Let her watch a movie or look at books.

- Go for a drive and park somewhere when she is asleep. Keep a pillow and blanket in the car and you can read, or sleep in the front seat while she naps.

- Give a back or foot massage to relax her and keep her horizontal. The more she lies down the more likely she will nod off. Even when watching a movie, get her horizontal.

Toddler Sleep - Dropped Naps

"My toddler no longer naps. How can I keep him busy so I can rest or take a nap?"

Brain development stage: Toddlerhood is the most active, busy stage of childhood. Unless they are napping, they are on-the-go busy. Their brains are driving them to explore and they don't understand danger. Supervision is a must, but a conflict of needs arise when the parent needs rest and the toddler doesn't.

Suggestions:

- Use technology. Go to the library and stock up on videos. Get out the tablet, computer or whatever. Sleep makes this necessary!
- Rotate toys and bring out a fresh bucket of non-messy toys when you really need a one-eye couch snooze.
- Use some drop-in daycares. Keep a pillow in the car and snooze in the car while he is being cared for by adults in the daycare.
- Arrange a alternate afternoon play-date with another parent in the same situation so every other day, you have the afternoon off.

Toddler Sleep - Late to Bed

"My 17 month-old girl stays up too late at night, and wakes late in the morning."

Brain development stage: Every child has their own inborn sleep needs and schedule. Parents can't force sleep but can facilitate it.

Suggestions:

- Get her to have a good nap during the day.
- Wake her up earlier and earlier while putting her to bed earlier and earlier. Shift her schedule by little bits every night – 15 minute increments are best.
- Put her in the crib awake but with some toys.
- Use music with a beat similar to a heartbeat to lull her to sleep.

- Routine is so important. Have a regular bath/teeth/pajamas/book/cuddle time routine and do it every night. Shorten it but don't eliminate bits if you are rushed for time.
- Try giving her a heating pad to keep warm.

Toddler Sleep - Night Nursing

"How do I stop night nursing my 18 month-old when I co-sleep?"

Brain development stage: Children who nurse into toddlerhood find comfort in nursing as well as nutritional benefits that continue even though they are on solid food. There are several reasons that a toddler might continue nursing. Night time comfort is given in the form of nursing. Nursing could also be a sleep association which cues the child to go back down into another sleep cycle. Or nursing could just satisfy the need for calories that the toddler is too busy to eat during the day.

Suggestions:

- Have your partner give him a bottle with breast milk in it. You stay in another room.
- Dilute the breast milk so that more proportion of water decreases the proportion of breast milk.
- Give your son a shirt or something that smells of you while he has the bottle.
- Give him a comfort item such as a stuffed animal or special blanket.
- Tell him that your breasts have to go "Night-night."
- For a period of two weeks, perhaps sleep in another room after he is asleep and have your partner comfort him during those times he wakes up wanting to nurse.
- Have a small snack of juice or cow's milk for him to drink from a cup.

Toddler Sleep - Shared Room Party

"My toddler and preschooler share a bedroom. They take a long time to settle down and are sometimes so noisy at bedtime, they wake the baby in the next room. What do I do?"

Brain development stage: Young children do not understand quiet or "settle down." They feel excited when they are excited. They need an adult's help in settling down, and facilitating a quiet environment.

Suggestions:

- Give sleep inducing snacks – milk, cheese, etc.
- Use lavender aromatherapy or use a homeopathy spray to induce sleep.
- Put them to bed in sequence. When one is asleep, put the other to bed. Share duties with your partner and each take one. Switch the next night.
- Put one in the guest room or your bedroom to separate them. Move them back to their room later.
- Put black paper in the window or buy black-out blinds.
- Put a white noise machine in the baby's room so she can't hear the party.
- Put them to settle down, with book-tapes or a video. Insist that they have to be horizontal for the stories to continue. Eventually, one will fall asleep.
- Let them play until they drop, as long as they stay in their rooms. Or, as long as they stay in their beds.
- Set a time to "turn the house down" which is turning off quite a few main lights, quiet down the house and put night lights around the halls and rooms. It cues everyone that it is "settle down" time.
- Start bedtime earlier – perhaps 7 p.m. instead of 8 p.m.
- Commit to new habits for 30 days. Often we toss out good ideas after two tries of "not working" but don't give new routines a chance to work.
- Cuddle or lay down with each child for about 10 minutes every night. They often like to chat and open up about a lot of issues.
- Stay in the room if that is what it takes to settle them down. Move in a table and do some work.

Toddler Sleep - Night Waking

"My 2 year-old keeps waking me up at night. She cries for me to tuck her back into bed."

Brain development stage: Toddlers miss their parents and caregivers, especially at night. Night waking gets better after the teeth molars come in.

Suggestions:

- Leave the door open so she can come and crawl in with you.
- Give her high protein snacks before bed.
- Put her crib or a mattress on the floor next to your bed.
- Get up, lead her back into her room and say goodnight, if you don't want to co-sleep. Be boring, kind and don't talk or engage at all. Repeat as many times as necessary. Keep it dark.
- Make a bedtime photo-book of routines (this can be done for most activities that you would like them to do – getting out the door, toileting process, eating process, play-date etiquette, etc) Take photographs of your child doing activities and upload them into a store that makes the books. Write captions of what you want them to do such as "wash hands," "share," "food stays on the plate," "we stay in our bed at night," or "we can cuddle our bear," so the photo-book will read as a story book. Or, you can have the child do the drawings instead of taking photographs. Books cost about $20 and are a very nice keepsake.
- Remember that this stage shall pass too.
- Avoid giving excessive cuddles and rewards for waking up. Be boring and bland.
- Give her your shirt or something that smells of you so she can cuddle that in bed. Get a big body pillow and put 2 of your worn shirts over each end.
- Send in your partner instead of you.
- Give her a bottle or breast to go back to sleep. Finish the bottle - don't let milk pool in her mouth while she falls asleep.
- Use white noise to keep her asleep.
- Use lavender oils.
- Set up a digital photo frame in her room with big head-shot photos of you and your child together or just smiling headshots of you or your partner.
- Tape a lollipop to the top of the door and promise that she can have it the next day if she stays in bed.

....

Toddler Sleep - Won't Sleep Alone

"How can I encourage my child to go to sleep by himself?"

Brain development stage: Toddlers go through separation anxiety where if they don't see their loved ones, they are anxious of where they are and feel afraid.

Suggestions:

- Find a toy glowworm or lighted cuddly.
- Have some "me-time" for you before the bedtime routine so you won't feel frustrated when he is not giving you space for "me-time" later.
- Talk to him about how we need sleep.
- Be consistent in taking him back to bed.
- Make the bed special with bedding or a canopy.
- You could take extra naps on weekends.
- Do something noisy in the next room so he is comforted by the sound of you moving around. Sing so he can hear you.
- Talk about what you are going to do tomorrow.
- Use a white noise machine to lull him to sleep.
- Get a gate to keep him in the room, but he can see you.
- Get your partner to go in and put him back to bed.
- Give him a little tent on top of a toddler bed on the floor of your bedroom. Gives him (and you) privacy but he is near you for comfort.
- Find a sibling for him to sleep with.
- Let him start in your bed and move him to his bed when you go to bed.
- Let him sleep on the couch if he promises to be quiet. Move him back to his bed later.
- Set up a desk in his room, and do some quiet work there while he falls asleep.

Toddler Sleep - Wakes Early in Family Bed

"My 19 month-old girl stays up too late at night, and wakes too early in the morning."

Brain development stage: Every child has their own inborn sleep needs and schedule. The trick is to keep her busy while you sleep.

Suggestions:

- Make sure the entire room is child-proofed.
- Be boring. Don't entertain her. Pretend you are asleep so she goes back to sleep.

- Have a basket of small toys for her to play with.
- Have a TV anchored to the wall and a remote close by, so you can flick on the TV and catch a few more Z's
- Have a small snack that she can access but not make a mess.
- Get up, make some strong coffee and know these nights will pass all too quickly.

Toddler Toileting - Won't Sit on the Potty

"My toddler won't even try to sit on the potty. How can I entice him to try it?"

Brain development stage: The average age to toilet train is 2 to 3.5 years and it takes cognitive development of the brain for the child to know when the urge is coming, and physical development for the child's body, to be able to run to the toilet in time. Every child is different as to when that takes place.

Suggestions:

- Treat toileting matter-of-factly and don't take setbacks personally.
- Give him a sticker chart, chocolate chips, or a reward system for trying the seat.
- Take a break from potty training. Let it go for a few months, so the power struggles are out of his memory.
- Let him play with the potty and put his dolls and stuffed animals on it.
- Read the books that he really loves, while he sits on there.
- Wait until he is ready. Use a big toilet so your options are wider when going out.
- Use a stool to support his feet. Many children want a stable base to put their feet on while sitting on the potty.
- Let him pick out his new underwear.

Toddler Toileting - Accidents

"My 2.5 year-old goes pee and poo in her pants and then tells me after she is done. Should I put her back in diapers or nudge her to toilet train? I have a new baby."

Brain development stage: The transition period of having a new baby makes toilet training hard, because the parent needs the toddler to be independent, and the toddler needs attention, which can be acquired through messing up toilet training.

Suggestions:

- Remind her to sit on the potty at consistent times of the day.
- Treat it matter-of-factly. "Oops, let's clean up. Get a cloth."
- Consider whether she is really ready. Relax and let it go. She is only 2.5 yrs.
- Make it easier for her to pull up her pants. Have an easy to reach step stool, pump soap, easy to reach towel.
- Get her stickers to put on a weekly calendar for those times she makes it to the potty.
- Make a big celebration of her successes.
- Ask her to help you clean up the underwear.
- Stay home for one week, put her in underwear and train her in boot camp timing.
- Get a potty seat that she really likes.
- Invite an older child friend over that she really likes and let her watch the other child use the bathroom.
- Put her in cloth diapers so she feels the wet sensations more than the "pull-up" type of diapers.
- Use underwear beneath the diaper.
- Use underwear but use liners so it's easier to clean up.
- Use bribery such as chocolate chips when she makes it.
- Let it go for a few weeks.
- She may need attention because of the baby, and soiling her underwear is one way to get it. Help her get attention in more positive ways such as one-on-one time with you and the other parent.
- Make a potty fort, house, or castle out of a really large appliance box and set it around the potty seat. Let her decorate it with stickers, sparkles, and that can be her special room.

Toddler Toileting - Tips for Easier Potty Training

"What are some tips to facilitate potty training?"

Brain development stage: Rewards work if the brain is developmentally ready to begin potty training.

Suggestions:

- Use insert seats and take them with you when you go out.
- Children will want to be wiped until they are older and can do a better job, around 5 years of age.
- Ignore advice from others. Do it when it works for you. There is no magic window for timing.
- Tell her that if she uses the toilet, she can phone "whoever is her current favourite hero or TV star" and then get an aunt or uncle to take the call and pretend to be the hero giving lots of encouragement.
- Put floating candles in the toilet and light them. Pretend that you son is a firefighter and can use the "hose" to put out the fire. This also works with cheerios floating in the toilet. Be sure to supervise!
- Use stickers if she is ready.
- Consider non-food rewards such as blowing out a supervised candle.

Toddler Toileting - Signs of Readiness

"How do I know my toddler is ready?"

Brain development stage: Sometime between the ages of one year and four years of age, your toddler will be ready to tackle the toilet. This is a process that often is two steps forward and one step back. Be positive, proactive and encouraging and toilet training will go smoother.

Suggestions:

Your child is ready when...

- He is uncomfortable in wet or dirty diapers.
- He is able to hold urine and stool long enough to make it to the toilet.

- He notices he is peeing or having a bowel movement.
- He can understand simple directions.
- He tells you by facial expressions that he needs to go.
- He is able to walk or run quickly to the bathroom.
- He is able to pull his pants up and down.
- He says and understands one-word statements – wet, dry, potty, go.
- He is able to stay dry for at least two hours, or wakes up dry from a nap.
- There are a few well-formed stools a day rather than frequent little movements.
- He wants to be trained, or asks to go, or tells you when he is about to go.
- He is anxious to please you.
- He has a sense of social appropriateness (wet pants can be an embarrassment).

Your child is NOT ready if...

- There is a change in his life: new baby, move, new caregiver, or divorce.
- He is going through a negative stage and resists cooperation with you.
- You want to train due to outside pressures: family, preschool entrance, friends.
- He has no interest or curiosity yet.

Are you ready?

- Can you drop everything when he needs to go, in order to help with wiping, hand washing, etc?
- Can you accept accidents and setbacks with patience and encouragement?
- Is this a non-stressed time for you?
- There is no magic window for toilet training. If it becomes too much for your child or you, there is nothing wrong with putting him back into diapers and trying again in a few weeks or months, when things are more positive in both your lives.

Toddler Toileting - Refuses Training

"My son doesn't want to pee in the toilet."

Brain development stage: Toileting is one of four things that parents can't force children to do. The other three are eating, sleeping and learning.

Suggestions:

- Let him see you do it.
- Treat it matter-of-factly. The more you want him to do it, the more power he gains by not doing it.
- Allow him power in positive ways such as giving him the power to choose between two options. Give choices as much as possible.
- Offer, "Would you like to pee in the toilet, or pee in the diaper?" One day he will eventually choose the toilet option. Or you could say, "Do you want to use the upstairs toilet or the downstairs toilet?"

Toddler Toileting - Holds Stool

"My 2 year-old is holding his stool. Our family has been travelling and he has just begun potty training."

Brain development stage: Toilet training should take place when the child is in a fairly cooperative stage, more toward the end of toddlerhood, and when there are no stress periods in the family. Travelling is a positive stress, but still one that impacts toilet training. Jet lag and change in water composition can make regularity difficult.

Suggestions:

- You are doing all the right things, just keep encouraging him to go.
- Feed him fiber rich foods like corn, vegetables, seeds, fruit and whole grains.
- Buy him a new "special" potty.
- Give rewards, incentives for going. Example: a jar with treats on the back of the toilet.
- Give him enough water to keep the fibre moving.
- Give him water with brown sugar mixed into it or prune juice.
- It will happen when it happens. Unless he becomes constipated, nature will ensure he empties.
- Use bottled water instead of tap water. Some places have very hard water.

Toddler Toileting - Wiggly Diaper Changes

"My 2 year-old moves while I try to change her diaper. How can I get her changed?"

Brain development stage: Toddlers' brains drive them to move!

Suggestions:

- Do up the diaper first and then slide it on her like a "pull-up diaper."
- Change her standing up on the bathroom counter while she faces the front of the bathroom mirror. You are standing right behind her. Pull down her pants so her legs are anchored by the pants around her ankles. Take the soiled diaper off by pulling the tabs and removing the diaper. Wipe from front to back. Stand right behind her and use your chest for her to lean her back on and position the back of the new diaper to her bum. Pull the front of the diaper up and seal the tabs. The mirror distracts her while you can change her from behind.
- If it's a urine diaper, change her on the run.
- Give her an item from a "forbidden item" basket that she doesn't get any other time. Old remotes, phones etc.
- Distract her with a toy, book or songs.
- Give her a lump of play-dough to keep her hands busy. Pull down her pants only to her knees so she can't run away.
- Set up a change station in front of the TV and only turn it on for diaper changes.
- Give a warning with a timer as to when you will start.
- If she really resists, have her undress for the bath and run a tub if you have time. This works well when the child has diaper rash from not allowing you to change her. Getting her into the tub and clean helps. Let her air dry her bottom by running around naked after the bath for a few minutes, to reduce the redness.

Preschoolers 3-5 Years

The stage of "Why?" and "No!"

....

What Can Preschoolers Do?

Preschoolers 3 to 5 Years: Pre-Operational Stage

Physical

- Can jump, kick, swing, skip, hop, run, and throw balls

- Shows intense facial expressions

- Can empty wastebaskets, bring in groceries, mop a floor, spray-clean surfaces, vacuum, pick up socks and library books, set table, help with recycling

- Sleeps twelve hours a night, drops daytime naps

- Can use a toilet independently by four years

- Active, energetic and moves body in coordinated way

- Can hold a pencil and scissors; can print name by five years

- Can fully dress and undress self; uses buttons and zippers

- Can cut food with a knife and use fork and cups; learns to pour

- Can ride a tricycle at three years and a bike with training wheels at five years

- Can brush teeth at five years but needs supervision until eight years

- Less physical and impulsive than toddlers but can still be overcome with emotion

Cognitive

- No understanding of safety considerations or what causes death

- Can't imagine logical outcome of certain actions (operations) on objects or people. Can't foresee consequences

- Intense imagination; magical thinking

- Animism: may have imaginary friends or pets; stuffed animals are "real" to them

- Can't see other's point of view at three years, but can at five years

- Doesn't understand lying as inappropriate, but as wishful thinking; tells tall tales

- Beginning to connect outcomes with actions (consequences) at five to six years

- Asks a lot of questions; wants to know how things work, including how babies are made; says "What's that?" a lot

- Manipulates objects to learn characteristics

- Stops putting things in his mouth to explore

- Needs to play; gets lost in play and is not distracted by other things

- Adults can understand 75% of speech

- Can say words for everything and use three-word sentences at age three and tell complete stories at age five

- Understands three hundred to one thousand words

- Knows his name and age

- May count numbers and know colors

- Can understand between edible and inedible substances: dirt, shampoo, toilet water

- Unaware of traffic safety; still impulsive

- Can sing, rhyme, and tell jokes

- Able to join in adult-guided problem-solving

- No sense of time or ability to plan; can't understand that adults need to adhere to time schedules; dawdles

- Has nightmares and night terrors

- Longer attention span of about fifteen minutes

- Can follow simple directions: "Put the toy in the box," but compliance still at 40% of the time

- Can recite past experiences but not in the right order

- Begins gender role identification at five years

- Beginning Executive Function skills at 3 yrs and increasing until 6 yrs

Social and Emotional

- Feels more complex emotions such as jealousy, pride, envy, sympathy, insecurity, and guilt

- Begins to express feelings in words rather than body language of tantrums

- Whines to communicate displeasure

- Imitates adult behavior

- Enjoys silly and nonsense poems, rhymes, and jokes

- Can be bossy; doesn't understand leadership skills yet

- Feels stress when loved ones are angry

- Anxious to please loved ones

- Power struggles over bedtimes, eating, toileting

- Can share, line up, take turns, compromise, and play cooperatively

- Imagination stirs up fears: animals, dark, carwashes, noises

- May begin tension outlets: nose picking, masturbation, nail biting

- Still has some separation anxiety, especially at night

- May prefer one parent over the other

- Begins to understand that others have different feelings

- Honest and blunt: "Why does your house smell?"

- Enjoys pretend play, role playing, and play dates with other children

- Cooperation increasing but still difficult to stop activities that are enjoyable

- Can delay gratification for five minutes at four years of age.

- Tapers off temper tantrums to once a week or less

- Tattles

- Likes to be independent and may refuse help

*Compliance is 40% successful in a respectful, non-punitive parent-child relationship.

Preschooler Behavior - Energy Spurts

"My 3 year-old gets unbridled energy when my partner comes home. He releases it by hitting the dog, jumping, and banging into walls. How do I handle that?"

Brain development stage: Children have incredible amounts of energy that absolutely needs to be released. They can't help it.

Suggestions:

- Have some "steam-off" games ready to play when he gets into that energy high.

- Have partner take him to the park for 15 minutes as soon as he gets home, so they have time together and energy is burned.

- Have a mini-trampoline to direct him to. Say, "Let's bounce off our energy."

- Text your partner on the way home, to meet at a playground before coming home.

- Collect about 4-6 old sofa cushions for rough play and steam-off games.

- Get some tumbling mats, or ride-on toys, or jumping balls that can be used indoor to expand energy. Clear a path through the house that is safe and out of the way of furniture.

- Sneak your partner into the house by distracting your son.

- Have a dance party. This is a good time to teach your child how to do the Macarena, Chicken Dance, and the YMCA dance.

Preschooler Behavior - Homebody

"My 4 year-old doesn't like to go out. He doesn't participate in getting ready and I end up dragging him kicking and screaming to get out to the car."

Brain development stage: Children develop their introversion or extraversion by age 4. They have definite likes, dislikes, and various levels of tolerance for outings, people, and socialization. Parents must respect a child's inborn personality trait.

Suggestions:

- Use bribery with a small treat that you can stash in the car. (Black licorice is somewhat healthy and keeps well summer or winter, in the car's glove box.) Stickers or a special movie for the journey might work too.
- See if you can make it his idea by offering a choice between something really boring or undesirable and going out the door to what you want him to do. Say, "Would you like to stay here and clean the toilet with the toothbrush or go out to get groceries and a possible treat?"
- Give a choice in time: "Would you like to go now or in 5 minutes?"
- Use a visual color timer. Green is first warning, yellow is second warning, red is go!
- Tell him how much fun it is going to be.
- Explain that sometimes he has to do things the adult way and adults have to do things they don't want to do.
- Talk about how much a problem it is and ask him to help you come up with a solution. This works better if you are not running out the door and are in a calm space.
- Empathize with his feelings. Say, "It's hard to leave when you are having so much fun. I wish I didn't have to leave washing the dishes too, but we have to go."
- Just be firm. Say, "We have to go. Get dressed." Bring clothes and shoes with you.
- Get the younger/other siblings out first and say, "Look, your brother is already in the car."
- Before bed, talk about what you are going to do the next day. Remind him shortly before it is time to go. Make him a weekly calendar so he can see the days that he has to go out.

- Once you are out, do all you have to do. It's even harder to come home and then have to get him out again.

- Have a "car treat" only for the car. Perhaps library books (you can keep them rounded up that way) or a hand-held game player that stays in the car and is something fun for him to look forward to.

- Tell all the children that the first sibling in the car gets the best seat if they are easily movable, like booster seats.

Preschooler Behavior - Separation Anxiety

"My 3 year-old son has spent the majority of his time solely with me. He is now experiencing some separation anxiety when I leave him. What can I do to help alleviate some of his anxiety?"

Brain development stage: For many "spirited" temperament children, separation anxiety from loved ones still occurs because of their "sensitivity" characteristic.

Suggestions:

- Know that this will get better. (This Too Shall Pass)

- See suggestions under Toddlers.

- Eventually children get better on handling their separation anxiety. It takes spirited children longer because of their persistence in holding on to you. Patience is the key.

- Take baby steps, and each time go a little further away for increasingly longer periods of time.

- Leave him for brief periods with caring family members, friends, and neighbors so that he gently and slowly gets used to being away from you, and also knows that each time you return back to him.

- Take him to play groups where parents are close by. It's a great opportunity for him to interact with other children and enjoy his time playing away from you, but where he can see you.

- Never sneak away! Always communicate to him that you are leaving, where you are going, and that you will be back once you are finished what you have to do.

- Have something really special planned that the caregiver can redirect him to as soon as you leave.

- Be consistent, kiss him goodbye, and leave quickly. Lingering conveys hesitation that he may pick up on and it may make things worse.

- Leave him with an item of yours to hold.

- Give him a locket or baggie filled with your kisses. Give him a small photo framed of you, or draw a heart on his hand with pen.

- Buy matching stuffed animals, jewelry, scarves or clothes and give one to him and you keep one. It's something he can touch and give love to that you will receive on your end.

- Leave him with the same adult caregiver all the time if possible.

- When you leave him, walk away with confidence and know that he is safe and he will adjust to his new surroundings

- Acknowledge his feelings by saying, "You are sad Mom is leaving. That's okay to feel that way and I will be back in two hours." Give him hugs before leaving.

- Limit separations as much as possible until he is more secure.

Preschooler Behavior - Separation Anxiety While Away Travelling

"My 4.5 year-old son is going to spend the weekend with my parenting partner while I go out of town. How can I make our separation smoother?"

Brain development stage: Even when children are left with one parent, they miss the other parent when absent.

Suggestions:

- Pre-write letters so that your partner can give one to your child each day, especially in the evening when children miss you the most. Include hearts and kisses.

- Prep your partner to acknowledge your son's feelings and give him hugs when needed.

- Take photos of your face and leave them as a screen saver in a tablet or computer so he can "see" you.

- Leave a T-shirt or something that smells of you, that he can cuddle.

- Let him watch you blow kisses into a baggie, so he can keep the baggie and take out some kisses when you are away.

- Bring him back a gift - but know that this sets a precedence!

- Skype or FaceTime often.
- Have your partner plan a full schedule of activities. Busy kids have less time for moping. Play up the "special twosome time" they will have.
- Have him draw a picture when he is sad.
- This is a good example of positive stress - he will get through this time, cope the best he can, and build his resilience by knowing that he got through it with adult support!
- Bring a photo of him on your trip for your separation anxiety too.

Preschooler Behavior - Baby Obsession

"My 4.5 year-old daughter is obsessed with babies. She is a strong-willed girl. How do I set safe boundaries?"

Brain development stage: Preschoolers love to play pretend and are in the fantasy, creative, pretend, and imagination stage of their development.

Suggestions:

- Negotiate so she has some control over what she can do with the baby.
- Have two lists - The "Yes" list, or a green list of things she can do, and a "No" list, or red list, of things she must get an adult to help with. Have "picking up baby" on the red list.
- Nurture the sibling relationship and encourage it. Supervise, but don't go overboard with anxiety that she may pick up on. Babies are not too breakable.
- Support her mothering - but give boundaries for her. Have pictures of those boundaries for visual learners.
- Keep facilitating interaction but don't let the two be alone together. Preschoolers still do not have a good grasp of what are dangerous activities.

Preschooler Behavior - Hates Clothes

"My son hates wearing certain types of clothes and goes outdoors improperly dressed."

Brain development stage: Spirited children dislike seams, certain fabrics and washing soap residue in their clothing, due to their "sensitivity" characteristic.

Suggestions:

- Turn socks inside out so the seams don't bother him.
- Give him 3 choices on what to wear.
- Use reverse psychology. Say, "I dare you to wear that coat!"
- Use when/then. Say, "When you get dressed, then we can read a book."
- Put an easel by the door to distract him with coloring while you put on his shoes, coat and hats.
- Let it go. Carry his coat and if he gets cold, let him have it.
- Invest in real good articles of suitable fabric clothing that you think he will wear.
- Give away articles that he doesn't wear, so you don't look at them every day and feel that you are wasting money.
- Most kids only wear three favorite outfits constantly, although they have at least thirty. It's annoying but we often only have about 10 favorite outfits too, even though our closets are stuffed.

Preschooler Behavior - Acts Out Hero Aggression

"My 4.5 year-old son re-enacts everything he sees on TV and movies. He pretends to be the villain and Dad engages in this type of rough play. How do I handle his aggression to other children?"

Brain development stage: Albert Bandera's Social Learning Theory explains why children act out what they experience. It's a normal way of processing their inner feelings and thoughts, and it helps them work through the idea of how the action they are imitating, such as the aggressive behavior, fits into their lives. As well, children don't understand the difference between real and pretend until about age 8.

Suggestions:

- Try talking to him during the movie and explain how movies are made and what is going on behind the scenes. Explain about real emotions and pretend actions.
- Tell Dad to watch more non-violent movies.
- It will slow down as he starts school and the behavior is not accepted in that environment, which reinforces it not being acceptable at home.

- Book play dates with friends where the ending is controlled, rather than the interaction spins into fights with playground peers.

- Outline the ground rules - no limits on feelings, but limits are on behaviors such as hitting, and pushing. If someone says "No," adults or children, then action must stop.

- Hang around with more adults that have boys. Boys really are more boisterous than girls.

- Find more ways to act out empathy.

- Children this age don't know what is real. Remind them.

- Channel the expression of feelings. Get a trampoline or take him to the park a lot, or other acceptable "place" where he can express and act out as much as he needs to in order to process his emotions.

- Give him sticks to use outside.

- Give him materials to build outdoor forts.

- Get him into team sports.

- Have a toy gun day where all his friends with toys guns are invited over to play guns. Supply all the foam bullets so that no one loses all theirs. You start with all the ammunition and keep all the ammunition.

- Make caring a family rule. No hitting, especially with toy weapons.

- Model kindness and resolving problems without violence.

- Avoid violent games, movies, TV shows for this age.

- Realize that young children don't know how delicate machines can break. Childproof by moving household items out of the way for a few years.

- Reinforce "acceptable" and "not acceptable" places and people to be aggressive with. For example, the playground is fine if all the boys and girls and their parents agree. It's not okay if people don't agree or the environment is not safe. Get consent first.

- Set boundaries - that kind of play is more for playing with toys, not other people. He could make his toy dinosaurs fight, but not do it to real people.

- Read books and watch the "offending" movie first before your child is exposed to it in order to see how violent the movie is.

- When children sit and watch a two-hour-long aggressive movie, their bodies absolutely have to move afterwards to burn off energy. Take them out to the park so they can kick and karate chop to their hearts content.

- Have a white board with the message, "Deep breathe. Say what you are feeling. Count to ten." It helps with pent-up anger for both parents and kids.

Preschooler Behavior – Masturbation

"My 3 year-old daughter has picked up some annoying habits from somewhere. How do I handle it when she plays with her 'private parts?'"

Brain development stage: Masturbation is very normal in childhood as children are sexual beings from the moment they are born. Some babies even have visual signs of erection while they are foetuses in the womb. Children touch their genitals because it feels good, just like eating chocolate cake feels good, and they are unaware of the cultural or social implications of such behavior until about the age of 6. See Teaching About Sex under General Parenting.

Suggestions:

- Teach your daughter that although touching her vulva feels good, it is her body and something to do in private. Talk about private (behavior done when alone) and public (behavior that is okay to be displayed when other people are around) behavior. Teach her which is which and keep repeating over and over.

- When she is touching herself, offer her privacy such as the bathroom or her bedroom. Say, "I know that feels good, but that is a private action and we need you to do that in private."

- Avoid shaming, teasing or punishing her. It is normal behavior just like using the toilet, but not meant to be shared with others.

- Teach her to not insert toys or anything in her vagina. Just like her nose, ear, or other body openings, they should be kept clear to function.

- If she does it in public, dress her in a onesie or overalls so she can't get her hand down her pants. Lead her to the bathroom and tell her why, if she continues.

- Give her a small carton of play-dough to keep her hands busy in public.

- Ultra secure her diaper with duct tape at the waist so she can't access anything.

- Give her consistent messages and she will soon understand.

Preschooler Behavior - Fast Anger

"How do I help my 4 year-old son manage his anger? He goes from 0-60 mph in a flash."

Brain development stage: Most children need about 13 years to learn how to handle anger. They are very physical from age 1-4 and then it subsides where they might hit about once per week from ages 4-6, then once every couple weeks from ages 7-9 and then once a month from ages 9-11 and then never from ages 13 on. In the teen years, they slam doors and use their words (swear) but physically hurting siblings or playmates is curbed. Handling anger is a life-long, ongoing skill.

Suggestions:

- Stay calm and stand your ground. Speak calmly so he knows that a stable force is in his life.
- Remember that time-outs don't always work to teach how to express anger, and can make children angrier.
- Say an inside joke, like "I love your butt," to put the humor back into the situation.
- Give him a hug.
- Offer him a drink. Say, "Let's go and get your cup," to divert his energy.
- Give him chewing gum.
- Get him to drink through a straw. Sucking helps calm children.
- Get the "Angry birds" stuffed animals. Say, "Lets bite the bird," or press the bird button.
- Get a bunch of tin cans for him to throw outside.
- Hammer a stake in the garden and let him use a child's hammer to pound it further into the ground.
- Active listen to his feelings. "You are really feeling mad!"
- Say, "It's okay to cry and be angry. I will help you through your feelings."
- Extract yourself from his anger by saying, "I'm going to go and get you some water," or "I have to go pee. I'll be back."
- Get him a batch of red colored play-dough to pound.
- Get a hanging bag for him to punch or a sit on ball to bounce around on.
- Have a white board with the message, "Deep breathe. Say what you are feeling. Count to ten." It helps with pent-up anger for both parents and kids.

Preschooler Behavior - Parent Forgets to Acknowledge Feelings

"I can't remember to actively listen in the moment when my child has a problem. What are some tips to help me remember?"

Brain development stage: When adults are angry, we need to express our anger and acknowledging someone else's feelings is not our first course of action. We have to train ourselves to do that when our children are experiencing problems. New habits take 21 times to reinforce.

Suggestions:

- Make it your first "go-to" response anytime your child is having problems of any kind. Repetition makes for habits. It takes 1500 times for it to come out naturally.
- Make sure that you are in the mood for active listening. When you are angry may not be the best time. Wait until you are calm and feeling empathetic, not angry.
- Write a reminder on your hand with washable marker ink.
- Keep your active listening response short.
- Don't beat yourself up over it.
- Remember that you don't have to active listen right away. It can be done in calmer times too.

Preschooler Behavior - Exuberant Baby Hugging

"How can I encourage appropriate affectionate behavior between my 4 year-old and her 10 month-old baby sister? Currently there's lots of exuberant hugging going on that usually results in a tumble."

Brain development stage: When children are excited, they don't understand their strength.

Suggestions:

- In one word - attention! Give lots of attention to your older child is what she is probably wanting but doesn't know how to communicate.
- Encourage gentle hugs and supervise whenever they are together.
- Encourage her to hold the baby while she is sitting down and you could even hold them both in your lap that way.
- Spend some one-on-one girl time with her.
- Play up her role as big sister. Encourage its importance.

- Keep your baby out of the older child's possessions by putting up a gate or putting all the valuable stuff in a separate room. Relax. Soon, they will be playing together!

....

Preschooler Behavior - Can't Decide

"My 4 year-old daughter gets really anxious when deciding what to wear. She often is only presented with two choices and still can't make up her mind. When I put my foot down and decide for her, she gets upset."

Brain development stage: Children can't think about two options, because preschoolers can't understand the effects of consequences. They don't have the ability to pre-plan or think too far ahead in terms of "what if?" They are worried they might make the wrong choice. It's why logical consequences are not recommended until age 6 and up.

Suggestions:
- Pack away her matched outfits in those big zip-lock bags. Sort them according to what goes best. Put top, pants and underwear in one bag.
- Put away a lot of her clothes. Too much choice can be overwhelming.
- Keep choices simple and down to 2 or 3 options.
- Choose outfits the night before and don't let her change her mind in the morning.
- Do away with pyjamas and let her sleep in her clothes to avoid the morning angst.
- Take photos of various tops and bottoms that she wears together and give her a photo collage of what works well together. (This works for adults too!)

....

Preschooler Behavior - Complainer

"How do I deal with my 5 year-old son who constantly complains?"

Brain development stage: Children complain. It's normal. Their level of patience isn't very developed like an adult.

Suggestions:
- Acknowledge your child's feelings of unhappiness, boredom, or sadness.

- Don't make it personal. It's not about you. As the helper person, just validate his feelings and let him solve his own problem of unhappiness. You can't control his level of optimism.

- Model optimism yourself – remember that children who live with critical parents become critical adults.

- Say "Oh well. This is bad. But, we can..." This shows that you are optimistic and can make lemons out of lemonade.

- Ask your child what he would do as a solution; have him offer suggestions.

- Have patience. Accept it. Some people are just complainers, but may learn through natural consequences that it does not attract other people's time and friendship.

- Is he complaining out of boredom? What would he do instead? Perhaps he needs more stimulation for his level of intelligence.

- Organize more play-dates for him. He might be ready for more "outside the family" social activities.

Preschooler Behavior - Purging Toys

"How can I sort and give away excess toys and clutter without upsetting my 3 year-old?"

Brain development stage: Remember that children under age 7 have a childhood characteristic called animism which means that they "think" of inanimate objects as having real, human traits. That is why stuffed animals are so loved and real to them. So are other objects including toys. Most children are not ready to give away their possessions until the teen years.

Suggestions:

- Start phasing them out. Pack them up in a box and put the box in a garage for 6 months. If she doesn't miss them, give them away.

- Talk about reasons for de-cluttering such as space issues, people that need the items more, etc.

- Encourage the child to give to someone they know so that they can see the joy on the person's face when they receive it.

- Read about "minimalism" on the internet.

- Stop it at the source - talk to friends and relatives about buying too much stuff.

- Ask for "experience" gifts such as movies, theatre tickets, etc.

- Cut down on clutter by instituting a 5 gift rule - 1 from Santa, 1 to read, 1 to wear, 1 that they need, and 1 that they truly want.

- Be careful with children who have a sentimental personality or a love language that is "gifts." They value tangible items as a symbol of love and taking away their treasures can be extremely hurtful if done before they are ready.

- Most children are ready to clean out their rooms and purge by age 18. Not many are ready to consent to doing it before then.

- It's more respectful to ask the child's permission, but sometimes you just have to give it away because of allergies or throw it out if it's broken. Perhaps take a photo of it as a permanent memory. Sometimes you just have to keep it even if you don't want to, because it is so meaningful to the child.

- Have a general rule that when a new item comes in, an equal number of items goes out.

- Purging is a great skill that all children have to learn. Teach her to take a photo of it and then say goodbye to it. Let her grieve for the item. She will get through it with your support and it develops a useful skill for later on.

What are the toys you want to keep?

- Blocks, people, Lego, Playmobil, Hot Wheels, kitchens, dollhouses, building sets, puppets, dress-up props, craft supplies, and musical instruments are great toys that grow with kids up to age 13. Get rid of toys with push buttons that just sit there and do things on command. Toys in which the child adds no imagination or energy to, get dusty and left un-played with pretty fast, so get rid of those ones first.

Preschooler Behavior - Bossiness

"My 4 year-old daughter likes to speak for the group. The group doesn't outright object, but when asked individually, they want different things. How do we curb this?"

Brain development stage: Spirited temperament children are natural leaders but come across as bossy before they learn true leadership skills.

Suggestions:

- Perhaps this isn't a big battle right now.

- Go to each child individually and see if they agree with what she has stated was the consensus.
- It's a good sign of confidence for her. Don't squelch it, just channel it.
- Give her a lot of choices.
- Remind her to ask others for their vote and opinions. Show her how to write them down by doing it for her.
- Say, "You want to ..." so she understands the words people use, instead of her saying, "We want to..."
- Say, "Let's check and see if everyone wants to do that."
- The others will eventually assert themselves when they need to.

....

Preschooler Behavior - Shyness

"My 4.5 year-old son is shy and sensitive with other adults. How can I help him with this?"

Brain development stage: Some children are naturally shy (and may have low social needs) and that is fine as long as they speak up when they really need to. Like anger, managing shyness is a skill that is developed over childhood. Some children grow out of shyness and some don't but they will need to learn to advocate for themselves as adults.

Suggestions:
- Get him to pay for items in stores.
- Don't pressure him when he retreats. Keep encouraging but respect his "No. Not now."
- Get down to his level and ask him questions.
- Gently nudge him, but don't force him when he is not ready to challenge himself, as that could set him back.
- Respect your child's feelings if he doesn't like certain strangers.
- Honour who your child is. He may be a quiet introvert that is happy with one friend and a lot of solitude. It may not be a problem.
- Use Good, Better, Best: Say, "It would be good if you say "Hi" behind my legs and it would be better if you could come out and say "Hi" and it would be best if you could say "Hi" and shake hands with the person. You decide."

- He is young. Being cautious is a good thing. You probably want him to be more shy than overly friendly.

- It's okay to think of answers before responding.

- Try to hold back on answering for him. Give him time to say something.

- Give him a security item to feel better when you are out together. Perhaps a favorite jacket, hat or something.

- Have a little conversation before you go out about how he would like to deal with strangers. Practice social skills. What can he do and what does he want you to do?

- Let him set the pace. Ask him how much social time he can handle for the outing?

Preschooler Behavior - Dawdles

"My preschooler and toddler hinder my efforts to get out the door in the morning."

Brain development stage: Children are very ego centric until age 6. Their needs are first in their mind, ahead of other people's needs, and they learn to begin thinking about other's during the school-age years. They are most focused on playing at this point.

Suggestions:

- Don't look at the time. Just keep moving.

- Have a picture checklist of tasks that need to get done: teeth, clothes, breakfast.

- Give them control by allowing them to choose what gets done in what order.

- Get up earlier to get yourself ready first.

- Have a longer breakfast together to get some attention time in.

- Dress them yourself to fill attention needs. Build in time for it.

- Build some fun things into your routine. Have a play set of empty make-up containers for them to use, while you put on yours.

- Avoid commands from another room. You have to stay with them to keep them moving.

- Keep distractions that hinder their action, to a minimum, such as electronics.

- Have special treats in the car such as music, food, games and books.

- Put the clothes on once. Warn the kids that if they take them off, they stay off.
- Carry kids out to a warm car and have boots, mitts, and hats in a bag that they can put on in there.
- Use a timer.
- Get kids' outerwear on first and then get them strapped in their seats and then get your outwear on. That way, you don't get too hot.
- Have the older children dress their siblings.
- Have a bag hanging on a hook with their outdoor pieces that they can grab and go.
- Accept that small children take longer to do things and change your schedule and stress level.

Preschooler Behavior – Destroys Property

"My 5 year-old son is clumsy and very explorative. He doesn't realize that he wrecks things by using them."

Brain development stage: Young children don't understand how machines work or how they are damaged.

Suggestions:

- Give information about proper care of machines.
- Show how to use gently.
- Show how to fix broken items if they are fixable.
- Don't leave out any items that are precious.
- Supervise play. If it becomes rough, move the children somewhere else.
- Pack away any delicate items until he is older (age 8) and can understand.
- Get help from him to clean up so he knows how long it takes.

Preschooler Behavior - Temper Tantrums

"My 3.5 year-old has tantrums. I thought they only had these as toddlers. How do I handle them?"

Brain development stage: Many children still have tantrums into the preschool and school-age years due to their self-control not being well developed yet.

Suggestions:

- Get eye contact, get her attention, get close to her, and talk quietly.
- If you have said "no", you have to stay with your "no!"
- Stay calm yourself!
- Say, "I wish I had a magic wand to make it better," when she feels she never gets her way.
- Leave the shopping cart and take her out of the public place and calm her down in private.
- Make a figure 8 motion with your hand while rubbing her back.
- Be consistent in how you handle it. If you are going to ignore it, always ignore it.
- Acknowledge her feelings after she is calm. Say, "I know you feel sad."
- No talking during the tantrum. Children are too out-of-it to listen. Try to hug, touch and hold her to let her know you are there.
- Validate her feelings. Feelings have no limits. Behaviors like throwing have limits.
- Say, "It's hard being three."
- Think of how you, as an adult, want to be treated when you are angry. We want to be listened to, be given time, space, and items to calm down, have our feelings validated, and be given ideas for solutions when calm. We want comfort and not judgment, rationalizing, blame, punishments or justifications. Children want the very same things!

Preschooler Behavior - Imaginary Friends

"My family moved here 3 months ago. My 3.5 year-old daughter seems to be having trouble adjusting to the change. She misses her old friends and has little desire to make new ones. She has made "imaginary" friends (the ones she left behind) in her new home. She has also become increasingly defiant and has started acting out."

Brain development stage: Children who are spirited temperament have a harder time with transitions than easygoing children. They are in the brain development stage of pretend, fantasy and make-believe, and they come up with "let's pretend" to make things easier for themselves. When children reach their half birthdays (3.5, 4.5, 5.5 years old) they can become very defiant and moody due to emotional growth spurts. This is called disequilibrium. They can be overwhelmed with all that they are processing throughout the day.

Suggestions:

- Know that this is a normal stage of development with children ages 3-5. Their cognitive skills and social skills are growing all the time.
- Be aware of how you are feeling with the big move; take care of yourself through all of this. Use this time to bond as a family and take the pressure off of yourself and your daughter to make new friends; it will happen naturally. It is very common and very natural for a child at this age to only have 1 good friend.
- Communicate, age-appropriately, to your daughter about how this move has made you feel.
- Arrange to have online live sessions with her friends overseas.
- Age 3 can be a very challenging age for both the parent and the child; add to that a move to another country, it can completely overwhelm everyone involved. It is important for you to be very gentle with yourself at this time, and allow your own process of adapting to a new country evolve. Try to laugh and have some fun with your precious babes and know that this is only a phase, and it too shall pass.
- Join a group for you and her so that you will both make friends. Volunteer for her preschool or playgroup administration team and you will have many impromptu play-dates when you have organizational meetings. Both of you will benefit socially.

Preschooler Behavior - Hates Tying Shoes

"My 5 year-old hates tying her shoes."

Brain development stage: It takes practice and many children can't tie their shoes until the school-age years.

Suggestions:

- Teach by using long strings of licorice and the back of a chair.
- Buy velcro shoes until you can't anymore and then she will have to learn.
- Tie her shoes loosely so that she can put them off and on without doing the laces up. Buy buckles only.

Preschooler Behavior - Won't Brush Hair

"My 5 year-old hates brushing her hair."

Brain development stage: It hurts when children's hair gets tangled.

Suggestions:

- Consider a short cut.
- Braid long hair at night before going to bed.
- Buy a silk or satin pillow case.
- Show her how to brush every day.
- Brush her hair while she is watching a movie.
- Slather long hair in conditioner and comb out tangles gently from the bottom and work your way up the hair. Hold the hair in your other hand, so it doesn't pull at her scalp. Rinse out conditioner when you are done.

Preschooler Behavior - Won't Gather Things to Go

"My 5 year-old son ignores my request to get going in the morning. How do I motivate him?"

Brain development stage: Routines help children remember what they need to do in order to go out. Remember at this age, it is still your agenda rather than theirs and they do get distracted.

Suggestions:

- Say, "After the show is done, we have to leave."
- Say, "When the timer goes off, we have to go."

- Have bins by the door with the day's necessities such as water bottles, juice boxes, snacks, socks etc.
- Hang jackets on small hooks so they can reach them.
- Have sun screen and bug spray by the door.
- Have a photograph checklist so they can see what they need to do and bring.
- Buy velcro or slip-on shoes.
- Tie her shoes loosely so that she can put them off and on without doing the laces up.

Preschooler Behavior - Fears

"My 5 year-old son has a lot of fears. How can I help him?"

Brain development stage: Fears at this age show a sign of brain development. Children understand that some things in the world are dangerous but not why they are dangerous, or what safety cautions are needed. You are their lifeline to safety.

Suggestions:

- Don't belittle their fears or patronize them. Take their fears seriously. Say, "It's okay to feel scared of dogs. I used to be scared of dogs too when I was a child. Dogs are mostly friendly though."
- Don't take away security items. A child that feels secure gets over fears faster.

Vacuums

- Use a backpack to carry him while you vacuum.
- Vacuum when he is out of the house.
- Let him use it and try turning it off and on.

Monsters

- Acknowledge the fear but not the monster.
- Leave a nightlight or overhead light on.
- Get a fish tank as company.
- Leave music playing through the night.

Dark

- Go on regular night walks, night skating or skiing, and point out the stars and moon. Pretend the moon is a friendly item looking over us.

- Celebrate the night with candles and magic sparkles (stardust sprinkled outside).
- Avoid scary movies or books about darkness.
- Have a special night picnic.
- Give him his own flashlight.

Dogs

- Avoid dogs at this age.
- Model cautiously reaching out to dogs and petting them.

Events, car washes, movie theatres, etc.

- Ask, "What if?" to understand their fears.
- Don't take the child or take them out if you are already there and they are scared.
- Give plenty of cuddle time.

Preschooler Behavior - Too Friendly With Strangers

"My 5 year-old son is much too friendly with strangers. He talks to them and accepts gifts from them."

Brain development stage: Some children are naturally friendly and can't distinguish between adult social categories of people such as friends, acquaintances, and colleagues.

Suggestions:

- Preschoolers need 24 hour supervision.
- Give him information about his feelings. Talk about "funny feelings," "tornadoes in the tummy," or "creepy feelings." Tell him to trust his feelings.
- Enroll him in stranger danger classes.
- Don't instill fear in him. Talk to strangers yourself and assure children that most people are kind and helpful. Let your child talk to strangers when he is with you.
- Teach basic safety rules such as no one touches his body parts covered by a swimsuit and to get away from anyone (friend or family) that makes him feel icky.

- Teach him that if he needs help in public, go find a mom with children to ask for help, and he will be safe. Research shows that moms will stay and help a child.
- Teach him to run and scream if he is scared.
- If anyone grabs him, teach him to yell, "Stop. You are not my mom or dad!"

Preschooler Behavior - Loses Things

"My 5 year-old loses everything at preschool, shopping and friend's houses."

Brain development stage: Children commonly forget when they lay an item down until they are about age 8.

Suggestions:

- Teach him to keep everything secure in a zippered backpack. Get in the habit of putting things back in the pack when done with.
- Pin items together such as mitts.
- Make it a rule that special toys do not leave the car or home.
- Buy two of his favorite stuffed animals because he might lose one.
- If he bring items to daycare, camp or a friends, show him how to write a packing list. You will remember what he has brought and remind him to look for the items. This is a good practice to do for future summer camps, university dorms, etc.
- When your child's friend borrows things from your house, write it down as well, so you teach the kids how to keep track of their belongings and you will remember where it went to the next time they ask for it.

Preschooler Behavior - Hates Dentist and Doctor

"My 5 year-old son hates going to the doctor and dentist."

Brain development stage: Professionals with white uniforms and clinical smells coming from the office, can be scary for young children.

Suggestions:

- Appreciate any small steps; even letting the dentist look in his mouth.

- Hold him on your lap and then you sit on the table or in the chair.
- Take him along on your visits so he can see that it is what adults do.
- Warn him the night before and read books about going.
- Visit doctors or dentists that can wear colorful clothes instead of professional whites.

Preschooler Behavior - Refuses to Change Activities

"My 3 year-old daughter dislikes it when she has to transition to another activity. It usually spurs a tantrum."

Brain development stage: It takes practice and brain development for children to switch tasks and focus. Many children can't do it until the school-age years.

Suggestions:

- Teach her to take a break by enticing with a snack. Then change activities after.
- Warn her of the transition. Show her how much time left, with space between your hands.
- Pick her up and carry her out after the warning time is up.
- Acknowledge her feelings of frustration with, "I know you are upset we have to leave. It's okay."
- Have a good-bye routine. Say to the toys, park, or the building, "See you later, Alligator." Wave.
- Say, "Lets rock and roll!" Leave with the "roll."
- Give one or two "last times." Really leave.
- If she really hates transitions, consider how really necessary they are and limit them. All kids handle them better as they age.

Preschooler Behavior - Refuses Medication

"My 3 year-old son refuses to take medication orally."

Brain development stage: Many children hate taking medication but it is important that they do.

Suggestions:

- Crush the pill and put it in a teaspoon of applesauce or yogurt if it doesn't say to take it whole.
- Crush and put in a bottle nipple of apple juice and let him suck it out.
- Pour the liquid medicine with an eye dropper at the side of his mouth so he has to swallow.
- Acknowledge his feelings. Say, "You are scared of the medicine?"
- Explain the need as best as you can. These are one of those parenting moments you just have to do.

Preschooler Behavior - No Boundaries

"The 5 year-old boy that I care for has been diagnosed with ADHD. He has very little body awareness and boundaries of others. He can't sit still for any period of time and is struggling with potty training."

Brain development stage: 5 year-olds are in the process of developing boundaries according to social rules. Some are better at it than others. Children this age still pick their nose, have their hands down their pants, and chew their nails with very little awareness of the social impact. The ADHD may complicate things.

Suggestions:

- Make sure the child is getting plenty of exercise and is involved in an array of activities.
- Try some kid-friendly yoga videos.
- Play soothing music, and also some fun dance music.
- Have him tell you how he is feeling, when appropriate (but not in the middle of a tantrum). Get him thinking out of his head and into his body.
- Make sure you are taking care of yourself and finding time to relax and replenish your reserves.
- Ask the parents what would help him.

Preschooler Behavior - Prefers Other Parent

"My 4 year-old daughter only wants me to brush her teeth, and read her a story. My husband isn't allowed to do anything. How can I get her to let my husband to do the bedtime routine? I also have a toddler and a new baby."

Brain development stage: The preschooler age is one where it is common for children to temporarily prefer one parent over another. Having a new addition to the family is an unsettling time of transition and one where everyone needs security and comfort.

Suggestions:

- Your daughter is looking for security, possibly because of the new baby, and she wants you to do the bedtime routine because she spends the most time with you and temporarily feels attached to you the most.

- Perhaps ask Dad to take care of the baby and spend some quality time with your toddler while you have some "big girl" time with your preschooler.

- It's a stage and in a few years, Dad will be the preferred parent. This is a totally normal period and we ask Dad's (who are most often the shunned parent) to be patient. Meeting children's needs for security makes them more independent.

- For the tooth-brushing issue, have family brushing time where everyone is in the bathroom.

- Perhaps get an electronic brush so that in your limited brushing time, you can get a better job done.

- If you are doing all the giving, be sure to give yourself some time off to fulfill your needs.

- Don't pressure her into accepting the less-preferred parent. Nudge her but don't force it. Perhaps send the preferred parent out to walk the dog or get some private time. It might be easier if the parent is out of the house.

- Get Dad to be the first parent to pick her up when she cries or when she is hurt or upset. He can hold, hug and use comforting words for her pain.

- Dad should be the one to care for her when she is sick.

- Get Dad to do the bedtime routine every second night. Acknowledge her feelings of unhappiness, but send in Dad. It will do no harm and give Mom a break.

- Get Dad to do the bedtime routine every second night.

- See if partner is too authoritarian. Make sure he gives treats and fun outings too.

Preschooler Behavior - Sensitive Feelings

"My 4 year-old daughter is very sensitive to other's actions like teasing, and can also pick up on other's feelings very well. How can I help her to be less sensitive?"

Brain development stage: Spirited temperament children can be very attuned to other's feelings as well as their own. It can be a real gift or disadvantage depending on how they are taught to handle their emotions and other's emotions through respectful communication.

Suggestions:

- Decide if her "being sensitive" is a bad thing. It will serve her well in life. She will be ahead of the game in terms of emotional intelligence and being able to "read" people and respond to them.
- It can also be a disadvantage if she is too caught up in what people feel and if she thinks she is responsible for making them feel better. Assure her that people own their feelings and that she is not ultimately responsible for their well-being.
- If she takes their joking too seriously, tell her that sometimes she needs to laugh at herself.
- Assure her that people like to joke and are not intentionally being mean to her.
- Role model how you react to people.
- Learning resiliency takes time and practice.
- Put her in martial arts lessons and classes that will build her confidence.
- Get her involved in drama for her inner "drama queen."
- Tell her about her "protective armor" and to imagine that she has a protective shield around her, so when people say or do something to her that may hurt, she can visualize that she has a shield protecting her.
- Build her assertiveness skills. Teach her the words to use to and how to say it politely, if she doesn't enjoy jokes about herself.
- Recognize that sensitivity is one of the eight characteristics of temperament and that it is normal and natural for her. Help her to handle it, rather than to hide from it. Sensitivity truly is a gift when well managed.

Preschooler Behavior - Bothered by News

"My 4 year-old daughter is very sensitive to media images and videos of people being mean to each other or reports of natural disasters. I try to shield her from what I think will bother her, but even in media geared to kids, she finds things that are upsetting. How can I help her to work through what she experiences?"

Brain development stage: Spirited temperament children can be very sensitive to what they see or hear. You can help her express her feelings and move on.

Suggestions:

- If she asks for the show or news report to be turned off, respect her by turning it off.
- Pause the show and talk about it or explain it to her. Ask her if she wants to continue.
- Acknowledge her feelings. Say, "It was scary, wasn't it?"
- Fast forward through the upsetting part.
- Have her draw a picture of what she thought of the show, movie, news item. Give her paper and markers and it will help draw out her feelings.
- For upsetting news items, focus on action - what can you do as a family to help?
- Connect their emotions to real life. Say, "Remember when you felt sad? The people on the TV are feeling sad too."
- Take your child's lead. Avoid over-talking and let it go if you think they need to let it go.

Preschooler Behavior - Learning Phone Number

"How can I help my 4 year-old girl learn my phone number?"

Brain development stage: As soon as they can talk, children can memorize your name and phone number.

Suggestions:

- Pick a favorite song to recite the number too. People tend to remember music and numbers.
- Make a poster in big letters to recite once a day.
- Give her a rubber wrist band and write your phone number on the inside in case she forgets.

Preschooler Behavior - Teaching Giving

"How do I teach my preschooler to be more giving?"

Brain development stage: Children are beginning to develop empathy and now is a good time to set the stage for pro-social behaviors.

Suggestions:

- Have her tag along with you when you reach out to people. Let her chat to people when you give the homeless a food gift card or a neighbor a plate of cookies.
- Let her come when you visit relatives in the nursing home.
- Bring her along when you help a friend clean her house before moving.
- Encourage your child to help others in the family. "Please help your sister bring in the groceries." "Does Dad need help weeding the garden?" "Please take this bread to the sick neighbors next door."
- Help her sort through old clothes, toys and come with you to donate to the depots.
- Help her give some of her allowance to a favorite charity.
- Plan gifts for relatives and friends and help her see the whole process - shopping, wrapping, and giving.
- Talk about why you are doing all the above.

Preschooler Behavior - Hoarding

"My 4.5 year-old daughter likes to hoard things. She loves to keep everything from the recycling, walks, and especially outgrown items. She remembers them if I try and hide them to dispose of them. The house is piling up!"

Brain development stage: Some children's love language is "gifts." Not store bought gifts, but objects they find outside, and everywhere around them. As well, preschoolers tend to think that objects are alive, complete with a personality and feelings. They do not want to "hurt" objects by abandoning them. They are in the brain development stage of "pretend" and "make-believe."

Suggestions:

- Sneak the recycling outside without her knowing.
- Keep a recycling box of goodies just for her.
- Take photos of the stuff before saying "Goodbye" to things.
- We all are either purges or keepers and have to find ways to live with each other.
- Ask her to let go of one item when another comes in the house. She could choose.
- Make a memory box of her special things.
- Is she uneasy about any transitions in her life that she is finding it difficult to deal with? She may need her items as they bring her security and comfort.
- If it is a blanket or piece of clothing, cut a little piece off the fabric every day until it is a manageable piece to store.
- Let her keep things but organize it better.
- Give her control over when to dispose of the items. When she is striving for autonomy, she needs security of familiar and loved things. Most children in their late teens let go of even special childhood things.
- Make a special place in her room or garden so she can put collected rocks, shells, sticks etc.
- Tour the city recycling plant so she can see how new materials get made from old ones, and tour second hand stores so she can see how other people need the items more than her.

Preschooler Behavior - Nail Biting

"My 3 year-old likes to chew her nails. It's becoming a chronic habit. She has a new sibling. I provide her with objects to chew such as teething rings. How do I get her to stop chewing her nails?"

Brain development stage: Children often develop nervous, stress-releasing habits. If you are wanting to stop one habit, substitute another.

Suggestions:

- Give her a chewy substitute.
- Don't make a big deal of it.

- Give her a worry ribbon to rub.
- Give her worry stones to feel when she is stressed.
- Get her a nail file - big and soft.
- Ignore it and stop mentioning it.
- Try to keep the nails short.
- Boys tend to bite nails more and it will pass when the peer group pressure kicks in.
- Is it worry? Give her worry balls to squeeze.
- Try painting her nails or buy some special nail wraps for her.
- Have a manicure, spa, or pedicure session - real or pretend.
- Have her do your nails.
- Emphasize that hands are pretty.
- Say "We don't want you to do that."
- Talk about how germy it is. Germs live under the nails.
- Let it go if you can't change it.
- Don't worry - at 3 years, she is still very oral and tactile. She will grow out of it and it won't hurt her even when she munches on a few germs. Remember that the more germs she is exposed to, the better her immune system will be.

Preschooler Behavior - Transition Energy

"My 5 year-old son has a hard time with transitions. He acts out (plays silly, pushes, runs around) as soon as we get somewhere for the first 15 minutes, until he settles in."

Brain development stage: When children are unsure, uncomfortable or uneasy, they act out in ways that are annoying to parents, although the child doesn't mean them to be. They need parents to look under the behavior and see what the child needs, since they have a hard time verbalizing their feelings.

Suggestions:

- Acknowledge his feelings, "You are really antsy right now," or "You are feeling uneasy going here?"

- He could have extra energy that he needs to dispel. Give him a job to do such as: Let him hold a digital camera or cell phone and his "job" is to photograph the new place. Give him paper to draw on. Allow him to tape record his thoughts on the phone.

- Give him a container (or baggie) of birdseed and he has to run around and feed the birds, if you are outside.

- Get him to run up and down the sidewalk once each way to let off steam.

- Get him to do 10 jumping jacks on the spot.

Preschooler Behavior - Warming Up to People

"My 4 year-old son is having transition difficulties and tends to initially 'growl' or 'hide' upon arrival in new places and with new people. He takes a long time to warm up. Is this something I should worry about?"

Brain development stage: Young children do need a period of time to warm up to people, especially those they haven't seen in a week or two. They don't remember relatives' status such as "Grandma" if they haven't seen them in a while. Most children take about 10 minutes to hours to warm up. It is very individual.

Suggestions:

- Get the child involved in an activity upon arrival. Bring one with you.

- Let the child take the lead in how much initial contact there will be. Respect her need to not have attention focused on her if she hides.

- Don't force the child to kiss, shake hands, or touch anyone they don't want to. Nudge them to offer a "Hi!"

- It is normal for children to have their own coping mechanisms. If he settles down and stops the growling once he is there, it should be okay. Keep repeating that growling at people is not nice and find another action he could do, such as hold your hand.

- Ask him for ways he can settle in right away. Getting a drink of water at the new place is a good activity and one that is always available.

- Always acknowledge his feelings and teach the "adult" way to handle the situation. Go right to an activity and get involved. A group facilitator once said, "When we do adult education classes, we put out reading books and materials on a table, so that participants who are introverted can spend the first few

140

minutes (where everyone new is getting seated at the class) engrossed in a book. This helps with their comfort level in getting settled."

- Be sure to let the visited person know that your child needs time to warm up.

....

Preschooler Behavior - Interrupting and Excessive Talking

"My 3 year-old daughter talks nonsense when I am trying to hold a conversation with a friend or my partner. She is loud and intrusive. It is driving me crazy. Sometimes she talks my ear off when we are alone."

Brain development stage: Most children gain enough self-control to wait for their turn, and recognise how to interject in the conversation by age 8-10. It's hard for little ones to hold on to their thoughts while they wait for you to finish talking. They don't have the working memory (executive function) for that to happen yet.

Suggestions:

- Hold her hand and touch her when you know she wants to say something. Tell her you know that is her signal that she wishes to talk and you will honor it as soon as the other person is finished talking.
- Practice, practice and more practice.
- Let her hold the floor and talk for a few minutes to the other person.
- Some children are just born to talk. They need to be taught how to hold a conversation and talk for 15 seconds and let the other person have a turn. These are part of social skills.
- Give her a recorder so she can talk into it.
- Say, "Time-out!" and explain to her that you need a ten minute break to talk to your partner or the other person. Use a visual clue such as a colored stoplight or a timer.
- Honor your word and really keep to time limits.
- Provide snacks, toys or diversions.
- Reinforce effort. Say, "Thank you for not disturbing me while I was talking to Lynn. I have some extra time now and would like to read to you."
- Have her express herself in ways other than talking, such as drawing a picture.

- Get her talking on Skype with a grandparent or a senior friend who would love to chatter with a preschooler.
- If you are losing patience, give yourself the pleasure of earplugs.
- Let her talk on the phone whenever telemarketers call.
- Use a talking stick at home. Give a stick to whoever holds the floor to speak.

Preschooler Behavior - Embarrassing Comments

"When kids point out body differences such as color, shape, nationality, tattoos, or disabilities, and they are loud and obvious, how do I handle it?"

Brain development stage: Children are brutally honest until they learn the art of social lying - about age 7.

Suggestions:

- Acknowledge differences. Say, "Yes, some people have big bums and some have small bums. It's all good."
- Be honest and matter-of-factly. "Isn't it great we are all different."
- Talk about it later in the car, so that they know that any topic of conversation is open with you privately, but some restrictions apply in public.
- Don't punish them for what she said.
- Encourage compassion. Model talking to people who look different. They are people first.

Preschooler Development - Is Preschool Necessary?

"I can't afford preschool costs. Is it really necessary?"

Brain development stage: In Canada, only about half of preschool children attend preschool. Yet, Canada most often is in the top 10 countries in the world showing excellence on the worldwide PISA exams in math, science and reading.

Play-based preschool is a great option for children from ages 3 to 5 years, whose brain development is progressed enough to allow them to practice sharing, take turns and play with other children. It also give parents a few hours break. However, a home program can be just as good in fostering a child's social, physical, cognitive and emotional development. The most important factor, whether in preschool or at home, is not so much toys but the attention of one caring adult. Most preschool activities include a mix of free play with the unstructured toys below and a small amount of "circle" time which includes reading, singing or sharing in a group. Provide unstructured play at home with a variety of toys and be an attentive adult. Build in time to read and sing to your child as well as outings to the park or playground and arrange some play-dates with your child, and your child will have everything at home that a preschool offers.

Suggestions:

- Have a sand/rice/lentil table or box that children can play in.
- Set up painting station - all you need is newspaper, paper, paints, brushes and lots of patience.
- Set up water play in the sink or backyard pool.
- Have play dates in your home, in the other parent's home or meeting at an indoor play-place – you control length, company and activities. Don't worry too much about groups of children - your child has plenty of time to learn how to line-up and sit to listen when she attends Kindergarten.
- Have as many open-ended free play toys on hand as possible, but rotate them often, so every week is a new-to-them bucket of theme toys or old favorites.
- Have a building block station with wooden blocks, Legos, K'nex or Meccano pieces.
- Assemble a dress-up tickle trunk with hats, shoes, belts and shirts obtained from the local goodwill store.
- Set up a play dough table with cutters, rollers, pans, etc.
- Set up a "kitchen" or "workshop" centre with toys.
- Have a "garden" centre with seeds, planters etc.
- Have a "workshop" centre with nails, hammer and wood.
- Have a "music" centre with instruments to play.
- Read to your child every day until they ask you to stop. (They won't.)
- Let them explore. As long as it is safe, allow them to take the toilet tank cover off, mix soda and vinegar potions, or build a potato blaster. Feed their curiosity.

- Live in the physical world. Take them to the zoo, science centre, and museums. Go to the nearby park or playground every day for thirty minutes.

- Have conversations everywhere. Turn off the screens and ask open questions that begin with How... and What... Talk while driving, sitting in waiting rooms, and at the dinner table.

- Listen when your child talks. Make eye contact and repeat back what you think you have understood what they have said. Children live in a world where everyone talks at them, but don't really listen to them. Listening builds their confidence, self-worth and encourages conversation. Giving a child your attention is the most precious gift.

- Fill waiting times with games. Play "I spy," Rock, paper and scissors," and bring a deck of playing cards or Uno to play a multitude of games.

- Don't entertain your kids. Boredom breeds creativity. Have lots of building supplies around such as paper, cardboard, tape, packaging, and markers, and ensure they clean up the mess.

- After age 3, invite other children over for play dates. Supervise and teach social skills as the need arises. (It will!)

- Drop all punishments and look at misbehavior as a conflict of needs. Together with your child's input, solve the problem so that both of you win. These are good people skills that they need to practice often.

- There is some evidence that shows that too many years in structured learning leads to burn out in the teen years. Peter Gray, PHD and Professor at Boston College, did a survey in 2013, that showed the more years a child was in formal classes, the less likely they were to go on to post-secondary education.

- Answer all questions thoughtfully. You can never give too much information as your child will only process what their brain can handle. Your child should know that no question is off limits from you - his information lifeline.

- Remember that you are your child's first teacher. Think of all those homeschoolers who excel at academics and socialization. Keep on these practices even when your child begins school. You are still their primary educator. Start saving money for those college savings plans!

Preschooler Development - Allowance

"What age should I start giving an allowance, how much should I give, and any tips for success? My child is 5."

Brain development stage: 5 is a great age for learning about money and allowance. Be sure to keep track of the wallet or purse for him as he will probably not remember where it is until the age of 8 or older.

Suggestions:

- Decide with your partner and child what items he will pay for the first year. Birthday gifts? Treats? Video games? Re-evaluate the list as he gets older. Clothing beyond the base level? Cell phone?

- Have three categories for divvying up allowance: spend, save, and share.

- Give $1 per year of age, once per week. It's enough money to save for special purchases in a reasonable amount of time, yet not too much that he blows it only on junk toys and candy. Besides, you will spend that money on him anyway. This way, you are handing over the control, which he needs to make good and bad choices.

- Give him total control over decisions of what to spend the money on. Natural consequences will teach your child about quality, and the value of purchases while the amount is still low enough to not have huge impact. Allow the child to make financial mistakes while he is still young which is better than when he is in college. Don't stress about the bad choices.

- Don't tie it to chores (duties) if you don't want the child to "buy" his way out of doing them. He may not need the money and opt out of chores. Chores should be done regardless of allowance.

- Keep an eye on your child's coin purse when out shopping. It's a good idea for you to keep an eye on his purchases when out shopping together as well.

Preschooler Development - Living with Grandparent Criticism

"My children are ages 4 and 2.5 years, and their grandparents live with us. Grandma is displaying signs of Alzheimer's and can be curt and sometimes mean to the children. How do I build their resiliency with her?"

Brain development stage: Your child at age 2 won't be affected if she is treated kindly and warmly by other adults in her life. Your child at age 4 might remember Grandma's behavior for a while and stay clear of Grandma. Either way, all children need is one adult to be warm and structured with them, so if the grandparents aren't but the parents are, it won't hurt their social and emotional development.

Suggestions:

- Encourage contact on days that Grandma is feeling better and more kind.
- Continuously offer comfort and a sounding board for your older son to vent. Validate his feelings as being real.
- Assure him that Grandma's brain is not working properly and she acts that way because of her brain. It is not the child's fault at all. Keep reminding him of that fact. Assure him that Grandma still loves him.
- If Grandma snipes at either of them, offer hugs, cuddles and reassurance that when she behaves that way, she is doing it because she is sick, not because she wants to hurt people. Grandma owns her feelings and behavior and reassure your children that they are not the problem.

....

Preschooler Development - Siblings Bathing Together

"Kids that bathe together. When should they stop? When should parents start covering up?"

Brain development stage: Children naturally become more modest and start requesting cover up by age 7.

Suggestions:

- Say "hands to yourself" when children want to explore each other in the bath.
- Use proper vocabulary to name all body parts.
- It's appropriate to bath together until one child feels that it's not right.
- Whoever says "No" rules, and should be respected whenever it comes to nudity, bathing, etc. If kids want parents to cover up, the parents should. If the parents want kids to cover up, the kids should.
- Suggest boundaries, "These are my private parts and are only for me to touch," when a child wants to touch your parts. This should be started at any age when they are curious.
- Have an open door policy for discussions. Start early. You have to throw out conversation starters or they might not happen. "Mommy is menstruating this

week and needs to wear special underwear." You can't give out too much information. They will take in as much as their cognitive development will allow.

- Have many conversations over the years, not just one.
- Any books by Meg Hickling are excellent for both children (Body Science) and parents (More Speaking of Sex and Speaking of Sex).
- See "Teaching about sex" under General Parenting Tips.

Preschooler Development - Religion Questions

"My 4 year-old has a little friend who talks about God and now she is interested in religion. She was told that God is a "he" and he lives in the sky. My partner and I are atheist and agnostic. How do I approach this situation?"

Brain development stage: Children don't understand abstract concepts such as religion, faith, and spiritual beliefs until they reach puberty.

Suggestions:
- Ask her "What do you think?" Stress that what other people think is not right or wrong. What is important is what she thinks.
- Religious icons are all around us. Point them out and say "That is a cross. Some people believe that such and such is..." And be sure to add, "I believe that..." When she begins to know what others believe and what you believe, she can begin to formulate what she believes.
- Age 4 is a time of asking questions. Answer her as matter-of-factly as possible, in simple language and you give her the message that no question is off the table.
- Be sure to teach tolerance and etiquette. For example, if she swears, you could say, "That word can be very offensive to people who believe in God."
- Go on field trips to different places of worship. Read books about different religions.
- Ask reflective questions. "Where do you think heaven might be?" "What does God look like?" Have her draw pictures of what she thinks.
- You can't control what the outside world tells her. Use them as talking points. You can set a climate where you and she can discuss her feelings and thoughts on anything and you will accept all her answers even though you may not always

agree. Ultimately, she will make up her own mind on her values, although, if your relationship is a good one, you will have a heavy influence on her beliefs.

- Age 12 is the age of abstract thinking, and she can develop concepts such as religion and death easier than when she is younger.

- Respect is universal. Keep teaching that virtues are not the domain of any one person or belief system.

- Model open-mindedness, tolerance, learning and asking questions when you don't understand concepts.

Preschooler Development - Teaching Assertiveness

"My 3.5 year-old daughter was playing in a play place and another child pushed her away from a toy. My daughter was upset and started crying, but didn't do anything. How can I teach my daughter to stick up for herself?"

Brain development stage: Aggressiveness is an ingrained trait. We need to socialize kids to be assertive which is standing up for themselves in a polite and respectful way and they need a lot of teaching and practice with parents help in order to do it well by themselves.

Suggestions:

- Wait to see if she truly is upset over the incident or are you more upset for her? If she is upset, then you have to intervene.

- Enroll her into sports, ballet and activities so she can feel more confident about herself.

- Speak to her about how she felt towards the intrusion. Did it bother her?

- If she didn't have the words to say "It's still my turn," then teach her simple words to say. "No, mine." "I'm not done yet." "Don't butt into line."

- Teach her to put up her hand to ward off space invaders.

- Observe her in other situations. What does she do at the park? At preschool? At playgroup? With siblings?

- Teach her I-statements. "I don't like that." "I want a turn please." "I need more time." "I'm not done yet."

- Model the words when you interact with her. She copies what you say.

- Try role-playing at home.

- Respect her "No's" at home and she will come to expect respect outside of the home.

- If the other child doesn't listen, appeal to the program staff or the other parent.

- Order of addressing the problem: The first rule of conflict resolution is to address the direct parties involved. Help your child speak to the other child. If that doesn't work, then you as a parent should step in and speak to the other child. If that doesn't work, speak to the parent of the other child. If that doesn't work, then you have the choice to leave, negotiate some more with staff involved, or put up with the status quo.

Preschooler Development - Teaching Empathy

"How can I teach my daughter empathy and compassion for other people's welfare and situation?"

Brain development stage: Children under age 6 are still quite egocentric and think more about their needs than other people's needs, but we can begin to teach them how to help others and nudge them to do it.

Suggestions:

- Modeling is the best way to teach. Parents and teachers show how to be compassionate through their actions. Respond to your child's needs. They in turn, will learn to respond to others.

- Choose reading material that teaches moral lessons like helping each other.

- Go visit hospitals, nursing homes, and places where you can distribute a little joy either through singing holiday songs or bringing cookies.

- When you donate, talk about why you are donating, rather than just silently doing it. Emphasize the good feelings you get from helping someone else.

- Mention it out loud if you missed an opportunity to help someone. Express your regret and answer your child's questions.

- Welcome all feelings in your home.

- Bake cookies, shovel a walk, help a neighbor with a project, give blood, formally volunteer at an organization. These actions teach the act of service without pay - a harder lesson for children to learn than service for pay.

- When someone is nasty to you, say to your child, "We don't know what kind of day that person is having. Let's show him some kindness." Perhaps give a coffee gift card or something to help turn their day around. This is also great in teaching children to not take other's anger personally.

- Talk to strangers. Use their name if they are wearing nametags. Be kind to people who serve us.
- Give kids more power to trust. Encourage them to talk to strangers in your presence.
- If shopping and not buying too much, pick up something for a less privileged child too.
- Rather than giving cash to panhandlers, give a gift card which allows them to buy the food they want and use the washroom as a paying customer.
- Have an advent calendar of activities for the holidays - donate to the food bank, buy for the less privileged, or make cookies for staff at the fire hall.
- Model kind behavior - say "Hello" to people who are homeless. Ask how they are.
- Appreciate people and acknowledge it in words.
- Keep up consistent contact with absent family members.
- Live in someone else's shoes for an hour or day.

Preschooler Development - Refuses Preschool

"My 3 year-old hates going to preschool. Should I force him to go or not?"

Brain development stage: Preschool should be totally play-based. Children at this age need to move, play and explore without being forced to use a desk or worksheets.

Suggestions:

- Set up play dates with some friends from preschool.
- Leave him there and wait to see how it goes. Evaluate in a month.
- Perhaps stop for a month and start again later when he is more ready.
- Stay with him as long as you wish until he is more comfortable.
- Give him a calendar and let him choose 1 day (out of the three he is registered) to go. He has the power of choice which may reduce power struggles.
- Ask every week, "Do you want to go this week?"

- Pick his favorite things to do after preschool and set them up to do when he gets home on preschool days.
- Follow your intuition on what to do. If it doesn't matter to you if he goes or stays home, leave it be for awhile. Children change fast.

Preschooler Development - Preparation for Hospital

"My 3.5 year-old preschooler is having surgery in 3 weeks. How do I prepare her for that?"

Brain development stage: You can talk and read books about what will happen, but each child reacts differently to an impending hospital visit.

Suggestions.

- Buy a book about hospitals and read it to her. Say "We are going to get this done and then you will feel better."
- Be there for the initial anesthetic if you can. Some hospitals have policies, but if you insist, they might let you come in. You will have to wear mask and scrubs.
- Talk about it often and be honest about it. Put it on par with grocery shopping. The more anxiety you feel, the more she will pick up on the "scariness."
- Check with the hospital – they may have suggestions for you.
- Check movies on YouTube that are appropriate for your child about going to the hospital.
- Get a mask and scrubs and wear them around the house, so they don't look so scary to your daughter at the hospital. Let her play with them and wear them too. Pretend you are doctors and help the dolls feel better.
- See if you can visit the hospital before the actual day. Children's hospitals have many play stations and welcome visitors.

Preschooler Development - Handling Grief

"My 5 year-old is struggling with the death of his Grandma. How can I help him cope?"

Brain development stage: Children need honest, matter-of-fact answers and support from adults when faced with their loved ones dying. Children grieve in different ways.

Suggestions:

- Answer his questions as much as possible.
- Give him paper and markers to draw his feelings.
- Ask him to keep a journal and you can scribe/write for him.
- Read books about loved ones passing and talk about them.
- Use language that indicates the finality. Don't call death "sleep." Say the words "died, passed away, left us."
- Give him extra hugs and cuddles.
- Alert his teacher and adult people in his life that he is dealing with a traumatic event. Remind them that kids grieve in different ways and he may act out his anger or sadness in his own way. He needs gentle correction rather than punishment.
- Spend extra time with him.
- Talk about the spirit of Grandma and when he might see her again if that is your belief system.
- Have a photo of Grandma or a shrine so he has a tangible place to "talk" to her.
- Acknowledge his feelings of sadness.
- Tell him when you feel sad so he knows he can share feelings too.
- Go easy on all of you. It's a hard time.

....

Preschooler Behavior - Funerals

"Should I take my preschooler to a memorial service for an old friend?"

Brain development stage: A preschooler will not understand the abstract concept of death or why everyone is so sad. The meaning and purpose of church or a funeral will be lost on a child so young.

Suggestions:

- Yes, people will enjoy her and she won't remember anything.
- Prepare yourself that you may have to leave if she acts up.

- No, leave her at home with your partner or a babysitter.

- Yes, it might provide a focus for you so that you can hold it together, if that is what you want.

- Be sure to bring along some diversions to meet her needs for play.

Preschooler Development - Child Has the "Gimmes"

"My son wants everything when we go into a store. How can I curb the "gimmes" and "I want that!" whenever we go shopping?"

Brain development stage: Young children are fascinated by objects in stores. Even if it is something they own, to them, everything is new if they haven't seen the exact same thing. They can't wait. They want the immediate satisfaction of playing and exploring an object right away. They don't understand time until about age 7, so they can't understand how far away a "birthday" or "holiday" is. They want it NOW!

Suggestions:

- Leave him at home until he outgrows this phase or can wait a few weeks to get something.

- Clarify before you go, exactly what you will and will not purchase. If you plan to give him a treat or small toy, tell him now.

- If he wants things, put it in the cart and take them out at the checkout if you can divert his attention. Many times, the items are forgotten once they are in the cart and you can give them back to the clerk and say you don't want them.

- Give him an allowance so he can see how his money accumulates and he can pay for the item. Put a photo of the object on his piggy bank.

- Take a photo of the item or write it on a list and say, "I will keep this for your birthday wish list." Chances are by the time of his birthday, he will have forgotten it.

- Perhaps you shop and your partner can take the child somewhere else.

- If it's a real problem store, don't take him there for a few years. It gets better.

- Give him a camera to take a photo of it so it can go on his birthday wish list.

- Limit television viewing which stimulates this behavior with a lot of commercials promoting consumerism.

- See if you can find a second-hand version of the item.
- Begin a "gratitude" jar where every day you and he can write down or draw a picture of what you are grateful for.

Preschooler Development - Crankiness

"My son is going through the half year disequilibrium stage where he is cranky, uncooperative, and argues with attitude. "How do I handle this? He was fine at 2, 3, and 4 years, but seems extra challenging at 2.5, 3.5 and now at 4.5 years."

Brain development stage: All children go through periods of crankiness and uncooperativeness. It can last for months.

Suggestions:

- Be careful how you word requests. Try "I need you to ..."
- It's a definite stage, defined by Pam Levin as Disequilibrium.
- Pick your battles. Enforce the ones you really want to see happen.
- Standing there enhances power struggles. Go away for awhile and come back.
- Speak to him about how it hurts you, so you don't feel walked over. Do it in a connected time. Say, "I feel hurt when you scream at me when I ask you to put your boots on."
- Give choices – this really helps by giving him control when he feels that he doesn't have any.
- Reinforce the times he shows good behavior in a loud voice.
- Make statements, not questions. "We need to put our boots on." Instead of "Let's put our boots on, okay?"
- Make requests a game. "I bet you will beat me if we race to put our boots on!"
- Don't worry, in six months he will grow out of it!

Preschooler Development - Chores

"I threaten my 6 year-old daughter with consequences too much, and I notice that she is doing the same to get cooperation from her brother. Sometimes, I don't even know what the consequence will be. What can

I do instead to get her to do things around the house such as homework, emptying her lunchbox and backpack, getting ready for bed, etc?"

Brain development stage: Children can start simple chores such as putting blocks into a bin by age 18 months. They still need reminding and help up until the age of 12 when they should be able to do most chores on their own.

Suggestions:

- Use "when/then" and promise something positive if she cooperates. "When we get the backpacks put away, then we can have a snack." "When your homework is done, then we can watch TV."
- Give lots of appreciation for when she does do what you ask. Lay it on really thick!
- Try and turn the request into a game. Make it fun or silly for her to cooperate.
- If you threaten a consequence, then you must follow through, or it will not have credibility next time. Consider problem-solving with her next time instead of consequences.
- Take a photo of the job and make a book, so she can understand the steps in the routine.
- Try to respect your needs for getting things done, but also her needs for doing things in her own time frame. Give her a time frame window.
- Teach, but without expectation that she will understand or do it every time.
- Don't phrase the request in the form of a question that she can say "yes" or "no" to. "Do you want to feed the dog?" Better to make a statement. "I need you to feed the dog in the next ten minutes."
- Ask reflective questions, "What would happen if all the lunch containers were never removed from backpacks and the food residue was left in them?"
- Make some things routine, such as when homework is done, when backpacks get emptied so that you don't have to nag. It just becomes automatic.
- Pick your battles. Does she really need to do the task a certain way, or is there another way? For example: Put clean clothes on instead of pyjamas, so it is super easy to get dressed in the morning.
- If she is protesting a certain step in the routine, such as not brushing her teeth while getting ready for bed, go on to the next step – read a book. she might remind you about the "missed" step, when the power is taken out of the power struggle.

- Just do the job. A 6 year-old is still pretty ego-centric. If you do it for her now, it doesn't mean that you will always do it for her. It might be beyond her capabilities to expect her to remember to empty her lunchbox every day.

- Do the job together. Make it a bonding event by having a conversation while working side by side.

- Be short with requests. "Dog's hungry!" "Backpack, empty!"

- Use "I-statements." "I am worried the dog will starve if he isn't fed."

Preschooler Discipline - Doesn't Listen: No Executive Function

See also explanation under "Toddler Discipline - Doesn't Listen"

"My 3 year-old won't listen to me. She complies when I threaten, but I hate to do that. Are there any other ways to motivate her?"

Brain development stage: 3 year-olds have other things on their minds. They are still very ego-centric in the here and now, and focused on what they want; not on what you want.

Suggestions:

- Use the "When/then" phrase. "When we clean up your toys, then we can have a snack."

- At three, they are just beginning to learn natural consequences. Use sparingly and give a lot of warnings.

- Make it a game. Make it fun.

- Give a positive reward.

- About 60% of children under 5 do not comply to requests, so she is behaving normal developmentally. Children can generally do tasks on their own by age 12 so she has a long way to go yet.

- Work together and talk about why the task is important.

- Pick your battles.

- Be consistent. Emphasize she is part of the family and we all pitch in to help out.

- Practice self-control through play and games. Play "Simon Says," "Bingo," "Red Light, Green Light," and Freeze Tag to learn how to stop when appropriate. Practice taking turns by doing things with her.

- Take photos of things you want her to do and not to do and make a photo book from those photo uploading sites. You can "print" a book for any lesson you want to teach! Read the books at night during bedtime cuddle time.

Preschooler Discipline - Dictator

"My 4 year-old son can often behave like a dictator. I pick my battles, and give in to his wants quite a bit, and then I feel like I don't get any respect as the "Alpha Dog" because he doesn't listen to me. My partner thinks I am too soft. Where is the line between being too much of a pushover, and too authoritarian?"

Brain development stage: Young children don't have much power. As parents who have money, transportation and decision-making opportunities, you have a lot of power! Always remember that!

Suggestions:

- Good leaders rarely need to wield the power of control. They listen and guide most of the time, about 90 percent, and then firmly take control when they truly need to about 10 percent of the time. You are a good leader.
- Pick your battles and stay with them.
- Choose what you are going to do and mentally know where your limit is.
- You always have the power of controlling yourself. Say "No!" if you don't want to do anything. Your son owns his reaction to your limits. You are not responsible for how he feels.

Preschooler Discipline - Handling Defiance

"My 5 year-old daughter reacts to most of my requests with defiance. She is constantly pushing back. I'm losing my mind and my patience."

Brain development stage: Young children don't have much power and some children's personalities demand more control over their lives then we can imagine. When we instruct over and over, and it feels like a broken record to us when we observe that the child is still not listening, we must remember that we are still reinforcing pathways between brain neurons which will eventually take hold and shape future behavior. It will happen.

Suggestions:

- Don't give up. Keep teaching over and over again. Someday, you will see the fruits of your labor!

- Give 2-3 choices of which all are okay with you.

- Problem-solve with them. Be open to helping them get their way. On the other hand, insist on them helping you get your way at other times. Remind them that it is reciprocal.

- No doesn't work for these "spirited" kids. Explain and reason with them.

- As much as possible, put things she can't have, out of site.

- Pick your battles. Give in on the small things, so you have more incentive to hold your ground on the big things that matter.

- Phrase everything in the positive - "We walk." "We help out." "We pat the dog gently."

- On days where there might be endless battles, as much as possible, distract. The child might not notice they are not getting options.

Preschooler Discipline - Tosses Clothing

"My child leaves clothes all over the house and socks all over the floor."

Brain development stage: Children live in the moment and don't think much about finding items in the future or cleaning up.

Suggestions:

- Buy socks all one color such as white or black. Then you don't have to sort and they are easy clean-up. Have a big bin of clean socks by the door and an empty bin for all dirty socks.

- Have children pick up all socks once per week as their chore.

- Have a specific drawer or cubby for each child's outerwear (and later school) items.

- Hang a basketball hoop over a laundry basket in their rooms.

- Hang a colorful pillowcase over the door that they can use for laundry tossing.

- Make it routine that coats get hung up, (put hooks at their level) as soon as they come home.

Preschooler Discipline - Lies

"My 4 year-old lies about a lot of things. I want to nip this in the bud."

Brain development stage: Preschoolers are in the magical thinking stage and may or may not understand that lying is not telling the truth, but telling their perception of reality.

Suggestions:

- Describe what you see rather than trap them into a lie. Say, "I see that you have the toy from Liam's house. We need to give it back to him." Don't say, "Did you take that toy from Liam's?" You are setting them up to lie.
- Read books about lying.
- Help her find a way to get her needs met without lying.
- Don't ever punish. Children lie because they fear punishment.

....

Preschooler Discipline - Refuses to Sit Quietly

"My 4 year-old daughter won't sit quietly when in church, at concerts, or adult places such as the train station or court. She isn't interested in using the tablet."

Brain development stage: Children don't have the self-control or brain development to sit quietly for more than a few minutes at this age. You have to constantly entertain them or go home.

Suggestions:

- Appreciate every minute she is quiet.
- Bring distractions such as quiet toys like markers, paper, stickers, books, magnetic boards and quiet food that takes a long time to eat such as raisins, cereal, juice boxes.
- Find little jobs for her such as "count the blue hats" or "count how many times the minister says 'we'."
- Practice whispering on a tape recorder so she can hear what being quiet sounds like.
- Sit in the back for quick escapes.
- Sit in the front so she can see if it is a more child-friendly venue.

- Sit between siblings so they don't fight because of boredom.
- Do a physical activity like going to the park, just before she is expected to be quiet for a long time.

Preschooler Discipline - Nags for Treats

"My 5 year-old son nags me when he wants something. He never gives up!"

Brain development stage: Children don't know when they are being annoying to us.

Suggestions:

- Never buy a treat when they nag and clarify the rule every time before you go out.
- Consider buying a treat when they ask politely.
- Ignore the tantrum when you say "No."
- Decide before you go into the store on what you are and are not going to do.
- Scoop them up and calmly leave. Just look straight ahead. Don't look at anyone else or you will feel judged.
- Good for you. Pat yourself on the shoulder for being an awesome parent!

Preschooler Discipline - Won't Carry Items

"Our 5 year-old daughter refuses to carry her backpack and her items when we are out."

Brain development stage: Preschoolers have to be reminded to carry their things.

Suggestions:

- Make it routine that she goes everywhere with a backpack. She can carry her shopping, library books, lunch and coat in there.
- Ask her to bring in her personal items from the car; coat, lunch containers, swim and snow gear.
- Use a wagon or sled to bring her and all her stuff around at outings. Preschoolers do get tired easily in places like the zoo where there is a lot of walking.

Preschooler Discipline - Runs Away

"My 3 year-old son bolts every time he gets the opportunity when we are out in public and I have to leave the baby in his stroller or high chair while I run after him. It's getting worse."

Brain development stage: Running is a very fun game to young children who can't comprehend the danger of it. They need parents and caregivers to keep them safe. Preschoolers may find the "run and chase" game fun. They also run because they are physically active and they find items very interesting and want to run and touch them. They are old enough to understand your concerns if you tell them, but lack the self-control to follow directions when it goes against what they want.

Suggestions:

- Safety first. Get a leash and don't worry about what it looks like or what other people think.
- Some of those child leashes are very short. Get a longer, retractable dog leash and tie it to the child leash for extra length.
- Get those ropes with rings so your son will hold on.
- Constant supervision is required.
- Get a big shopping cart where you can contain him and the baby bucket and he can't easily escape (unless he jumps).
- Have a natural consequence. Warn him before you go to a public place that if he doesn't stay close by you, he will not go the next time.
- Leave him at home with your partner and stick with your "No."
- Read a book or story about children who run away from caregivers so he might understand the seriousness of it. Most kids just think it is fun as it turns into a chase game for them and a nightmare for you.
- Stop going to places for awhile, where you don't have to bring him. It's a phase and he will gain the self-control needed to overcome his urge to look at things, run and instead will stay with you.
- Get your baby out of the car first and settled into the stroller/cart and then get the runner in the cart and settled.
- Use a whistle to signal "Freeze" and that you are serious about him stopping. Play the game before hand so he understands how it works.

- Don't let him loose even once in a store, even if that particular store is safe, because then he will always want to run free for the next couple times, no matter what store he is in.
- Put a lock on the top of your front door so you control when everyone leaves the house.
- Role play before you leave the house. Go over what could happen if he gets away from you.
- If he runs, give the baby to another mom to watch and run after him.
- Give him a special reward for every two times he stays with you. Don't worry – you won't be doing it forever.
- Give him a job to do. Give him a clipboard with paper and pencils and he has to draw the things you want to buy.
- Go early in the day when stores are less crowded.
- Shop at stores with in-store daycares.
- Bring snacks and distribute when you don't want him to run.
- Buy online as much as possible.
- Leave him home and go shopping at night when your partner is home.
- Make sure your child has labels on him such as a rubber bracelet with your cell phone written in permanent ink on the inside of the bracelet.
- Make a plan with him in case he gets lost.
- Take a photo of him each time you go out in public in case he gets lost.
- Get a double stroller.
- Distract him with a movie or tablet. Only promise him the item if he sits still in the cart or stroller.

Preschooler Discipline - Not Listening in Public

"How do I get my child to listen and obey the adult in charge while he is out on a play date?"

Brain development stage: Children generally behave better for someone else (an unknown person) than someone they love and know well (a family member) because they feel safe with the familiar. Children are also able to learn about different expectations in different environments as young as 18 months.

Suggestions:

- Talk to him before you go to someone's house, about expected behavior and also stranger danger.

- Go over specifics – "Is throwing toys something we do in other people's houses?" Let him figure out the answers.

- Instill that it's someone else's house and we are the guest. We have to abide by certain rules.

- Have chats about the rules before you go in. Tell him that if he doesn't respect the rules, he will have to leave.

- Talk about your feelings on the way home, when he acts that way. Say, "I feel embarrassed when you explore other people's fridge without asking."

- Be specific – he probably doesn't understand words like "respect" or "appropriate." Use words he will understand. "We don't go into other people's bedrooms. It's a bad thing to do."

- Separate him as a person from the action. It is "bad" to explore bedrooms. He is not "bad."

- Offer suggestions of how to act. "We can play in the playroom, living room or outside."

- Talk about respect and what it is:

What is respect?

Treating someone the way you want to be treated.

A mutual common ground of treating people well.

Treating people and belongings kindly.

Using manners.

Being kind to people with your mouth, eyes and hands.

Encarta Dictionary Definition: A feeling of deference, admiration, thoughtfulness and consideration.

....

Preschooler Discipline - Refuses Sharing

"My 3 year-old son will not share with his younger brother."

Brain development stage: Children begin to have a sense of ownership around age 3, and really care about possessing certain items in their grasp. They also have no idea about how long a "turn" is or how long "5 minutes" are. Children younger than 3 should not be expected to share, as it is a confusing concept and their brains can't understand it yet.

Suggestions:

- Bring in the concept of negotiation. If he wants something that the other child has, teach him that he has to find some item that will catch the other child's attention and the other child will want to trade for it.

- Tell him to "work it out" and then teach ways how to.

- Keep precious items that are not sharable, tucked away in a locked room.

- Assure him that if another child breaks it, you will replace anything he shares.

- Limit play-dates to the playroom only and not your child's bedroom where his special things are.

- Show how much you enjoy sharing with your friends. Point out how sharing is reciprocal and benefits you and him.

- Have patience - it will come.

- Spend more time with him.

- Role play how to give up a toy and how to ask for it back.

- Problem-solve who gets it and for how long, so that everyone is happy. Perhaps the first person to get it, gets a shorter turn.

- Allow him to say "no" to sharing and he soon learns that if he says "no" too often, the other child will say "no" too and no one wins.

- Ask the child to state how many more minutes until the other child can have a turn. Allow him the ability to control time. Set the timer and remind him to hand it over when the timer goes off.

- If he doesn't hand it over, say the toy has to go at the count of 3. Say "I will count to 3 and you will give it back, or I will "help" you give it back." You may have to pry the toy out of his hand, and help him through the resulting tantrum or crying. Support his feelings. Give hugs and acknowledge that it is hard to let something go.

- Remember that children under age 5 listen only 40% of the time. He will get better at sharing.

- If the other child doesn't care about a turn, let it go. You will have many opportunities to settle sibling squabbles in the future.

Preschooler Discipline - Screaming

"My 3 year-old daughter screams."

Brain development stage: Screaming is common in the years between birth and 6.

Suggestions:

- Wear earplugs when she screams.
- Talk about strategies she can try when she is calm.
- Give her positive feedback for the acceptable behavior, such as when she doesn't scream.
- Track her days of non-screaming on a chart and give her gum as a reward.
- Talk to her about the different types of voices there are when you and she are calm - model the "inside" voice, the "outside" voice, the "normal" voice and the "screaming" voice.
- Encourage your partner to get involved.
- Use the shock factor – drop to the floor when she does it.
- Video tape the behavior and show it to her.

Preschooler Discipline - Uses Slang Words

"My daughter's vocabulary is growing and she is using undesirable words to express herself, such as, 'I don't want to go to the dumb park.' How do I get her to choose her words differently?"

Suggestions:

- You could have an authoritarian figure like a teacher talk to her about her choice of words. Sometimes our children will heed the advice of another adult over ourselves.

- When your daughter uses undesirable words to express her wishes or feelings, communicate further with her and try to get her to feel into what she is really trying to say; When she says "My brother is dumb," look around and see what the issue really is. Did he take her toy? Is he sitting on her doll? Take in the whole picture and communicate back to her what you see and think is going on. Use your active listening skills. Say, "I can see that you are angry with your brother for taking your toy." Teach I-statements such as "I want my toy back please."

- Keep adding new words into her vocabulary that she can use other than "dumb." Replace the word with a more appropriate one.

- Set up a reward chart with her. Use stickers or smiley faces to show when she is using new, appropriate, words. Don't punish her when she uses an inappropriate word, but don't reward her either. If she is earning more 'sad faces' than 'happy faces', let her know what she needs to do in order to earn a happy face.

- Go over any family ground rules that you have; what is acceptable in the house and what is not acceptable, and draw pictures of them or photographs rather than a list. Post the "rules."

- Breathe deeply, play fully, and enjoy your little angels; even when they act the opposite.

- Tell your friends that you are aware of her language and are working on it.

- Ignore the word. If it is not reinforced, it loses specialness.

Preschooler Discipline - Power Struggles

"My 5 year-old daughter is in an ornery stage. How do I stop getting into power struggles over everything?"

Brain development stage: 5 year-olds are starting to want control over their lives and make more decisions. It's a good sign of brain development.

Suggestions:

- Give choices and allow her as many age-appropriate decisions as you can.

- Say 10 "Yeses" for every 1 "No" that you have to stick to.

- Make sure that she gets enough sleep and eats regularly.

- Rephrase your "No's". Say, "later," "not now," "let me think about it," etc.

- Acknowledge what she is saying and ask, "What is your idea? What is your point of view? What do you think?"

- Remind her of the rule.

- Curb the TV, and movies. The characters can be catty, snarky and full of attitude - all behaviors that young children pick up on and try out with family members.

- Warn of the parameters of what is coming. "We will have to leave in 30 minutes and we need to get dressed for Winter. We have to go right away, so please don't start a computer game that will take too long."

- If they are upset because you said "No," don't worry about it. They own their feelings and reactions which you can't control. Just stick with your "No" and let the reactions fall where they will. The more they can see that you are upset with their anger, the more they will express their anger loudly. Don't change your ruling of "No" and they will understand that you mean what you say.

Preschooler Discipline - Stealing

"My 5 year-old daughter took an item from a store. She also has taken toys from friends' houses and playgroups. How do I handle this without punishment?"

Brain development stage: 5 year-olds are still in that wishful thinking stage where they wish they owned an item. If they see no other way that they can have an item, they may just take it. It's normal for them to have difficulty letting go of toys at this age. They are not in the adult space yet, where people ask for things they want. They may know it is wrong to just take it, but struggle with self-control.

Suggestions:

- Insist that she give it back to the rightful owners and encourage an apology. Phone the victim ahead of time to let them know what is going to happen.
- Ask that she write or draw a picture to express that she is sorry.
- Don't ignore it or worse, let her keep it. This is a appropriate teachable moment.
- Don't rescue her from the scolding the store or friend's parents might give her. Let her hear "the victim's statements."
- Emphasize empathy. Ask her how she feels if someone took her things?
- Watch her closely in stores and at friends houses. Check her pockets on the way out until you can trust her again.
- In stores, don't let her have the item until she has paid or seen you pay.
- Give permission to have things as much as possible when she asks, so that she learns that asking permission gets her needs and wants met.
- Always ask her permission when you take her things.
- Read books about stealing.
- Teach her how to ask to borrow items from friends' homes. Write down the toy borrowed and be sure to return it.
- If the friend doesn't allow borrowing, say, "That toy doesn't belong to us. We can leave it here to play with next time. It will miss it's family if we take it with us. Let's say good-bye to the toy. See you later toy!"
- If it happens at a playgroup, model the act of asking for permission to take the toy home for a week. Be sure to bring the toy back next week.

Preschooler Discipline - Child Says "NO!"

"My 5 yr-old daughter retorts, 'NO!' when I ask her to do something. She adds, 'That's my choice and you have to respect that!' What do I say and do?"

Brain development stage: Preschoolers are figuring out how to use what little power they have. They hear the "No" word so much from adults and recognise that it is a powerful word and like to use it for themselves too.

Suggestions:

- Acknowledge her feelings of not wanting to do the duty or job. Say, "I understand that you are busy and don't want to clean up."
- Say, "We need to clean up our toys or we can't use them."
- Say, "I need you to help clean up."
- Don't give her choices about if she should clean up, but you can give her a choice on how or when to clean up.
- Use a kitchen timer or clock or some other audio or visual clue that it is time to start a job.
- Use construction paper in red, yellow or green to cue her that it is time to end playing and start clean-up.
- Help her and do it together. It's more fun to work alongside each other.
- Keep at it. Perhaps she picks up one toy today and 20 next week. Be consistent in insisting that she helps no matter how much. It's not the severity of clean-up but the certainty.
- Make it fun or a game.
- Scale down expectations.
- Hold a contest. Nothing motivates kids more than a friendly competition.

Preschooler Discipline - Misbehavior After Vacation

"My 3 year-old acts up the first couple of days we are together, after we have been apart, such as when I have been away on a trip."

Brain development stage: Preschoolers still are in the stage of separation anxiety. When children reunite with parents, they often don't know how to express their fear and anxiety of being left, and show it in behavior – clinginess, tears, misbehavior and refusal to be independent. They often revert back to not being able to brush their teeth, get dressed, pour their own juice, etc.

Suggestions:

- Ride the wave and pump up the "I missed you!" acknowledgements.
- Give up and do it for them. The attention you give is what they need. They will fill up on attention and go back to their independence of doing things themselves.
- Say, "Let's do something together."
- Clear your schedule and read on the couch and reconnect.
- Play games, bake together and spend a lot of focused time together.
- Try to work on your own patience.
- Let her know that you will always be there.
- When she is clingy, sit and hold her. It takes forever, but then she will know she has your attention and she won't have to act out to get it.

Preschooler Discipline - Makes Messes

"My 4.5 year-old is being contrary all the time. He gets into things like toilet paper and duct tape and makes things without asking. He even goes into the bathroom and mixes liquids for perfumes and concoctions. How can I channel this?"

Brain development stage: Children love to explore as their brains are driving them to use all 5 of their senses to discover the world around them. They have no concept of "mess" but can learn about it and help clean up.

Suggestions:

- He sounds pretty creative. Hide the items that he tends to use if you are feeling like you don't want to deal with a mess that day.
- Lock away items you absolutely don't want him to use. Use baby gates and locks.

- Get him to help with clean-up. Play a five minute song and race to clean up before the song ends. Or use a timer.

- Teach him to clean up before the next activity gets set out.

- Sing and talk while cleaning up.

- Give appreciation for any small effort he makes.

- Use when/then. Say, "When we clean up, then we can have snack."

- Be specific. Say, "You pick up all the blocks and put them in this container. I'll pick up the rest."

- Get a clean dustpan to help scoop up the small toys.

- Have visiting friends help with clean-up.

- Write these words in big letters and post on your fridge, so you can remember the positive side of his actions: "Creative", "Initiative", "Problem-solver", "Inventor", "Resourceful", or "Scientific."

- Consider putting him in a science class as an outlet for his creativity.

- Get him outside with fresh air and exercise.

- Say, "Yes, we can play this, but with supervision." Make time and space for him to experiment under your watchful eye.

- Take photos so you have memories of his creativity.

- Find the need. Does he need attention and "gets into things that are inappropriate" to get your attention? If so, give positive attention when he is doing non-messy things.

- Buy him a lab coat and safety goggles and set some "lab" parameters or rules for how much stuff to use and how to clean it up.

- Consider pre-school – perhaps he needs more things to do.

- Give a warning and then put it away.

- Bake and cook with him – he can mix the "potions."

- Recycle and roll up the tape and toilet paper.

Preschooler Discipline - Name-Calling

"One or both of my children will sometimes be mean to me by saying "Stupid Mommy," or other name calling. Then they giggle and show no remorse when I get upset. How do I handle this?"

Brain development stage: Children are watching to see what reaction comes out of that. A firm, but respectful response is helpful in stopping that behavior.

Suggestions:

- Give it very little attention in the moment, so it doesn't escalate.
- You could distract them to take the focus off the situation.
- It's probably "try it out" behavior, so address it right away and say, "That is NOT acceptable!"
- Keep them busy; perhaps they are bored.
- In a calm moment, talk to the kids and tell them how hurtful it is for you.
- Say in a loud, upset voice, "Ouch, I feel hurt!"
- Read books about children teasing.
- Model respect. Don't call them nicknames if they don't like them
- Teach them what is name-calling, slang, swearing and teasing.
- Recite the family rule, "In our family, we don't call people that!" Say it over and over again.
- Don't worry about "the talk" not being in the moment – it will sink in better in a moment that you are connecting – like before bedtime. Bring up the matter then.
- You decide what you are in control of. If you feel you are being abused, stop doing favours for them. Tell them why.
- Keep calm. Don't react in anger, but be firm.
- Have a family meeting – talk about a special code word that everyone in the family can use to tell others that the teasing is crossing over to hurtful behavior. It could be something simple like, "ouch!" or "purple peacock!"

Preschooler Discipline - Whining

"How do I cut down on whining from my preschooler?"

Brain development stage: Babies cry, toddlers shriek, preschoolers whine, school-agers speak with attitude, and teens swear. It's a normal developmental stage to try out vocal variety. Children whine more when they are tired.

Suggestions:

- Copy her and say "That doesn't sound very nice, does it?"
- Change your tone of voice and say "Stop Whining."
- Acknowledge what she is whining about, and say "Ask again," or ignore it.
- Say, "Can you tell me in a real voice?" Then give what it is that she wants when she uses the real voice.
- Distract with another activity.
- Say, "Take your whining voice out of your mouth, and put it in your pocket. Let's try again."
- Say, "Can you ask me nicely?" "Please use big girl words."
- Get her to take deep breaths and calm down.
- Reframe it, "Is this what you mean?"
- Acknowledge feelings, "It looks like you are getting angry."
- Say "Help please – Mom?"
- Practice with her favorite stuffed animal and model different voices: outdoors, indoors, whiney, normal, shouting, whisper, etc.
- Say, "It hurts my ears."
- It's okay when she asks for something you can give, but harder when it is something you can't give. Try to give another alternative.
- Pretend that you can't hear when the whining is occurring.
- Remember that she is not doing it on purpose – she genuinely wants something.
- Leave her at home if shopping is a major problem.
- Say, "If you whine, you will definitely NOT get it. If you use a normal voice, like this, then you will get it." Give it as soon as you can if she doesn't whine.

Preschooler Discipline - Back-Talk

"My son is 5 and is constantly talking back to me. He tells me I'm wrong and says it in a snarky voice. How do I stop this?"

Brain development stage: Children are great imitators and like to copy the adults they see in media, school and around them. They try it out at home and those they feel the safest with.

Suggestions:

- Say, "I won't interact with you, when you speak to me that way." Then, stop talking.

- Say, "Enough!" Don't engage, don't talk.

- Don't punish him. Not talking to him while you are angry is enough of a natural consequence and very real.

- Deep breathe.

- Don't let him see your reaction. That may be the payoff he gets for attention. He is getting you riled. Say, "I'm not engaging." Then walk away.

- Tell him how you feel in an "I-statement", when you are connecting with him in a good space, such as playing ball at the park or going for ice-cream. Say, "I feel discounted when you speak to me with back talk." Then explain what it sounds like. Brainstorm ways he can communicate without the snarkiness.

- Reinforce praise when he does or says things that respect you.

- Say, "No!" "Stop it!" These are times you really need to use your "No!"

- Be consistent on this one!

- Have your partner talk to him about respecting you.

Preschooler Discipline - Acting Out in Public

"My son, 4.5 yrs, was whining and acting out, because he was required to share. Normally, I would have taken him to a quieter place and calmed him down, but I felt watched and judged and so I thought I should do a harsher type of time-out, then I normally would have in private. How do I deal with my feelings?"

Brain development stage: Children don't understand social rules. We have to explain and remind them about it. It's also normal for us to modify our parenting depending on the group situation we are in.

Suggestions:

- Scoop him up and carry him to a quieter place that is out of hearing and sight of other people. Go to another room, or your car, where you can both calm down and talk. He can try to come back. If it looks like it might just be a bad day, go home.

- Take your groceries to the customer service and say you will be back. Leave.

- Switch gears and try to imagine some compassion for the child.
- Talk in the quiet place after you have calmed down.
- Get comfortable with how you want to parent.
- Stay with your plan, no matter who is watching.
- People who already have kids are very empathetic. Remember that!
- Try distracting him while in public and then in private, deal with the real issue.
- Say in a loud voice, so onlookers can hear, "Let's talk about this in private."

Preschooler Discipline - Stop Yelling at Child

"My older children don't listen. I am reduced to yelling all the time, and I really want to stop. What can I do?"

Brain development stage: Children under age 6 are very egocentric and are focused on their needs rather than other's needs. They are reminded to care about others and learn empathy as they grow.

Suggestions:

Reducing yelling takes a lot of practice, but it can be done, so congratulate yourself for every yell that was turned into a calm response!

First, separate your frustration from your commands to motivate.

Deal with your frustration/anger first:

- Grit your teeth.
- Stomp your feet.
- Yell into the toilet and flush the negatives down.
- Drink water.
- Breathe.
- Play some music.
- Have a cup of tea.
- Check your social media site.
- Clean something.
- Phone a friend.
- Walk away – go to the bathroom and tell your child where you are going. Say, "I'm taking a time-out to calm down."

- Use self-talk. Think, "She is distracted. She is just doing what children her age do. She is not being malicious."
- Take a Mommy or Daddy time-out and do whatever makes you feel good. Make sure the kids are safe if they are young.

Next, deal with the "not listening":

- Go directly up to your child and whisper in your child's ear.
- Gush when the child does follow directions.
- Use simple one, two or three word directions.
- Give one direction at a time.
- Or go directly up to your child, get eye contact, state your request and put your hand on her shoulder and stay there until she complies. Or gently take her hand and lead her to what you want done.
- If she refuses, avoid power struggles. Leave for a few minutes. Come back in ten minutes, connect with her and ask again. Try again in a few minutes, hours or a day.
- Declare your feelings with "I-statements;" "I'm feeling really angry. I'm frustrated that you are fighting. I'm angry that nothing is happening and I don't wish to yell."
- Don't talk at all. Just do what you need to do. You can only control you. Stop doing things, or change things around or take action. If daughter doesn't pick up some toys and she wants you to take her to the park, just tell her that you had an extra 60 minutes but it was taken up by cleaning up the mess. Just do it! Be real, not vindictive. Be open to her suggestions to problem-solve it.

Preschooler Discipline - Wants Own Way

"My 4 year-old son always wants his way. He says "No" a lot to me. Some issues are very important to me and I don't want to lose those ones. I'm an empathetic person, but how do I stick to my guns when it really matters like in areas such as tooth brushing or car seats?"

Brain development stage: There are four areas that preschoolers and parents get into struggles over and are all within the control of the child - eating, sleeping, toileting and learning. Parents must step out of the power struggle as children control those areas. Parents can facilitate those but can't outright control them.

Suggestions:

- Repeat your ruling. This is more for you to stick with it, than for him. "Teeth need to be cleaned." "The car doesn't drive until everyone is buckled in!" "Dishwasher gets emptied before we play."

- Wear earplugs to lessen the loud sounds of crying and protest.

- Stop talking and just do it.

- Acknowledge his feelings but continue the action such as putting him in his carseat. "I know you feel restrained in this seat. We need to be safe."

- The more the routine, the less the struggle. They get used to it.

- Say, "Here are your two choices," or "Let's make a deal!"

- Never ask a question where they could give a "yes" or "no" answer such as "Let's get your boots on, okay?" Say, "Will you go and get your boots or would you like Mommy to get your boots?" Either way, they are getting their boots.

- What is their true need? Behavior is only a symptom.

- Use distraction for yourself – music player, drinking water, reading a magazine – anything to take the focus off the child.

....

Preschooler Discipline - Handling "I hate you!"

"My 4 year-old son loves to say "I hate you!" Our 2 year-old is picking up that language. How do I stop that?"

Brain development stage: Hate is a flippant word for children but a strong word for adults. We learn to attach meanings to words. Children don't get this, and only understand it as a power word, not what it means to us.

Suggestions:

- Talk to him about how you feel.

- Explain that it hurts your feelings and that those are cruel words.

- Say, "I love you. But you can't have all the cookies." Don't give him the cookies.

- State the rule, "We don't use the word 'hate' or 'stupid.'

- Say, "That's okay. I love you."

- Tell him to use the words, "I don't like it when..." instead of "I hate..."

- Use colors to describe feelings. Red is mad, blue is serene, yellow is happy. Ask him, "Are you feeling red right now?"

- Push the I-statement. Say, "You need to say this in an 'I-statement'. Say 'I don't like this!'" Say to him, "Repeat after me..." "I feel................when............. because............." Allow him time to fill in the blanks so he gets the format of the I-statement.

- Acknowledge his feelings but continue the action, such as not giving him the cookies. "I know you feel angry right now. I will help you through your feelings."

Preschooler Discipline - Taking Toys

"My 3.5 year-old son takes toys from other kids. How do I stop it?"

Brain development stage: A child is naturally possessive over objects he touches. A 3 year-old is just beginning to learn ownership and lending.

Suggestions:

- Give him more one-on-one time.
- Teach him to ask for a turn. When the other child says, "No", teach your child to ask again or ask for a time that he can have a turn. Go with him to assure him of your presence. If he doesn't ask, you model asking for him so he learns how.
- Give more attention when he does positive things like sharing.
- Try to talk to him. Ask "Why?"
- It is developmentally appropriate behavior but needs to be addressed.
- Could be due to poor impulse control, power struggles or lack of knowledge of how to channel anger.
- Give him positive physical ways to handle anger from rejection, such as feet stamping, breathing, banging his hands, etc.
- Get your son and go for a walk together. Come back when he is calm and has a concrete tool such as deep breathing to try when he is angry.

Preschooler Discipline - Hitting and Attitude

"What can I do for the really big two discipline issues of hitting others and attitude statements, instead of using time-out or spanking?"

Brain development stage: Attitude is assertive language that is packaged wrong. Children of all ages need to be taught assertive language that is respectful and that adults will listen to. Hitting is misplaced anger. Preschoolers are still developing the art of self-control and they make mistakes. Teach that hitting is not okay, and eventually the brain will reinforce those pathways of learning and the teaching will stick. See hitting under toddler section as well.

Suggestions:

Hitting, biting, and spitting

- Teach how to handle anger and frustration - give her tools to calm down. Make a "yes" list of all the things she can do in order to get a grip. Post the list somewhere that she can see it in the moment of anger.
- Try to understand her feelings and talk about what she can do when she is feeling angry and frustrated. Don't talk until after she has calmed down.
- Role play the words and physical actions to express the anger.
- Remind her about what is acceptable. Tell her it was a mistake and you expect her to do a bit better next time.
- Teach her the words to us in order to express her anger without hitting
- Give information. Say "Mommy is a person and we don't hit people."
- Say, "NO!"
- Don't hit, bite or spit back. Model what she should do, not what she shouldn't.
- Get her to clean up the anger mess after she is calm.
- Work on empathy skills. Ask what she thinks the victim might be feeling.
- Be present and vigilant for a while. Keep reinforcing the teaching. She can't be charged with assault until age 13, so she has lots of time to practice.
- Get her to ask for a "High five" so she can hit in an acceptable way.
- See "hitting" under other age categories as well.

Disrespect, attitude, mocking

- Selective ignoring sometimes works.
- Use I-statements such as "I don't like that."
- Say, "Try saying that again but in your respectful voice."
- Model kind language.
- Show her how different voice tones sound.

*For both, remember to keep "teaching" them that it is not acceptable. You don't have to punish them for it, but you do have to keep reminding children that it is not the acceptable way to treat people. That's the essence of discipline versus punishment. Discipline is on-going teaching and eventually, by the teen years, they will get it.

Preschooler Discipline - Spitting and Spilling

"My 3 year-old is normally quite well-behaved, but he is in this exploratory spilling stage. I take away the liquid and now he deliberately spits at people. What can I do?"

Brain development stage: Deliberate spilling is science in action. Many children love to play with liquid and experiment with its properties. Or, it is a desire for attention. Spitting is also science but needs to be curbed. He still has little self-control and wants to explore, but these behaviours are difficult for parents and their needs for clean can also be respected.

Suggestions:

- Ignore it and don't give it attention. Leave the mess be, to clean up later so it doesn't add to the drama.
- Use natural consequences. Steer the child to "clean it up." Problem-solve any resistance.
- Remember that this too shall pass.
- Allow open cups at the table and sippy cups anywhere else.
- Use cups with suction bottoms.
- Just serve water, which is much easier to clean up than milk, until the behaviour runs out of steam.
- Just hand him towels to clean up. Don't say anything. Keep repeating the handing of towels, so children know that they have to clean up their messes.
- If it happens while driving, give no food or water in the future. This is a safety issue too so children don't choke while you are occupied on busy roads.
- Allow the behaviour, but contain it: allow spitting in the bath tub, sink, or toilet, but not at people. Sometimes if the child has to leave the playing area to go do it, it might not be worth it then.

Preschooler Feeding - Picky Eating

"My 4 year-old daughter won't eat much. She loves noodles and cheese but not much variety. How do I get her to eat?"

Brain development stage: It's normal for young children to have food jags, where they only eat a certain type of food for months on end, and shun all others. They are still developing taste buds so may have certain preferences.

Suggestions:

- She might like smoothies.
- Don't overload her plate. Put small amounts on her plate, (teaspoonful) and replenish as she eats.
- Insist on setting a time that she can finish.
- Don't show her the preferred food until the yucky food is eaten.
- Ask for help in cooking and shopping.
- Back off and don't pressure. She will get what she needs.
- Make it a rule that everyone comes to the table for social reasons even if they don't want to eat.
- Limit juice, milk and liquids. Serve only water between meals and snacks.
- Be sure all snacks are healthy.
- Hide the junk food or don't buy it.
- Sneak in vegetables so she doesn't know they are there.
- Don't prepare food just for her. Have something on the table that you know she will eat such as apples, cheese and bread.
- Adapt dishes. Serve your curry but leave out the spice. Serve your noodles but leave out the sauce.
- Don't worry. Kids get all they need over their monthly food intake.
- Check for cavities - sometimes toothache will cause loss of appetite.
- Have a "No thank you," bowl where she can spit out food she tries but doesn't like.
- Give raw vegetables a grown-up name such as "veggie capers" so it sounds more appealing.
- Each child can pick a small piece and say "Cheers" while clinking the food together. You can do it with your child too.
- Have a "No manners," night or hour. Eat with fingers, burp, don't say "please" etc. Lots of fun!
- Also see "Picky Eating" under the Toddler section.

Preschooler Feeding - Craving Candy

"My 4 year-old daughter craves candy. She hunts around the house looking for it."

Brain development stage: Some children love sugar and some can take it or leave it.

Suggestions:

- Provide structure. People should eat by the 80/20 rule of 80% healthy foods, and 20% "less healthy" foods.
- Don't bring treats home if you don't want the children to eat it.
- Give her a small piece of candy at every meal. Put it on the plate with the dinner so it doesn't elevate the status to "treat."
- Give her sugar-free gum regularly.
- Make your own healthy candy.
- Help her say "no" to the craving. The more times she can resist the urge, the brain makes pathways that make that outcome more likely as a first choice of action.
- Replace candy with her favorite fruit.
- Just say "No."
- Show her photos of rotten teeth.
- Get a doctor's opinion. Sometimes people are missing nutrients in their diet when they crave a certain food.

Preschooler Health - Refuses Hand-Washing

"My 4 year-old son forgets to wash his hands even after eating sticky foods."

Brain development stage: Children at this age are forgetful and often don't have adult standards of cleanliness.

Suggestions:
- Make it routine to wash hands before and after eating at every meal and snack.
- Get some fun bathroom soap dispensers and a stool.
- Sing the Happy Birthday song so he learns how long to scrub.

- Watch a video about germs.
- Always carry wet-wipes and use them to wash sticky fingers.

....

Preschooler and Parenting partner - Partner Doesn't Engage Children

"My partner doesn't seem to connect, play with or communicate with his 1 year-old or 3 year-old daughters even when he is tasked with parenting them. The kids vie for his attention, but he is always on the computer or phone."

Brain development stage: Young children need at least one engaged, nurturing parent in their lives. If they have more than one, that's good, but they just need one.

Suggestions:

- Dad probably needs downtime or stimulation, so perhaps discuss how he can have it in chunks of time and then provide chunks of time with the kids that are screen-free.
- Each parent controls their relationship with each child. Nagging him may produce a divide between him and the children, and also you and him.
- Verbally praise him when he does engage - such as reading and paying attention to the girls.
- Remember that some dads are uncomfortable with babies and toddlers. They often develop better relationships with older children that can talk and share interests with him.
- Let natural consequences run its course. He may notice that you have a better relationship when he observes you and the children and make a conscious effort to build his relationship with them patterned after yours.
- Don't project ahead. Relationships change and can improve in months and years when motivation is there.
- Ask him for a specific job and time period. Say, "Can you take the kids to this movie on Saturday afternoon, so I can have a bath?"
- Use your "I-statements", by saying, "I need some time to myself. Can you please take the kids for a quick walk after you get home from work and have shifted gears yourself."

- Buy them season passes (so they have to go regularly) to engaging places without you. Sometimes Dads don't know how to play with children at home, depending on how they were raised. Get passes for the transit train, science centre, zoo, theatres, concerts, festivals, or museums. Sign them up for Daddy and children swim lessons, or story time. Later, perhaps he could volunteer as the soccer coach or beaver leader.

- Have an activity for them to do together and then leave the house. Board games for little ones are great - Hungry Hippos, Bumblebee, Candyland are some suitable for young children. 20 - 100 piece puzzles are great too.

- Home building stores run Kids Building Workshops on Saturdays that are free and drop-in. Dads are mostly there! Some theatres do family movies every Saturday morning at 9 am that are very cheap.

- Use your velcro lips (don't say anything) about how he interacts with them. Dads have to find their own way with kids, and overcoming their nervousness and parenting problems allows them to build confidence and engage more with their children. There are many, many great ways to do things that may not be how you do it. It's okay. Avoid criticism. It's more important that they develop a relationship, than if the kids have sunscreen on!

Preschooler Play - Child Won't Play Alone

"My 4 year-old doesn't play by himself. How can I encourage independent play?"

Brain development stage: Children are still very attached to family. They are mammals that function well in groups and are very social. As well, extraverts love to have company whereas introverts are very happy with alone time.

Suggestions:
- Say, "I'd love to play right now but I have to go do... Do you want to come and help me?"
- Get him settled in an activity and then try to leave with an excuse.
- Provide cool options for alone play time, and offer boring time with you.
- Tell him to start playing and then you will come and join him so he has something to look forward to.

- Put him in a supervisory role. He can be "the teacher" in charge of the stuffed animals and help them with an activity.
- Play for 10 minutes. Set a timer. Warn him that it will be 10 minutes.
- Don't feel that you have to entertain him. Let him help with chores and the things you have to get done.
- Schedule a play date at a friends home if you need to get something done.
- Bring out a packed away toy bucket so he will have some "new" things to play with.
- The person who hasn't seen the kids all day tend to do the "sprint" play where it is concentrated, fun and short, and the person home all day does the "marathon" play where it is long-running and paced. The person with the kids all day might wish to alternate the sprint and marathon play during the day.

Preschooler Play - Outdoor Play Diminishing

"How can I encourage outdoor, unstructured or active play?"

Brain development stage: Children are wired to play, anytime and anywhere.

Suggestions:

- Encourage them to walk or bike to indoor activities, or on errands with you.
- Let them play in the fenced back yard with anything they can find.
- Encourage problem-solving in daily parenting, so they learn how to be resourceful when out in the world on their own.
- Teach them to trust their inner feelings about people and strangers.
- Find a peer group of parents who encourage outdoor, unstructured play and take turns supervising each other's children.
- Take the children out to natural areas, parks and outdoor settings. They will find sticks, stones, insects and a lot of natural things to play with and observe.
- Don't worry about them getting dirty. It's worth it.
- Camp.
- Join an organization that does family outdoor fun such as Junior Forest Wardens or Girl Guides or Boy Scouts. Become a leader so you or the whole family may join.

- Cut down on screen time. Children don't need cell-phones until they are 13 and are out travelling on their own. Screens such as tablets and phones compete with natural outdoor active play.

- Ensure a quiet time after lunch for children who are too old to nap, to entertain themselves with toys at home, perhaps in their room or on their bed.

- If other parents at the park are helicopter parenting your child, tell them, "Thank you, but it is my child." Next time, go with a tribe of like-minded parents or go to a different part of the park.

Preschooler and Siblings - Sharing Toys

"How do I handle it when my two children will not share? How do I handle ownership and fighting over toys?"

Brain development stage: Children don't begin to understand sharing until age three and beyond. Sharing is a confusing concept that sometimes mean one will get the item back (like a toy) and not get the item back (like a cookie). As well, parents have unspoken rules regarding sharing such as who owns the item (birthday gift) or what the item is (many pieces of building block sets versus one ride-on toy).

Suggestions:

- We have no separate belongings. Everybody owns everything.
- Keep teaching. Say, "Your sister is more important than things."
- Help them take turns and teach sharing but don't expect it under age three.
- Give them ownership and the ability to say "No" to each other. They soon learn that the more they cooperate, the more they get cooperation back.
- Teach that if they say "No" to sharing, then they have to play with the toy by themselves in private, so they don't tease the one they said "No" to.
- They can decide how long a turn is.
- Put a timer on.
- Buy more toys the same. If the coveted toy is a birthday gift, buy a cheap second hand one for the other sibling.
- Give a toy that you know will be popular, but can only buy one of, to your partner so he or she 'owns' the toy and can lend it out to any of the children.

Preschooler and Siblings - Time With Each Child

"I have 3 children close in age. How do I carve out time with each child as an individual?"

Brain development stage: Children crave individual attention from each parent when they are young.

Suggestions:

- Whenever a parent needs to run an errand, take one child along. Children don't care what the activity is; they just love to be around you.
- Join a babysitting co-op and drop the other kids off to play while you do something special.
- Interact with one child while the other is in a registered class.
- Stagger bedtimes, bath times and nap times so you are only dealing with one child at a time.
- Pull one child out of school and do something special for the day.
- Occupy one child with books while you play a game in another room with the other child.
- Read bedtime stories separately, or have some cuddle time with each child before bed. Spend some time while you tuck them in by talking and singing with them.
- Play with each child separately 15 minutes a day - can be toys, games, singing, crafts or whatever you like to do. Perhaps use screen time to keep the other child occupied.
- Hire a teen to play with one child while you play with the other child. Take turns.
- Do the bedtime routine conveyor belt-style; have one parent bath and dry and one parent dress and feed each child, one-by-one, through the bedtime routine.

Preschooler and Siblings - Desires Sibling's Toys

"My preschooler wants to play with her sister's toys when she is away at school. How do I handle this?"

Brain development stage: Children do not want their-aged toys for themselves when they have older siblings. The sibling's toys are more desirable to play with.

Suggestions:

- Buy two of everything. You can always sell it, or pass it on to your grandchildren as each child will want something to pass on.
- Have the younger child ask permission each day.
- Buy some second hand toys that are the same - designate them family toys so everyone can play.
- Take a photo of how the toys are placed in the older sisters room and let the younger sister take them out to play with and put them back according to the photo when she is done.
- Give the "hot" toys to the parenting partner for holidays so no child owns them and all can play with them.

Preschooler and Siblings - Tattling and Complaining

"How do I handle complaints when I don't see what happened between two siblings? They are 3 and 6."

Brain development stage: Tattling is common among preschoolers and school-aged children as they begin to internalize group rules and norms.

Suggestions:

- Active listen (acknowledge the feelings) of the complainer. Offer suggestions on what to do if he agrees to hear them. Send him on his way.
- Attend to anyone who is hurt and separate them physically from each other.
- They may be looking for attention, so give some one-on-one time to each child.
- Don't assume. There are always three sides to every story, two views and one truth.
- Is a child telling you the story to get someone in trouble (tattling) or to get someone some help (telling).
- Deal with the problem without bringing attention to the tattling.

- Show empathy but don't punish the other child. Acknowledge both siblings feelings and offer suggestions on how to problem-solve. They need to learn the process of brainstorming ideas early.

- Encourage and appreciate their uniqueness.

Preschooler and Siblings - Annoys Siblings

"My 3 year-old middle son doesn't know when to stop. He gets into his siblings' faces and hits, runs and deliberately tries to annoy everyone. He screams and throws things and perpetually wants what he can't have. What is going on? He is the middle child of two brothers and a sister."

Brain development stage: The middle child draws the toughest birth order card in the family. He is not the oldest son, or the baby son, or the only daughter. He may be trying out behaviors to find out how he fits in the family constellation.

Suggestions:

- Spend some one-on-one time with him. It doesn't have to be a special outing at the playground. When you or your partner has to run to the store to get something, grab him, and only him. He will cherish the time with you alone and become a totally different child. It will also spill over into better behavior around his sibs.

- Check to see what family stresses are going on. Move? New house? New job? One parent travel a lot? He may be expressing his stress resulting from the family stress. Help him find alternate ways to express his negative feelings: coloring, talking, playground.

- Talk to the siblings in order to give them strategies when he gets into their space.

- Give him other ways to seek attention. Is he funny? Play up his strength as the family clown. Is he thoughtful? Praise him for that.

- You're a good parent. Keep doing what you are doing. You will figure it out. You have the right tools. Most siblings love each other into the adult years.

- Don't compare. Encourage their uniqueness.

- See "Sibling Conflict" under General Parenting.

Preschooler and Siblings - Competition for Attention

"How do I balance attention and playtime among three children with the oldest being the most demanding (he is 6), articulate and wanting immediate playtime as soon as partner gets home from work. My partner spends a whole hour playing and still it is discounted by my son, who says 'But we didn't get to play!'"

Brain development stage: A young child's needs for attention can be overwhelming for parents, but it is a valid need and children will get their needs met through positive attention or negative attention.

Suggestions:

- Stagger children's naps so that you get alone time with each child.
- Enroll one or more children in preschool.
- Find an adult "buddy" (aunt or uncle) who will spend some focused time with him.
- Accept that he just needs a LOT of attention so give it to him. If the other sibs are not complaining, let go of the guilt of trying to even things up.
- Tell him, "We just played for an hour. We will play again soon."
- Do lots of one-on-one time with him, even when out doing errands.
- Make him your special chore helper. Give him things to do alongside you and talk while you work.
- Keep him engaged in conversation. He might feel that you and your partner are "with" him physically, but not engaged in mind or emotion.
- Meet your partner somewhere after work, and have the partner just take him home so they have alone time to talk in the car.
- Set a timer for playtime.
- Acknowledge his feelings that he never gets enough attention. Say, "I can see that you feel upset because our playtime was not long enough." Acknowledgement doesn't mean agreement. It means that you understand.

....

Preschooler and Siblings - Ignores Baby

"My 3 year-old son is aggressive and doesn't want to have anything to do with the baby, who is almost walking at 9 months."

Brain development stage: Sibling rivalry is the worst for the first three months after the new sibling is brought home, and then again during the last three months of the first year when the sibling is crawling, walking, and getting into the older child's things. The predominant feeling is jealousy but children are still unable to express feelings verbally so may act out aggressively.

Suggestions:

- Take your older son to parks or out of the house as much as possible to burn off energy.
- Use the drop-in daycares for your baby for even 30 minutes so you can give your older child focused attention.
- Have your partner take the baby for an hour or two.
- Hire a pre-teen to come to your house several afternoons a week to play with the baby and give you twenty minutes to cuddle, read with, or play with your older son.
- He is craving attention. Give it to him in as many ways as you can.
- Block off his toys and special items in a separate room or space away from baby.
- Don't make him share his stuff. He already has to share his parents.

Preschooler and Siblings - Baby Regression

"My 3 year-old daughter is bossy and demanding since I have had the 3 month-old baby. She sees the baby cry and get picked up, and that has increased her crying because she wants to get picked up. She says "You do it!" and "Help me!" when she can do things herself."

Brain development stage: Children with new siblings crave attention and will regress in eating, sleeping, toileting and many other areas they have control over.

Suggestions:

- Explain baby's needs and limitations to her. Say, "It's okay if someone is crying. We pick them up and comfort them." Or, "He is a baby and can't talk so I have to guess what he is saying. You are a big girl and can talk so please use your words and I will listen."

- When she is crying, you comfort her too. Perhaps get down on the floor and give them both a hug and cuddle as they both have differing needs, but they are needs.

- Give her more big girl one-on-one time.

- Do a lot of deep-breathing exercises! Bite your tongue to avoid yelling at her.

- Don't project - she won't be bossy at 15 years.

- Lower your expectations of what she is capable of. Right now, she doesn't have much impulse control.

- Give specific instructions such as "Let's get our coats on." If she refuses, you do it. She is needing the attention and you are filling her love tank. It will pass.

- Tell her that you used to comfort and cuddle her too when she was a baby.

Preschooler and Siblings - Personal Space

"My house is small. How can I give each child some personal space?"

Brain development stage: Humans are territorial and want some control over their belongings and the space where they are kept. We love to nest and this is the beginning of that behavior for children. This begins around age 2 when they begin to learn the concept of "mine!" 3 year-olds don't have as many belongings or privacy issues as a preteen but they still need a bit of space.

Suggestions:

- Each child can have their own space in a house – perhaps "their" shelf in a bathroom, or "their" cupboard or drawer in the kitchen. Give them a corner to themselves if they have to share a room, or a blocked off area of the family or living room that is totally theirs to control.

- Many children under age 12 share rooms. There are a lot of upsides to this. Room sharing helps kids sleep when they are experiencing separation anxiety from parents or fears of the dark. Having someone else to talk to at night is nice and comforting. It facilitates play as they can share toys and games and it obviously saves space when siblings share a room. Toy clean-up is easier if toys are taken to one room. It is the same with laundry.

- The downside of room sharing is that kids are harder to settle down for bedtime as they want to play, talk or wind each other up in a game of the sillies. One child may want to read while the other wants to go to sleep (get a portable reading light). Noise, light and activity such as sleepovers are all sources of conflict and problem-solving. (Have a guest room for sleepovers or camp in the living room.) One child might be messy and the other neat. (Problem-solve this.) Children should be allowed to control how messy or neat their space is. It's theirs after all. Communal areas should be kept to the overall standards of the house.

- Children can have separate shelves, areas of the closet, and areas in a shared room. Obviously, the bed and space underneath can be personal space, but also bookcases and wall space can be designated as their own without having to put masking tape down on the floor to designate boundaries. Boundaries should be discussed among children so that each knows what area is off limits and what is communal space. Have a rule that permission must be received before a sibling (or sibling's friend) touches or uses items in the boundary space. This also includes computers and video game consoles.

- Does drawing a territorial line in the room or dividing the room in half so each child has a half of the room make sense? If kids are fighting over space, a line may help at first, to establish boundaries and may be removed later.

- Bunk-beds are a great idea for saving space. They allow for the children to have more essential floor space to play. They can be used as a puppet theatre with sheets around the bottom bunk area. Also if the older child wants to read on top, the younger one can have dark by hanging dark sheets under the top mattress to hang over the lower bed. If the opposite occurs (younger child wants to read), get a little reading light or a top cover from a bedroom store to keep the top area dark. If one child wants to watch a movie, they can use the small players and headphones for noise. Children younger than six should not use the top bunk. Bunk-beds are not really great for when a child is sick and parents need to attend to them. The bunk-beds with a single on top and double below are ideal for sleepovers and attending to sick/scared children.

- A common question is; when should siblings move to a separate room? The answer is; when they want to. Many teens naturally want more privacy at age 13 away from parents and siblings, but sometimes due to small space, they still have to share a room. That's okay. It will do them no harm unless boundaries are not respected. Many teens are okay sharing a room until they leave home, depending on the size of the room and space limitations.

Preschooler and Siblings - Sibling Fighting: When to Step in?

"How can we help our children with sibling conflict? When do I hold back and when do I step in?"

Brain development stage: Angry kids become physical because they are still learning to express their feelings in words instead of body language. Always step in when conflict becomes really nasty, either verbally or physically.

Suggestions:

- Ask them, "What do you think a good solution is?" See what they come up with for problem-solving.
- Say, "It's quiet time!" and insist everyone be quiet.
- Put on music and turn it up.
- Put them in a room together, and make them find a solution.
- Break them up when they get disrespectful, name call, bully, or hit each other. Also, when you can see that something is going to get thrown or wrecked.
- Distract to a snack. Hunger increases irritability.
- Pull out an activity. Say, "You seem bored. Let's do this."
- Don't own their conflict. Give it back to them. "What can you come up with for a solution?" Show them how to problem-solve.
- Give yourself time to be calm first.
- Let them each fully tell their story. Acknowledge each of their own feelings, and then move forward to working out solutions that both will be happy with.

Preschooler and Siblings - Bossiness

"My 3 year-old daughter, yells at my 6 year-old son and bosses him around to do her bidding. He usually does what she asks. I'm upset at her bossiness and his unassertiveness."

Brain development stage: Children in the preschool years try out different ways of using power.

Suggestions:

- Pick only one child to work on first – probably the daughter's bossiness.
- Teach her to ask nicely and be respectful.
- Give her a reward chart with stickers every time she is kind to him.
- Coach your son to respond with assertiveness. Give him stickers if he is kind and respectful.
- Get her to do nice things for him: bake cookies together, write a "thank-you" note, or make something for him.
- Give her control over small things; choosing what is for dinner, what movie to watch, or care of a pet.
- Acknowledge both children's feelings. State how upset you are that they treat each other that way.
- Model assertiveness and asking for things to be done respectfully.
- Decide if it really is a problem for him. Encourage him to stand up for himself if he really feels trodden upon.

Preschooler and Siblings – Occupying Child While Nursing Baby

"My son is 3 and very active. What do I do with him while nursing a new baby 16 times a day?"

Brain development stage: 3 year-olds are very active. Newborns eat every 2 hours.

Suggestions:

- Figure out how to breastfeed and baby-wear so you can feed on the go.
- Give him a special box of toys just for nursing times. Put it away when you get up to do something with him.
- Make nursing time a reading-out-loud time. Pick an interesting storybook.
- Get him to be your helper and fetcher.
- Give him a bouncy ball with handles so he can blow off steam indoors while you sit.
- Explain to him the needs of his sibling. He may understand a bit.

- Childproof consistently. Make sure all the cupboards are clear and he can't drag chairs to the countertops to explore or get into things.
- Accept that he may have a bit more screen time during the first six months of adjustment with a new baby. Give him the tablet, or put a video on that is only watched during nursing times.
- Try and get outside to outings. Outings tire out preschoolers. Go with a friend so that you can hand off the baby when you need to corral him.

Preschooler Sleep - Cry-it-Out or Wait-it-Out?

"My two older sons are great sleepers but my youngest son, 3 years, is not. Is it damaging for him to cry a bit when I put him to bed?"

Brain development stage: Most children don't sleep very well until age 5 when teething, night terrors, nightmares, and separation anxiety have lessened. Most children cry for about 5 minutes before they drop off to sleep. It doesn't damage brain development to let children cry a few minutes before they go to sleep. Systematically letting them cry for an hour or more every night can be damaging as it constitutes toxic stress when not alleviated by a comforting adult.

Suggestions:
- Get an music player and play the same music every night.
- Try a white noise or sleep machine.
- Try a nightlight.
- Sleep with him and remember that it will be a passing thing.
- Get a digital photo frame with up close facial pictures of you on a slide show.
- Make him comfortable, warm and cosy.
- Perhaps get a twin bed into your master room. Then he can crawl into bed with you if he needs it.

Preschooler Sleep - Nightmares

"My 4 year-old daughter has nightmares. How do I handle it?"

Brain development stage: A preschooler's brain is fine-tuning its imagination, creative thinking, and fantasy thinking. Nightmares are common at this age.

Suggestions:

- Say, "Look down at your hands!" You want to see if she will wake up to see her hands. If not, she could be having night terrors, which is like sleep walking.
- Say, "There are no monsters in the bedroom, house or world."
- Reassure her that it's not real.
- Tell her it happens to you too, so she is not as scared of them.
- Ask her to call for you when it happens.
- Tell her that her brain is playing and is showing her how it's playing.
- Tell her to flip the pillow over for a better next dream.

Preschooler Sleep - Can't Sleep

"My 4 year-old son has trouble sleeping at night. What are some calming activities to get him to sleep?"

Brain development stage: Children begin to develop sleep habits at this age. Some children need less sleep and others need more.

Suggestions:

- Relaxation – try guided meditation for children. Read some visualizations for him.
- Give him a music player to listen to – with meditation music, nature sounds, and classical music too.
- Lie down and talk with him for awhile. Try not to fall asleep yourself.
- Do some deep breathing with him.
- Back rubs are nice. Draw on his back or massage his back with lotion.
- Use Lavender Epsom salts, or a facecloth with lavender drops that he can smell.
- Use mindfulness meditation. Say, "Visit your happy place."
- Teach him to shake out his tension.
- Teach him to replace the thoughts with something more calming.
- Let him look at books.
- Let him listen to books read on a music player.

- Let him play in bed with Lego or stuffed animals.
- Help him visualize sheep jumping over fences.
- Use a worry catcher, worry stones or worry dolls or a special worry chair that he can sit in and do his worrying.
- Help him with guided prayer.
- Help him write down or draw his worries and put them away in a worry box.
- Stay away from screens which have blue backlight that can keep them awake. No movies, games or anything that revs up his adrenalin.

Preschooler Sleep - Night Terrors

"My 3 year-old son has night terrors between 11PM and 1AM.

Brain development stage: Night terrors are common in children from ages 1-15, more common in boys, and most children grow out of them. Night terrors differ from nightmares in that children are in a "sleepwalking state" that doesn't include dreaming. They look like they are awake, but really are not.

Suggestions:

- See a pediatrician, naturopath, or sleep clinic if they persist.
- Put a movie on to try to distract him, hold him and wait it out. He will eventually "come to" so you can put him back to bed.
- Use lavender and essential oils to help him sleep better.
- Use some ambient music for sleep.
- Use white noise for soothing.
- Put an alarm or a bell at the door top, so you know if he is leaving his room or house.
- Sleep beside him and it might make him more comfortable.
- Take him to the potty when you go to bed, even though he may be half awake and groggy. It might stop him from waking up later.

Preschooler Sleep - Bedtime Stalling

"My daughter, 3, is hard to get to bed. She uses all stalling tactics. Naps are no problem. How can I get her to bed?"

Brain development stage: Children have separation anxiety at night and are very reluctant to leave parents to go to sleep.

Suggestions:

- Sit in the doorway with your back turned to her, read a book, and reassure her that you are there. When she gets up, just tell her to go back to bed.
- Take her to the park after dinner so she is really tired.
- Make no eye contact, no talking or interaction, and just keep taking her back to bed.
- Move a desk into her room and while she falls asleep, you can do paperwork. Use a night lamp.
- Warn her first that this is the new plan.
- Get good blinds for the windows to block out light.
- Sleep with her. It's just for a short period of childhood and she needs your security.
- Put a baby gate in the doorway and she can hear or see you but can't get out.
- Get her into the tub or shower before bed, to tire her out.
- Use your voice to calm her. Keep backing out of the room and talk through the door.
- You can't make her sleep. You can only facilitate sleep. Have her stay in her room and she can just play until she is asleep.

Preschooler Sleep - Won't Stay in Bed

"My preschooler won't stay in bed at night."

Brain development stage: Separation anxiety is what causes children to come up with excuses for not staying in bed. They want to be with parents.

Suggestions:

- Watch for tiredness cues instead of the clock.
- Lie down with him.
- Give him "get out of bed" tickets – 2 per night to spend on any excuse to get up: water, hugs, bathroom breaks. When the tickets are spent, no more getting

up. The benefit is that the tickets give him control on how to spend them each night.

- Hang a sucker on the doorknob and promise him that he can eat it in the morning if he stays in bed.
- Tell him that it's "Mommy time."
- Put on audio books, music or movies to keep him occupied in bed until he falls asleep.
- Do something in his room like working on a report or laptop. Be present but not engaged with him. If he talks, you leave.
- Have him sleep on the couch in the living room. He has to be quiet and still. He can see you for comfort. Tell him that if he gets up, talks, or engages with you, he has to go back to his room.
- Contain him to his room but he could get up and play until he is sleepy.
- Put a baby gate in the doorway.
- Incentive charts work for some children.
- Let him sleep with siblings.
- Have two family bedrooms; one is for quiet reading for those not tired, and the other is for sleeping.

Preschooler Sleep - Sibling Bedtime Stalling

"My two children, 3.5 years and 2.5 years, take two hours every night to go to sleep. They want Mommy or Daddy to put them to bed, depending on who isn't doing the bedtime routine at night. How do I get them to sleep?"

Brain development stage: Separation anxiety is high at this age. Children do not want to let go of the day without parents.

Suggestions:

- Let the siblings sleep together. Try it out first by moving one child's mattress into the other's room. It might be a party for the first couple weeks, but they will settle down eventually as they get used to sharing a room.
- Put the children to bed an hour earlier so you have more evening time.
- Put the youngest to bed first.
- Get some LED lights so they won't feel so alone in the dark.

- Leave them with a movie playing in their room. Use the same movie every night as part of the routine and they will nod off in the first 30 minutes.

- Go through the routine and be firm. Say, "Goodnight, I love You." Trade with partner next night.

- Make a poster of pictures of all the things you have to do in the bedtime routine (pyjamas, snack, teeth, story, prayers, hugs, then sleep) so they know what order they are in and the final goodnight is coming.

- Sticker charts, and checkmarks on a poster, might entice some children to stay in their room.

- Leave the room in baby steps. Stay in the bed the first night while they go to sleep, then the next night, stay next to the bed, and the next night, sit on a chair in the room. Then, sit in the doorway, and then outside the doorway.

- Get a paper calendar of the month. Let them color in red for the days they want Mommy to do the bedtime routine and black for Daddy. Choosing gives them power and when you and your partner alternate, you get a break and sometimes kids behave better with just one parent doing the routine.

- Use a timer app to visually count down the time to bedtime.

- Remember that 70% of preschoolers have bedtime or night-time problems getting up. It's a stage they will grow out of!

Preschooler Toileting - Refuses Toilet Training

"My 3 year-old is starting preschool in the fall and is showing very little interest in potty training. We are committed and have paid the deposit!"

Brain development stage: Many children don't train until ages 3.5 to 4.5 years.

Suggestions:

- Try the '4 days without diapers' method; allow your son to roam around without a diaper to allow him to feel more freely when he is wet. Its immediate cause and effect.

- Make sure that your son is exhibiting signs of readiness. Signs are: talking about going to the potty, staying dry for periods of time, regular bowel movements, can follow simple instructions, shows interest in the potty, can pull pants up and down.

- Try using cloth training pants. This allows the child to feel when he is wet, without all the bells and whistles of paper training pants which can distract a child from his goal of being dry.

- Lessen the frequency of potty trips; gear it towards his own natural rhythm such as every 2 hours, rather than every 15 minutes.

- Boys typically take a little longer than girls to potty train due to developmental stages.

- Provide choices in underwear, toilet paper, potty chairs.

- Have a "potty party." Invite other lagging children and get help from other parents. They all throw out their diapers in a garbage bag. Have cake and praise the "grown-up behavior."

- Investigate reasons for fear of the toilet.

- Discuss the preschool's requirements regarding potty training; most will accommodate a child that isn't quite fully potty trained even though they will present a blanket rule for everyone.

- Assure the preschool that he is potty trained, but be available to be summoned by cell phone if he is still having accidents. The preschool probably recognizes that potty training is two steps forward, one step backwards.

- Get your partner involved; "Ok, we're doing a Man-to-Man Potty Boot-camp". Make it like a rite of passage for your son. Send Dad and son camping and with lots of liquid and no diapers, and a potty chair, and he might come back potty trained. Do the same with Mom if you have daughters.

- Make it fun. Put some cheerios in the potty and let him play "Fire Fighter," by aiming at the cheerios.

- Dad can model using the toilet.

- Stop pushing it. Leave the potty out but wait for him to take the lead.

- Stickers, candy and rewards work if the child is ready and just needs a bit of motivation.

Preschooler Toileting - Accidents at Home

"My 4 year-old keeps having potty trainng accidents. She pees in her pants, but only at home and not out at activities. She also wets the bed at night."

Brain development stage: Toilet training is two steps forward, one step back. Each child has a different schedule for awareness, holding ability, and focus while using the bathroom. Children don't usually have night time dryness until age 6.

Suggestions:

- Give her a lot of water to drink and take her by the hand to lead her to the potty.
- Set a timer every hour or so to remind her to go.
- Back off. Don't turn it into a power struggle.
- Make suggestions to go rather than telling her to go.
- At 4 years old, she can help clean up. Get her to help every time.
- She is probably focused on playing so needs reminders to go. Invite her to go with you.
- Use sticker charts and candy rewards. She is developmentally ready and just needs motivation.
- Put her back in diapers for awhile.
- Don't make a big deal out of it.
- She could be jealous of the new baby. Give her one-on-one time other than giving attention just over potty training accidents.
- Use a bed pad for night-time accidents. Put some towels over the bedding so you can get back to sleep and change sheets in the morning.
- Get her up to use the toilet when you go to bed at night, even if she is half asleep.

Preschooler Toileting - Pee Accidents

"My 3 year-old son is potty trained for stool but not pee. My husband is getting frustrated."

Brain development stage: Children begin control of stool first, then urine, and then overnight dryness, usually around age 6.

Suggestions:

- Set a timer for every 30 minutes and put him on the potty. Don't let him get so full that he has accidents.
- Boys are usually later to train than girls. Average age of boys is 2.5 to 4 years.
- Get your partner to do the potty training if it is more important to him than you.

- Leave him naked for a day and let nature run its course.
- Kids are programmed to mimic adults. He will not go to college in diapers.
- Use a musical container toy that "congratulates" him with music instead of using treats.
- Start using smaller treats – chocolate chips instead of big chocolate wafers.
- Take him to the potty after every meal.

Preschooler Toileting - Holds Poop

"My 4 year-old holds her poop for days. She has no medical issues, but just doesn't like the feeling of going to poop."

Brain development stage: Motivation might be more of an issue than physical development. Most children at this age can learn to use the toilet easily.

Suggestions:

- Put her back into diapers for a few weeks and then start again fresh.
- Rub her belly or her pressure points.
- Increase fibre in her diet; give her prune juice, prunes, muffins, olive oil, bran buds with yogurt and lots of water and just put her back into diapers.
- Use suppositories for loosening up and making it runnier. Check with the doctor first if these are okay.
- Distract her while she is sitting on the toilet. Give her a video player to use.
- Make toilet time easy and positive. Have her sit in the bathroom, relax on the toilet and read books.
- Remember that the more you nag/want/tell her to go, the less she will.
- Make sure she drinks enough water to move the fibre. Give her some water flavouring to help her drink. Herbal or non-caffeinated tea might help.
- Put fake candles, soothing music, and low lights in the bathroom. Make it spa-like.
- Have her stand instead of sit and she won't feel so vulnerable.
- Don't turn it into a power struggle.

School-Agers 6-13 Years

The stage of "What would happen if...?"

What Can School-Agers Do?

Younger School-Agers 6 to 9 Years: Concrete-Operational Stage

Physical

- Totally potty trained including night dryness

- Can sleep all night for ten to twelve hours; once asleep, usually stays asleep

- Eats regularly: three meals, three snacks daily

- Can bathe alone

- Can tie shoelaces

- Can ride a two wheeler

- Can use all table utensils including a knife to spread

- Can use cursive writing by nine years

- Loses all baby teeth by eight years

- Can sit still for thirty minutes

- Can stand on one foot and skip

- Bone growth faster than muscle development; may have "growing pains"

- May have nervous habits such as nail biting, hair sucking, masturbation, nose picking, teeth grinding

- Can do most chores with help, direction, and reminding: empty dishwasher, take out garbage, sort laundry, water plants, pet care, meal clean up, recycling, and mopping

Cognitive

- Copycats; loves to imitate others

- Logical; understands that actions have positive or negative outcomes

- Understands operations (consequences)

- Questions; asks "Why?" and "What if?"

- Experiments by trying on behaviors from outside the family

- Rule-focused: loves rules and making sure everyone abides

- Negotiators; loves to make deals

- Concrete learners; understands what she has experienced personally

- Black-and-white thinkers; no gray areas in thinking

- Can work on projects and in groups

- Can sort items into groupings

- Can answer phone but may not take good messages

- Understands clocks and time representation

- Comprehends logical and natural consequences

- Understands that "No" means "Don't do"

- Can recognise ads from various mediums; can differentiate reality from fantasy

- Needs help with homework

- Understands money as a symbol for exchange; can handle an allowance

- Not good enough problem-solvers to stay home alone yet

- Loves new experiences and places: field trips, travel

- Understands jokes; loves potty humor

- Starts reading and writing

- Creative in visual and performing arts and crafts

- Beginning to understand time and the length of a certain block of time

- Can understand the basic mechanics of sexual intercourse and reproduction

- Executive function skills rapidly increasing

Social and Emotional

- Protective of belongings and territory

- Sore losers in games due to developing self-control

- Develops definite gender identity as a boy or girl

- May still have fears of dark, animals, sharks, heights, and losing parents

- Understands lying as deceitful and wrong

- Temper tantrums less than once a week if at all; rarely expressed physically

- Learning to recognise other's feelings and able to identify and label his own feelings

- Still hard to see other people's point of view over her own

- Developing social skills of empathy, listening and social "white" lies

- Can begin to use calm-down tools on her own and express anger in words

- Loves to help others and contribute

- Friends come mostly from shared interests

- Still lacks experience in handling conflict

- Good self-control; can wait for ten minutes or longer

- Play is more complex; still enjoys pretend play and loves games

- May prefer same-gender friends

- Not much regard for personal hygiene

- Still open and affectionate with family in public

- Can begin to reflect on own behavior and how it affects others

*Compliance is 60% successful in a respectful, non-punitive parent-child relationship.

Tweens 10 to 13 Years: Beginning Formal-Operational Stage

Physical

- May be beginning puberty changes: breast growth, menstruation, height increase. Belt of fat develops around the waist

- Growth spurts and extreme differences are evident in children of the same ages; girls tend to be ahead of boys

- Can mow lawns, do own laundry, wash dishes, cook with microwave, change bedding, answer phone and take messages, pack own lunch, clean bathrooms, and run to the store

- Ravenous appetite or picky eaters or peculiar tastes develop

- Sleeps ten to twelve hours

Cognitive

- Growing out of childhood toys that are becoming boring

- Can use a debit card to make his own purchases

- Needs help with homework and reminding

- Can cross a street alone and judge traffic timing at ten years

- Can stay home alone briefly if good problem-solvers

- Remembers where they left items

- Beginning to resist control by others

- Still black-and-white thinking; moral development progressing with increasing sense of right and wrong

- Attention span of one to two hours

- Knows difference between real and imaginary in digital and physical world

Social and Emotional

- Social relationships becoming more complex with feelings and nuances

- Friends mostly come from shared interests; may lose some as interests diverge; sticks to same-sex friends

- Becoming peer focused but family ties still stronger

- May exaggerate and overdramatize problems

- Certain topics, such as sex, are too embarrassing for discussion with family

- Attitude increases as peer behavior copied

- Learns to handle pressure and rejection

- Worries and anxiety increase as he becomes more self-conscious

- Sensitive to criticism and correction

- May move family affection to private moments

*Compliance is 70% successful in a respectful, non-punitive parent-child relationship.

School-Ager Behavior - School Anxiety

"My 6 year-old son is experiencing high levels of anxiety in Grade 1. He refuses to eat at school out of worry that he will be laughed at; he worries about the clothes he wears, etc. My son is naturally shy, but I feel he is regressing since we moved here from another country. He has experienced many transitions during this time, such as different schools, cities, and countries. Back home, he appeared to socialize very well in preschool. I need some help in easing his anxiety."

Brain development stage: Moves and different schools can take their stress toll on children. Even though it is positive stress, children need to be supported by caring adults.

Suggestions:

- Connect with your son's teacher and share what is going on with your son. Get her involved in the situation. This will broaden your son's support group and allow for additional support within the school system.

- Seek out other mothers and communicate your concerns with them. See if you can't encourage some friendships for your son to form with other kids.

- Involve your son in extra-curricular activities, and allow his passions to flourish.

- Some children have a very shy or introverted nature, and this may be who your son is. Always let him know that there is nothing wrong with him.

- Validate his feelings when he tells you he wants to go back to his home country. Say, "I understand you want to go back home. I wish I could sprout wings and fly us both there sometimes."

- You have the great gift of empathy with your son. You actually do know how he feels. Share this with him, and how you felt and what you did to cope with your own levels of anxiety.

- If his anxiety doesn't seem to alleviate at all, try contacting a child psychologist to set up an appointment. This can provide a safe place for your child to explore his feelings in a non-judgmental environment.

- Try some self soothing methods with your son; yoga, walking in nature, drawing, building, talking, etc. Let him know he is not alone.

- School doesn't work for every child. Investigate other options such as homeschooling, online, unschooling, or part time school.

- Remember to breathe deeply and stay present in the moment: allow your projections to come and go, let them flow through you like water. This too shall pass.

....

School-Ager Behavior - Feigns Illness

"My 5 year-old complains of sniffles and wants to stay home from school because she is "sick." Do I let her?"

Brain development stage: By age 5, children know they have power and how to use it. They understand that being sick means don't go to a place and may use "sickness" as a way of avoidance.

Suggestions:

- Keep her home but keep her bored. If she is sick, she must stay in bed and do nothing.
- Ask her what her needs are. Talk to the teacher and see why she doesn't like going to school. Focus on the ABC's: A for Autonomy, B for Belonging, C for Competency. Are any missing from the classroom?
- If you know an event is coming, talk it up. Pizza day, library day, etc.
- Investigate further if this continues. Something is keeping her from enjoying school.

School-Ager Behavior - Lying

"My 6 year-old lies. She knows it's not good. How do I react?"

Brain development stage: Lying is a common stage and shows a good level of brain development. A child needs an understanding of logic and consequences to entertain lying.

Suggestions:

- She might just be experimenting a bit. Say, "I'm not going to be mad at you, so I want you to tell me the truth."
- Help her get what she wants without lying.
- Focus on the lie, not the behavior. Separate the behavior from the deception and talk about trust.
- Never, never, ever punish the behavior or the lie. Talk about it. Assure the child that if they tell the truth, they will never be punished and that they can always come to you for help or advice. This assurance tends to breed truth telling.
- Read the book, "The Boy Who Cried Wolf!"
- As your child ages, have conversations about truth, embellishments and white lies (those told to save a person's feelings.)
- Call lies by another name. Say, "Is that a (child's name) story?" It gives room for creativity and storytelling but differentiates the deception from the truth.
- Model honesty. Tell the truth about child's age for entrance fees, etc. They are watching you.
- Encourage truth. Say, "I'm so happy you told me the truth, even though you didn't know if it would get you into trouble."

School-Ager Behavior - Anger

"My 5 year-old gets angry and defiant at times. My husband and I react back because we are dealing with our issues. Is my son normal? How should we all deal with this anger?"

Brain development stage: Children take at least 25 years to develop the reasoning, decision-making and self-control functions that originate in the prefrontal cortex part of their brain. It will take at least half that time to develop the self-control to stop aggressive expression of their anger. By the time he is 13, he should have stopped hitting. See all the other age groups as well for "anger" suggestions.

Suggestions:

- He might just want to be angry. Let him be while he is expressing it. Don't react back. Anger fuels anger.
- Don't clean up his anger messes. He will do it if asked when he is calmer.
- You are the safest place in the world for him to express his emotions. Teach better ways when he cools off.
- Mark off the good days with stickers on a visual calendar. You and he need to see that there are good days. It can also help you see patterns in his or your anger that are hormonal or food related.
- Ask him, when he is not angry, what you can do to comfort him when he is angry. Together, get those ideas ready.
- Ask your partner too. Perhaps have the conversation three ways.
- He could be picking up on your anger and anxiety.
- Active listen to him. "I can see that you are upset."
- We have a "no" list of things that can't be done in anger, but kids also need a "yes" list of things they can do with their anger. Have a "calm down" list of tangible activities he can do in the moment of anger to calm down. Revisit the list from time to time to add new things to it.
- Teach him some self-soothing methods; deep breathing, writing down anxieties and crumpling up the paper to put it in a worry box.

School-Ager Behavior - Hitting Friend

"My daughter is 5 and hit her little friend at a playgroup. The friend is now very upset and told her that she doesn't want to play with her anymore. The next day, the friend is still adamant against playing, even though everyone has calmed down. What do I do?"

Brain development stage: Children have 12 years to learn to control their hitting anger. Your daughter is not even halfway yet, but she is learning the natural social consequences that are very important learning tools. The school age years are great to learn relationship skills but children still need the coaching help from an adult.

Suggestions:

- Be honest with her and tell her what you know - that the little girl doesn't want to play because your daughter hit her. Actions matter and there are natural outcomes to choices.
- Make a list of "Yes" and "No" ways to express anger. (Look in each age group of this book under "anger" and add them to the yes or no list.) Go back to "helicopter mode" and hover to make sure she doesn't hit again and re-direct her anger.
- Practice deep breathing by the "candle app" on the phone. Get her to take a deep breath and "blow" out the candles.
- Perhaps talk to the little girl's parent and see if anything can be done such as a more formal apology and some restitution like a little gift of flowers with the apology.

....

School-Ager Behavior - Bossiness

"My daughter is 6 years old and is a bit of a bossy pants. She tells everyone what to do, including her friends and siblings. I need her to back off a bit."

Brain development stage: The age of 3-6 is the age of power. It can present in some children as bossiness, but really are the initial stages of leadership.

Suggestions:

- Ask her why she needs to direct.

- Perhaps she is trying to be like you. Sign her up to be a project manager on one thing only such as keeper of the snacks or pets in the home, planning a family outing or meal, or even an outside project like a lemonade stand.

- Give her a lot of choices.

- Let her be boss, but not if it is preceded by tantrums. Wait until she is calm and asks in a calm voice. Show her how to ask politely and assertively and give the desired result immediately.

- Have a secret cue that you can indicate to her about when to stop.

- Active listen to sibling's grumps about her.

- If she is just like you at that age, imagine what worked for you.

- Read a book on sibling rivalry.

- Role model bossiness, and leadership, and showing her what the differences are.

- You are doing right by telling her, "It's not her concern."

- Tell her the options, "Come to me, or leave the situation."

- Praise her positive comments to them, and step in when she gets bossy.

- Give her some one-on-one attention.

- Ask her to phrase things in an "asking" way.

- Talk to her, and find out why she does it. It might just be her personality.

- She is destined to be a leader. Teach her how to compromise.

- Don't call it "bossy." Say, "Let's work on your leadership skills."

- Ask her to "invite" people rather than "order" them.

School-Ager Behavior - Temper Tantrums

"How do I diffuse emotional outbursts of 6 year-olds and encourage more respectful behavior? How can I discourage manipulation and hitting me?"

Brain development stage: By school age, most children have a better grasp of self-control of emotions but some children are not there yet, especially spirited children who may still have temper tantrums.

Suggestions:

- Call her on the way you feel. Tell her "This is how I feel when that happens."

- Continue to let her know how it makes you feel when you are hit and that it's not allowed.

- Teach her to tell you what she really wants or needs directly using "I-statements." "I feel angry at you, Mommy!"

- Say, "Is that what you really think?"

- Celebrate her successes however small.

- Buy a trophy from the dollar store and giver her it after every anger episode if she doesn't hurt anyone or anything and works through her anger constructively.

- Remind her of natural consequences – people don't want to play with her if she continues the behavior. You don't feel like doing special favours when she treats you like that.

- Practice self-talk with her. Say, "Stop! Get calm. Breathe. What do I need?"

....

School-Ager Behavior - Social Skills

"My friend's 8 year-old son is very annoying. He needs to work on his manners and social skills."

Brain development stage: This is a great age for kids to model social graces. If they don't pick them up naturally, they can be taught them.

Suggestions:

- Allow yourself to feel angry and annoyed, but watch what you say.

- Separate yourself from your friend a little more and be around him less.

- Teach him manners. Say, "When you leave, it would be nice to say to the host (me), 'Thank you for having me over.' Can you try that now?"

- Say nothing. Kids will learn the hard way when they have no manners.

- Perhaps ask your child to say something to him about manners.

....

School-Ager Behavior - Homesick

"My 9 year-old daughter wants to go on a sleepover camp this weekend, but she has been very homesick in the past and will probably want a pick-up late at night."

Brain development stage: Some children are ready from about ages 4 onward for sleepovers and some are not ready until adulthood. Readiness depends on coping skills.

215

Suggestions:

- Allow her to make the choice on whether to go or not. Go over the pros and cons.
- Make the decision for her.
- Don't call her if the rules are "Don't call." Most camps will not allow children to phone home due to the fact that they have staff to help children through their homesickness.
- Perhaps just do a one-night sleep-over until she feels comfortable and builds her competency managing a night away from you.
- Pack her a picture of you and a zip-lock baggie of kisses. See "separation anxiety tips" for Toddler and Preschoolers.

School-Ager Behavior - Brags

"My 7 year-old son likes to brag to his friends about what he has, where he has gone, and how good he is at video games."

Brain development stage: This is a great age for kids to learn communication skills. Bragging is very common as they learn that it is not always welcome.

Suggestions:

- Teach your son how to ask questions of the other child, and practice conversation skills by listening.
- Give him the words on how to say compliments to others. Request that he try to give one compliment every day.
- Build his self-esteem. Comment on how much effort he puts into things he does well.

School-Ager Behavior - Argues

"My 8 and 10 year-old sons are constantly arguing with me when I ask them to do something. Or, when we have a discussion, they argue the finer points. They think I am wrong and they are right."

Brain development stage: The school-aged years of 5 to 13 are prime arguing years where children learn to question rules, traditions and ask how the world works. Sometimes they don't always use the most respectful language.

Suggestions:

- Don't take it personally. It is a valued development stage and demonstrates brain growth and social development. Your job is to fine tune the "respectful" part. Point out to them which part of their conversations are not respectful and give them the words to use, especially "I-statements," such as "I think..." or "I feel that..."

- Listen carefully to their point of view and acknowledge it.

- Ask them to listen to you and repeat back to you what they have heard.

- After you listen to them and they have listened to you, use the 6-step method (define the problem, explore needs, brainstorm ideas, evaluate ideas, pick an idea, and check back later) of problem-solving to resolve the situation.

School-Ager Behavior - Poor Sport

"My 7 year-old daughter is quite a poor sport. When she plays soccer, she won't shake hands if her team loses. She wrecks board games at home when she loses while playing with her siblings."

Brain development stage: From age 5 to about 9 years, children go through a stage of being poor sports. The frustration of losing is more than they can sometimes handle and they are not practiced at hiding their disappointment as much as adults can. Adults have had many years of self-control to hide their true feelings, but children haven't.

Suggestions:

- Allow her to use her I-statement. "I'm angry that our team lost." "I'm disappointed that I didn't win the game and the dice wasn't working for me today." She can express her feelings but not target anyone.

- Validate her feelings of frustration. "You are upset with losing the game today, even though you played your best. That's okay to feel that way."

- Emphasize her effort and not the result.

- Emphasize the moments of fun she had.

- Pack away board games for awhile until she has better self-control.
- Make a plan to escape the soccer game if she feels she can't shake hands. Go to the playground right after the game if she doesn't want to shake hands. Encourage her but don't force it. It will come with maturity.

School-Ager Behavior - Uses Weapons for Play

"My 8 year-old son loves to pretend play with toy weapons. I've tried taking them away but then he just makes weapons out of items from around the house, including food. What do I do?"

Brain development stage: Children under age 12 roleplay people and actions they witness from real life or media. It's a normal way for them to process how it fits in their life and is usually no cause for concern. They grow out of it. Around age 8, they also can distinguish between reality and fantasy and should begin learning what real behavior is acceptable in the physical world and behavior that must stay in the digital world (such as violent video games).

Suggestions:

- You could try to re-direct him to other forms of play and activities.
- Allow him 30 minutes of weapon play and then redirect.
- Be sure to live and model your values - if you don't like them, don't play violent video games, watch violent movies, or engage in violent sports.
- Don't buy them or give weapons as gifts either.
- Allow weapon play at friend's houses but not yours. You can control what happens in your house.
- Play more cooperative board games.
- Be sure to involve him in caring activities such as volunteering.

School-Ager Behavior - Quits Lessons

"My 7 year-old daughter showed a keen interest in playing piano. When I got her lessons, she showed less and less interest. Now it is a battle to get her to the lesson and to practice."

Brain development stage: This is a great age for kids to try out different activities that they wouldn't normally get in school. But "try out" means to drop those that don't catch any interest.

Suggestions:

- Go for a walk and ask her what she likes/doesn't like about lessons.
- If she has been at it awhile, let her quit. No one is benefiting.
- Show her a calendar and how many times a week she needs to practice and let her choose the days.
- Make a chart of the skills she has learned so she can see progress.
- If she is just starting, agree to go three times and see if things turn around. Then let her quit.
- The easier it is for her to stop, may mean that she will willingly take it up again on her own as she gets older.

School-Ager Behavior - Secretive About Outings

"How do I get my 12 year-old daughter to open up more about where she goes? She takes the bus and bike to places after school and won't share who she is with or where she is going."

Brain development stage: As children near into teen-ages, they become much more private about several aspects of their lives.

Suggestions:

- Get the whole family together around the table to have a conversation regarding communication. Ensure that everyone, (including you and your partner) lets at least one other person know where they are going and what time they will return.
- Ask each member to phone home whenever there will be a change in plans or location.
- Make your home very inviting for her to have friends over.
- Examine why you say "No," to her requests when she wants to go somewhere. Assure her that you trust her and build that communication flow so she trusts you enough to tell you where she is going.

- Avoid giving her the "Inquisition" when she comes home. Say Hi and let her volunteer information. If she doesn't, don't always ask. Practice letting go.

- Avoid constantly checking up on her. Trust her that she is telling the truth until she gives you reason not to trust her.

School-Ager Behavior - Stressed, Worried and Anxious

"My 11 year-old son is often worried about the next day. He gets stressed about upcoming events and sometimes goes through periods where he feels really anxious even though nothing is going on."

Brain development stage: Children that are out of the preschool years often experience worry and anxiety because their brains understand consequences and their creative imaginations feeds what negative, embarrassing or disastrous event could happen. Learning to cope with worry and anxious feelings is a lifelong skill and children need help implementing calming strategies and changing thought patterns.

Suggestions:

- Have a worry chair or room that he can go in and do his worrying. When he leaves the room or chair, he has to stop.

- Have him write down his worries on toilet paper and then flush them away. He could write in a journal too, or write on paper slips and put into a worry box.

- Have him focus in the moment. He could try some mindfulness meditation.

- Talk with him about what is the worst things that could happen. Help him see that it is not that bad. Share your experiences of worry and what didn't happen.

- Have him stay and "feel" his feelings even though he has physical symptoms. He will see that they can lessen as he works through things.

- Have two buckets: one labeled "Change," and the other labeled, "Can't Change."
  He can write down his worries and put into the appropriate box.

School-Ager Behavior - Cell Phone Obsession

"How do I get my 13 year-old daughter off her cellphone? She is obsessed."

Brain development stage: Children love, need, and crave their technology, but are also influenced by other's use of technology in our society. Children today are immersed in technology by their parents, culture, school and society. We need to model healthy boundaries.

Suggestions:

- Model healthy cell-phone use. Expect to have times that no one in the family is on the cell-phone. Dinner time, family movie time, social times, visiting with relatives time, restaurants (bring playing cards instead) are all good times to have a family rule of not being on the phone or screens. Interact with each other instead.

- Model restraint from texting and driving. Your child is watching your habits. Keep your phone tucked away in your pocket or bag while you drive.

- Have a basket or charging cupboard when all phones go to bed for the night about 1 to 2 hours before bedtime. This is good sleep hygiene for the whole family.

- Model turning off the email and social media by 6 pm every night. If you do it, you can ask your child to do it. Then you won't read anything disturbing that could keep you awake.

- If something is going on socially, and your child needs to check her phone, be sensitive to her needs. Ask if she needs to talk about anything that you might be able to help her with.

....

School-Ager Behavior - Mean to Parent

"My 13 year-old daughter is very mean to me. She swears and when she is angry, she tries to hit me. I feel scared of her."

Brain development stage: By 13, children should be able to express their anger in an adult way, such as words. They should be treating their parents with respect 95% of the time (they are still teens and mess up occasionally).

Suggestions:

- Use your I-statement. "I need to be spoken to politely if we are going to converse."

- Teach her to use I-statements and then change your behavior in response to when she says it to you, so she can see that they really work.

- Don't listen to rants or swearing. Walk away to allow cool-down time.

- Do spend more one-on-one time with her. She may need more love. She may open up more about her resentments with you causing the mean behavior.

- Give extra physical affection and build the relationship.

- Don't stay and take the mean behavior. Don't let her hit you. Get out of the path.

- If she says that you don't love her, don't defend that. Acknowledge her feelings and validate them. Say, "You feel sad because you think I love your sister more than you." Spend a lot of time listening. Say, "I love you," often.

- Don't take it personally. It's more about her, then you.

- Don't be afraid of her anger, but insist on her taking responsibility for what she wrecks after she is calm. She has to pay, clean, or fix.

- If she tells others you are a bad parent, say, "I can tell you have strong feelings about this and I accept it. But, I would like your feelings to stay in this family. It's not respectful to complain to others, while not coming to me directly."

School-Ager Behavior - Refuses Conversation

"How do I get my 13 year-old son to engage in conversation with me? I feel like I am losing him!"

Brain development stage: Children beginning puberty can sometimes become more aloof to parents, even when the relationship is good. They tend to put space in between themselves and the child in order to "separate" emotionally.

Suggestions:

- **Stop punishments.** All punishments: grounding, taking away privileges and electronics such as computers, tablets, phones, and everything. Give up "consequences" which are really a disguised punishment. Tell your child that in an effort to improve communication, you are giving up all punishments and just do it.

- **Listen without judgment and acknowledge feelings.** If you feel the overwhelming urge to give advice, ask your child if they want it first. Provide comfort when they need it. You can support them through anything.

- **Spend activity time together.** Play sports, gaming, do projects, contests, work out, walks, coffee dates, camping, concerts, theatre, restaurants, movies, together.

- **Problem-solve issues.** Really, really listen, clarify and listen some more, until you both can identify the real problem. Distinguish what your needs are and what his needs are. Brainstorm some possible solutions. Don't pooh, pooh the bad ones. Consider those too. Discuss possible solutions until you can narrow down a few that will fulfill both your needs. Give up your "position" (there are no absolutes in parenting) and really look at what your true needs are. Decide on the best solution that will meet both your needs and enhance your relationship. Check back later to see if the solution is working for both of you.

- **Share values in the no-problem times.** Even better, live and model your values.

School-Ager Behavior - Ignores Hygiene

"How do I get my 12 year-old son to shower and change his clothes? He is starting to smell like a goat!"

Brain development stage: Children beginning puberty need some basic hygiene requirements and reminders to use them. Soap, washcloths, razors and deodorant are some essentials.

Suggestions:

- Get your partner to walk him through some basic steps. You could do the same with your daughters. Make it a fun time. Let them pick out their own soap, razors, and essentials.
- Get competitions going. For example, play "mad dog" and see who can lather up the most foam at the mouth with tooth-brushing.
- Show pictures of bad teeth and ugly hair.
- Discreetly point out stinky people if you encounter any.
- Be aware it may be a sign of depression, if accompanied by other symptoms such as loss of sleep and appetite.

School-Ager Behavior - Wants to be Alone All the Time

"My 12 year-old daughter wants to be by herself most of the time. She dislikes seeing friends even when I make play dates for her. Should I make this an issue?"

Brain development stage: When children begin puberty, they really embrace their introversion or extroversion and will resist if you provide too much of either stimulation.

Suggestions:

- Let her decide how much friend contact she wants. You can't force friends on her.
- Find her a sport/art/music or job/volunteering activity that she loves. When social contact is the side effect, rather than the main event, she may blossom.
- Problem-solve time limits on solitary activities.
- Model an active social life.`
- Accept that teens want more alone time than family time.
- Set up unstructured time for the two of you to talk, preferably over an activity such as cooking, gardening, or driving.
- Encourage her hobbies and interests. Make space and items available for her.
- Keep encouraging her to join the family activities but dont force it.
- Avoid sneaking into her computer, drawers, or journal.
- Keep listening to her. Hold the comments unless they are supportive.

School-Ager Behavior - Suicidal Talk

"My 13 year-old son talks a lot about suicide. What do I say or do?"

Brain development stage: Suicide is a common word that children use. However, we must look for signs that they are serious about the action.

Suggestions:

- Speak the word. The more you talk about suicide, the more you give the go-ahead for him to talk about it. You are not putting thoughts in his head. You are giving him the opportunity to open-up and speak honestly if that is the way he feels and thinks.
- Notice if he gives away his possessions or says "When I'm gone..." "No one will miss me," or "You'll be better off someday without me..." These are serious red flags.
- Ask him if he is suicidal. Ask him if he has a specific plan or method.
- Listen to him talk. Provide silence so he has space and opportunity to talk.

- Talk about how final a suicidal solution is. Problems are always temporary.
- Tell him how much you love him and how much it would break your whole families' heart to lose him. Have the other family members say it too.
- Tell the siblings if he consents. Encourage them to share with him how much they love him.
- Assure him that things will get better and you will help him.
- Immediately get professional help. Even if he doesn't contemplate suicide, the notion that he is thinking about it, indicates a need for help.

School-Ager Behavior - Exposed to Swear Words

"My 7 year-old daughter has been exposed to swear words at school. She described the word to me and I told her I didn't want to hear her say it, just spell it. Did I say the right thing?"

Brain development stage: The early school aged years are when most children hear or see offensive language and begin to know what the meaning is behind it.

Suggestions:

- You did well saying, "I don't feel comfortable saying the swear word. Next time, just spell it or tell me you heard a bad word. Those words are not allowed to be said in our house." This lets her know your boundaries for swear words, but that you are open to talking about it.
- Tell her "That's an adult word - don't use it."
- It's good that she is comfortable talking about it to you.

School-Ager Development and Learning - Cheats on Schoolwork

"My son, who is 12 year-old was caught cheating on an exam. I found out that he has been using his friends to do his school work as well. How do I handle this?"

Brain development stage: Children may try cheating once or twice as an experimental behavior, but it should not be a regular occurrence. It could be a sign of a deeper problem.

Suggestions:

- Love him unconditionally. Does he feel he needs to achieve in order to gain your affections?
- If the school catches him, don't rescue him from consequences.
- Use your I-statement. Say, "I'm disappointed that you would cheat to gain a mark. How can you bring up your marks in an honest way? Can I help?"
- Problem-solve alternative ways to get an education such as homeschooling, online or another school.

School-Ager Development and Learning - School Behavior Problems

"How do I get my son to sit still in class? He is 7 years old and the teacher is complaining to me. He also doesn't follow directions."

Brain development stage: Children may or may not have the self-control to sit for long periods (30 minutes) of time at age 7. It will become better with age.

Suggestions:

- Ask the teacher what she notices. He might have a learning disability and doesn't understand what needs to be done. He might also be gifted and is easily bored. Or, he may simply learn more kinesthetically, which may require teaching adjustment.
- Ask the teacher to go over behavior expectations. Are they appropriate for a 7 year-old?
- Problem-solve with the teacher and your son together, to come up with some solutions.
- Be sure the teacher gets his eye contact while making requests.
- Use different colored sticky notes as reminders.
- Ask for a repeat of the request. "What are you going to bring back to me tomorrow, so I can sign it?"

- If he doesn't do something, don't let it go. Problem-solve with him to find a way that it can be done.

....

School-Ager Development and Learning – Teaching School Organizational Skills

"How do I get my 9 year-old daughter to stop dawdling to school? She doesn't seem interested to get out the door in the morning."

Brain development stage: Children at school-age are still not as anxious to get to school as you are, but they are very capable of making lunches, packing school bags, and learning organizational skills.

Suggestions:

- Have the same plan every day. Keep routines going
- Have a next day bucket with all items needed for school and activities. There should be a bucket for backpack and lunch container and shoes. A storage box for outerwear, and also one for papers will help keep things organized.
- Set a timer for gathering things in the morning.
- Turn off the TV and all distractions.
- Give her a paper towel tube to store papers coming home from school.
- Get your partner involved in preparation.
- Take pictures of items needed (papers, lunch, shoes) and paste them up on the wall or fridge. She can look and check them off as she packs her bag.
- Write down jobs that need to be done before school, on slim strips of paper. Take them around her wrist. After she completes the job, she can rip the paper off.
- Teach kids to make lunches for two or more days ahead. Have a special shelf for each child. Stock up on portable breakfasts, or snacks, and have a big bin by the door so that if she forgets to pack a lunch, she can grab a snack.
- Use a paper calendar in a shared space, or a shared electronic one so that everyone is aware of important appointments and events.
- Help her plan for events ahead of time, by reminding her of what she needs to do to prepare. Help her write a "to-do" list.

....

School-Ager Development and Learning - Prepping for a Move

"We are moving cities right before the holidays. What can I do to prep my 11 year-old daughter to make the move smoother?"

Brain development stage: Children at this age may grieve their old friends and community. They might have worries and anxiousness about their new place.

Suggestions:

- Enroll her in the new school even before the holidays because all the fun, informal learning happens then. She will have a taste of her new life and that snippet will ease her anxiety over the holidays.
- Let her cry and acknowledge how hard it is for her.
- Provide tangible ways to say goodbye, such as giving a party for all her friends to come, and they could sign cards for her.
- Help her keep connection via phone and social media.
- Let her do some artwork depicting the old house and garden and friends.
- Enroll her in new activities when you move.
- Expect that there will be an adjustment period. Some children take longer to settle in.
- Watch movies of children moving to help her talk about her feelings.

School-Ager Development and Learning - Peer Pressure

"How can I help my child deal with negative peer pressure at school?"

Brain development stage: Peer pressure is normal from ages 6-15 years and can be positive or negative.

Suggestions:

- **Look at your child's unmet needs**. Look beyond his behavior. Does he need more attention, self-confidence, encouragement, and understanding?
- **Build a connection with your child**. Spend time with him. Give him unconditional love.

- **Give respect.** Respect his space and belongings. Avoid criticism. Treat your child with politeness and kindness and he will come to expect it from his peers, too.

- **Build your child's healthy self-esteem.** Help him develop his talents and abilities to give him confidence. Every child excels at something. Encourage him, rather than praise him, to avoid over reliance on approval from others. Focus on the effort, not the results of his activities.

- **Don't overly value your child's outer looks.** Carol, a mom of 5 in my class says, "Does your child have a smart brain (and every child does excel at something) and a kind heart?" Emphasize those qualities that are under their control.

- **Choose your battles carefully.** Give your child small harmless rebellions. Teach your child to follow his instincts (his 'gut' feeling, or his 'spidey' senses).

- **Allow your child to say "no" if he wishes and you feel it's appropriate** For example: sharing toys, accepting rides, participating at an event. Teach your child to be politely assertive with peers, siblings, other adults, and you.

- **Keep communication lines open**. Listen, listen, and listen some more. Be non-judgmental and acknowledge feelings behind your child's words and actions. Seek to understand why your child wants the negative peer relationship.

- **Increase your child's decision-making.** Limit rules to ones that are necessary for safety and get your child's input on them.

- **Model handling peer pressure yourself**. Point out when you speak up in a group or in front of your friends.

School-Ager Development and Learning - Getting Ready for a New School Year

"How do I get my kids ready for a new year?"

Brain development stage: Children are still learning preparation and need a parent's help to get ready.

Suggestions:

- **Don't shop until the school supply list comes home.** It's tempting to get a heads up on sales and deals, but if you buy the wrong item, your child will refuse to use it.

- **When you shop, buy extras of the sale items.** Your child will lose things by Christmas or may want extra supplies for homework tasks at home. Especially stock up on loss leaders which are priced so low to get you in the store.
- **Get haircuts done early.** Most school photos are taken the first week and you want to avoid that just-cut look.
- **Get the doctor, optometrist, and dentist appointments out of the way early.**
- **Photos!** Don't forget to measure and weigh your child or take a photo of them next to the same object every year. You forget how quickly they grow.
- **Move back bedtimes.** Change the lights out time 15 minutes per night for the two weeks before school.
- **Pack away old school work.** Put in boxes and label.
- **New grade. New chores.** Celebrate the addition of another year and how capable your child has grown.
- **Tour the school.** The day before school officially opens, walk the halls with your child, get their timetable and map out the hallway and bathroom routes.
- **Arrange play dates**.
- **Draw up a homework contract.** Include stipulations that meet both your child's and your needs and both of you can sign it. Post on the wall for those inevitable whining moments.
- **Separation anxiety – handover or stay.** You must do whatever fits your parenting style. You know your child best. Stand your ground if you want to say. Say a firm and kind good-bye if you want to leave.
- **After the initial sales, stock up** on extra supplies like binders, which can be marked down 80% by the end of September. Kids lose a lot of things.
- **Clean up rooms at the end of August.** Pick up garbage, recycle old books, clothes and toys. Assess whether new furniture needs to be purchased.

School-Ager Development and Learning - Bullying Perpetrator

"We just found out that our son is a bully at school. He is 12 years old and the parents of the other boy contacted the school authorities. What do I do now?"

Brain development stage: Bullying is common in all age groups but most prevalent around childhood ages 9 to 16 years. Children discover the power of control from various sources in their lives and use it to target someone they think deserves it. Children who bully may have a big sense of entitlement and sometimes an unhealthy self-esteem. Although bullying is very common, it is still not acceptable.

Suggestions:

- Don't ignore the situation. You need to address it.
- Listen to all parties involved; the other parents, the school, and other people in your son's life.
- Confront your son: "I received a call from the school and they said that you and your friends are picking on so-and-so. What can you tell me about it?"
- Reiterate that it is not acceptable and you will not tolerate it.
- Expect him to provide an apology or some sort of retribution. He has to own his part in it.
- Monitor his whereabouts very closely for the next couple months.
- Talk to him about ways to help people. Get him to volunteer with you.
- Stop sibling teasing or put downs in the house.
- Speak to your doctor about counseling.
- Warn that if he doesn't stop, the natural consequence to cyber-bullying is to live without cell-phones and computers.
- Isolate him from his peer group (the henchmen who helps the bullying) by enrolling him in other activities or asking the teacher to separate them in class.
- Engage school personnel to help with the situation.
- Consider changing schools in order to have a fresh start.
- Meet with the bullied family (if they and your son agrees) so your son can see how it affects people.
- Help him find his power in healthy ways such as volunteering, job, or leadership activities like Scouts, Junior Forest Wardens, Junior Achievement, or Youth Toastmasters.

School-Ager Development and Learning – Bullied Victim

"How can I help my child deal with bullying?"

Brain development stage: Bullies are everywhere. Help your child minimize their effect.

Suggestions:

- It helps to understand what motivates each group:

What motivates:

Victims: lack of power

Bullies: power, make fun, popular, attention

Cronies: on the side of power, fear of bully

Bystanders: feeling inadequate, fear

- Provide emotional support. Spend more time with him and surround him with family friends and other groups.
- Build his self-confidence by encouraging his success in what he does well.
- Stay calm and validate his disclosure.
- Enlist help of teachers, administration and support staff.
- Devise a plan of action for safety.
- If it is cyber-bullying, **stop** looking and responding, **block** the bully and cronies and **copy** all emails, texts, etc. Screen grab and save on your computer.
- Put a "Google alert" on your child's name to see where it comes up on the internet.
- Don't take away his electronics. This is the major reason children don't tell parents they are being bullied.
- Ensure children don't use their real name on social media until they are 18. Search engines can't dig up dirt on your child if he changes schools or cities.
- Practice good comebacks, which deflate the emotional power of bully and hench people – self-deprecating humor gives power to the victim and engages sympathy from the bystanders. Role play. "Yep, I like my name because it's weird. No one else is named Meatball."
- Encourage eye contact with bully while standing up to them. Say, "So. My name is different. So what."
- Don't show anger or fight back.
- Try ignoring by walking away confidently – don't run or show fear.
- Don't go along with or give possessions.

- Round up the bystanders to stand up to the bully with a group. A group is safer because of less of individual targeting.

Comebacks for Bullying

Think self-talk

- "This kid has a real problem and I'm not going to let it be my problem."
- "I'm a good kid and I am not letting her win."

Instead of being defensive, agree. It takes the wind out of the bully's sails

- "Yup! I'm the freckle queen!"
- "Too many to count."
- "Yep, my glasses are geeky and they rock!"

Point out the obvious

- "Why do you want to pick on a shrimp when that won't prove anything about your strength?"
- "I must be really important for you to give me this much attention!"
- "Do you have anything better to do?"
- "Guess it's time to pick on me again. No one else smaller around?"
- "Yep, if you can't push yourself up, you want to pull me down, eh?"

Sometimes short and simple can deflate the emotional power of bully's comments

- "Brilliant."
- "That's creative."
- "You're right."
- "Get a life."
- "Whatever."

Try the direct approach

- "That's just mean." And walk away.
- "That's just lame." And walk away.
- "Get a grip." And walk away.

Self-deprecating humor is a trick that stand-up comics use against hecklers and win over the audience members (bystanders). It

shows you don't take things seriously. This really deflates the bully's power.

- "Big feet, big understanding!"

If the bully says, "Are you ugly or just plain stupid?"

You can say:

- "Actually, both!"
- "Stupid is as stupid does"
- "Yep. So what?"
- "Yep, I'm so ugly that when I was born, they put tinted windows in my incubator! So what?"

....

School-Ager Development and Learning - Chores

"How do I get my kids to do chores?"

Brain development stage: Children are still learning self-control. They will do chores if reminded from ages 6-11 and can remember to do chores all by themselves at age 12.

Suggestions:

Transfer characteristics from the concept of adult volunteering to the concept of kids doing chores:

1. Reasonable scope - small amount of work, definite finish, allow play during.
2. Group belonging - matching aprons, gloves, team name, etc.
3. Social - jokes, fun, talking, music, social atmosphere, give treat after as a group.
4. Choice - which job, scope, and time.
5. Recognition and appreciation - slather on the attention and thanks.

- Maintain the expectation that chores will be done, with no payment.
- Have a sheet that small pieces like Lego can be played in and clean-up easily.
- Use a clean dustpan to scoop up small pieces. Once a month or year, have a big sorting session.
- Give each child one job. Child A picks up all the socks and Child B picks up all the food plates.

- Have open shelves with photos of items so kids know where things go for clean up.
- Horizontal storage is always better than vertical buckets because small items get lost at the bottom of bins.
- You pick up big items and hand them to the kids to distribute to different rooms. They can set them down in the middle of the floor. Then you can finalize where they go in the rooms.
- Give each child a basket and toss everything in. Go together to each room to distribute the items.
- Work room-by-room.
- Have a small clean-up before friends go home from a play date or sleepover. Teach children that they are responsible for their friend's messes and they should solicit help or they will have to do it all by themselves.
- Make a bingo board and put chores on it. First line of chores that gets done, gets that family member a special treat.
- You could de-clutter and they could do the actual cleaning. Give them jobs such as vacuuming, floor-mopping, spray cleaning. After surfaces are clutter-free, cleaning is easier.
- See "age-by-age chores" under General Parenting

....

School-Ager Development and Learning - Teach Giving

"How can I help teach my child to be a giver?"

Brain development stage: School-age children are much less ego-centric and are naturally becoming more altruistic and helpful.

Suggestions:

- Involve or bring your child along with you when you help other people. Get them baking cookies with you for a hospitalized person. Have them come with you to the hospital or nursing home if possible so they can see the results of their efforts.
- Pick up litter at a local park.
- Volunteer to care for a friend's pet while they are away.
- Volunteer to get the mail for an elderly neighbor.

- Donate blankets to an animal shelter.

- Do yardwork or shovel walks for a neighbor.

- Organize a food drive for the local food bank.

- Have a garage sale and provide proceeds for a charity.

- Ask for donations for a charity instead of having birthday presents at his party.

- Let him chat with the people there. Don't worry that he will say the wrong thing - people are very forgiving with children and don't mind their natural curiosity.

- Have him help you in volunteering at a shelter for the homeless, the food bank, or sorting holiday hampers.

- Structure everyday helpfulness. Ask him to help Dad bring in groceries or run an extra loaf of home-baked bread to the neighbors.

- Give opportunities for him to directly impact other people such as saving his allowance or creating a lemonade stand for a charity. Give away his little-used old clothes, books, games or toys, with his consent of course.

- Help him pick a specific charity for the month or year. Research the charity online and go to visit it.

- Plan other people's birthday and holiday gifts with your child. Involve him in shopping, wrapping and most importantly, watching the giving!

School-Ager Development and Learning - When to Introduce Cell Phones

"Over half the children in my son's grade 2 class have cell phones, and now my son wants one. Should I give my 7 year-old a phone?"

Brain development stage: Children still forget where they left their possessions until age 8. Generally, most children don't really need a cell-phone until they are traveling on their own around the city, about age 13. Then they may need it to access route maps and bus schedules.

Suggestions:

- It's a personal decision. Decide if the risks and benefits are what you want.

- Parents worry about kidnapping on the way to school, or their child getting lost or hurt and not being able to contact them. How realistic are those worries?

- When children have cell phones, research shows that they lose out on their independence, creativity and problem-solving skills from figuring out how to handle situations on their own. At what point or age, do we allow children to "think" on their own, without the constant lifeline to parent's advice?

- Cell phones are expensive, and are easily lost, broken, or stolen.

- Parents like them because their children have something valuable that can be confiscated as a punishment. However, this is not conducive to open communication as a child ages.

- With smart phones, children have a window to the world (the internet) that can expose them to sexuality, porn, violence, bullying, advertising and nasty people, more exponentially than what they see in their daily life, without a parent's tempering and guidance.

- Decide what the true need is for a cell phone and talk together about the rules/ limits regarding its use.

- Explain how the data cost is calculated to lessen the likelihood of having an unexpected $300 bill the first month.

- If you decide on no-cell-phone, teach your child that everyone near him has one and if he really needs to phone you, he can ask a business or passerby to borrow the phone for a parent call. Making a call is even easier than it used to be, when we had to find a payphone, and coins to use it.

School-Ager Development and Learning - Teaching Kids to Say No

"My child's friends often gets him into trouble. How can I teach him to say "No" to negative peer pressure?"

Brain development stage: Children tend to want to do what their peers say and do in order to fit in. The school-age years tend to be ones that kids do not want to appear different.

Suggestions:

10 ways kids can say "No!"

1. Ask questions: "What if such and such happens?"
2. Give it a name: "That's stealing! No way."
3. Refer to the parent: "Nope. My Mom won't let me."
4. Get an ally: "No, Jason and I are going to the park instead."
5. Suggest an alternative: "Why don't we play Xbox at my house?"
6. State consequences: "I want a career in law enforcement and need a clean record."

7. Stall: "Hmm...maybe later."

8. Offer an excuse: "I have to go and meet someone."

9. Say "No" another way: "I can't." "I don't feel like it today." No explanation needed.

10. Make a joke: "Yeah, wouldn't that look great on YouTube!"

- If all else fails: ignore, act busy, or just walk away.

Helping your child deal with the possible fallout from saying 'No!':

- Help your child focus on other peer groups. Get her involved in groups outside of school such as church, scouting, cadets, or on-going classes or clubs.

- Acknowledge his feelings of loneliness and sadness. Share stories of times that you felt isolated due to peer pressure.

- Spend more time with your child and build her confidence and esteem. Notice and comment on her worth as a person, "I'm so glad you are my daughter," and also things she does well, "I noticed how much effort you put into studying for that exam."

- We all have times we need extra support. Make your family a soft landing place for the harsh realities of the outside world.

- We can't protect our child from the sanctions of refusing peers, but we can and should teach him how to cope with his emotions, pick himself up and work through the problem. This builds resiliency and parents are best able to help him. Kids need us just as much in the tween and teen years as the toddler stage!

School-Ager Development and Learning - Refuses Homework

"How do I get my child to do her homework?"

Brain development stage: Children often do not see the value of homework and may not want to practice skills or seek knowledge. There may be many reasons why they don't complete it and it's up to the parent to uncover those reasons and address them.

Suggestions:

- Give choices in subject matter, time, or place of study. E.g. Would the child like to do Math or English today? When is her best, most alert time of day? Would she like to study in her room, outside, or on the couch?

- Alternate bookwork days with outing days. Consider helping her learn in a different way with an outing or field trip instead of researching books.

- Consider giving tests first and if the concepts are mastered, eliminate the text material. Cuts down on boredom and busywork. If you know your child knows the material, talk to the teacher and request less homework.

- Present the material in a fun way and geared to child's learning style. Use learning aids such as movies, cookie fractions, board and action games such as multiplication tag. Children in elementary school love to learn through play.

- Follow interests as much as possible, if not in format, then in content. For example, if the child has to write essay or book report, perhaps she could choose the topic or book.

- Avoid rescuing from the teacher's wrath if the homework is not done. Let natural consequences occur.

- Make sure the child is fed and watered. Children don't learn on an empty stomach.

- Allow breaks every twenty minutes or so.

- Use rewards if they work for your child. Stickers, passes for fun outings and computer time are some choices from parents. Have a jar of 200 dimes (one for each school day). Any day the child does homework, put in one dime. The child can keep the money at the end of the year.

- Avoid power struggles. Put your relationship building first. Try and approach learning another way. Listen to why your child doesn't want to do the work.

- For those hesitant writers, try being the scribe while the child dictates ideas. Or try letting her write on the computer, which is easier on little hands.

- For those hesitant readers, try picking up an enticing children's book and reading out loud. Your child might come join you if it's not forced. Model reading yourself. Cuddle on the couch with your child and make reading a fun, cozy, exciting time. Use vocal variety and stop when the child is not longer interested.

- Keep a routine going when you figure out the best time of day for bookwork. This has to work for you and your child. Not all children are "get homework done right after school" kids. Be kind but firm in sticking to a routine that your child says would work for her. Children need some structure.

- Set aside a time for family quiet activities; she could do homework and you could pay bills, read, or do paperwork. All can work around the kitchen table.

- Discourage noisy fun activities like video games, if some siblings have homework.

- Have a written contract each week, month or year that is signed and agreed to by you and your child, about what work must be completed for that time period.

- Children often learn better by discovery than by being told. Lead her to an experiential activity that would reinforce concepts. For example, If she doesn't understand plotting coordinates on a paper grid, play Battleship instead.

- Show the child how to break up a big task into smaller chunks.

- Teach goal setting and scheduling.

- Talk to the teacher with your child present and have a three-way problem-solving session. Get at your child's true needs; is the work too boring? Too hard?

- Get your child assessed for a learning disability.

- Some months are better than others. Children go through spurts and plateaus and most do not learn in tidy sequential steps. During a plateau, trust that the desire and motivation will come back.

- Assimilation of material takes time. Plan for playtime, down time and many breaks (minutes, days, weeks and even months).

- Create a learning environment of fun, curiosity and good feelings. Make sure everyone is fed, rested, comfortable and non-stressed!

- Never punish for not doing the work. You want to create a climate for lifelong learning and enjoyment of the pursuit of knowledge. Remember, your job is to facilitate learning. Nudge, but don't force! A caring, loving relationship between you and your daughter will provide fuel for future learning. She can always learn math later. Build your relationship first.

School-Ager Development and Learning - Work Ethic

"How do I raise my child to have a good work ethic?"

Brain development stage: Children from birth to age 7 love to help out. Then they discover that some jobs are fun and some are not.

Suggestions:

- Give chores to do that are unpaid but contribute to the family unit. Include "cooperative living" chores such as bathroom cleaning, living-room vacuuming and not just their own little corner like "keeping their room tidy."

- Ensure they turn in homework on time. Insist the school doesn't give kids second chances.

- Avoid rescuing from other people's consequences imposed on them.

- Avoid rescue from experiencing failure. They need to develop the skills to pick themselves up and try again and experience the exhilaration of finally succeeding.

- Insist on cell-phone free times like family dinners, game night, socializing, family meetings etc. Kids need to learn where electronics are appropriate and where they are not.

School-Ager Discipline - Potty Mouth, Name-Calling, and Swearing

"My 7 year-old daughter has a bit of a potty mouth. We try and shield her from popculture, but she is the youngest of older siblings and she often hears swear words by accident. How do I handle this?"

Brain development stage: Like whining and swearing, children find power in words that adults give attention to.

Suggestions:

- Give alternatives of what to say when she is angry, such as "fudge", "shoot", or "what the heck."

- Say, "I don't like swearing/name-calling and we don't do that in our house." Keep declaring your values.

- Have conversations about how language affects how people view others.

- Ignore it if they are younger (under 4) so they don't attach the power to the words.

- Teach her "containment." Everyone swears, but there is a time, place and people that it is more appropriate for. Teach her to use alternative words when she is around Grandma, and perhaps she can use the swear words when she is alone and stubs her toe or whatever.

- Teach her to use "I-statements" when she is angry with siblings instead of calling them bad names. It helps her to express her feelings and gets at the real issue. So instead of saying, "You idiot! You wrecked my puzzle!," show her the words to use: "I'm really angry that you wrecked my puzzle!"

- Send her to her room and ask her to swear into a pillow if she must.

- Kids learn pretty fast that certain words have power. Studies have shown that swearing helps to reduce the stress hormone, cortisol, that we build up when we are angry or upset. Teach about the proper use of swearing. It's not the word itself, but the context in how it is used, that kids need to learn. Talk about when it is okay to swear and when it is not okay. Ask what they think.

- Model proper language.

School-Ager Discipline - Consequences or Problem-Solving?

"When I give my 11 year-old daughter a consequence, she insists that I am being mean to her. I believe that it is respectful discipline. What is the difference between consequences and a punishment?"

Brain development stage: Between the ages of 5 and 12, most children figure out that they are not choosing the consequence, and it is the parents imposing the order on them in the name of discipline. If the child doesn't see the point, she may experience it as a punishment.

Suggestions:

- Consequences are parent imposed. The conflict is now between the parent and child. Problem-solving is the parent and child working together to come up with a solution to fix the problem. The conflict is now between the parent-child team against the problem (even if the child caused it.)

- Problem-solving is a more real-world skill. It teaches kids how to fix things, make restitution, repair relationships and make things right.

- Consequences are focused on the child, where problem-solving is focused on the end result; a common goal.

- Consequences tend to be one solution (usually the parent's). Problem-solving can be many solutions (generated from both parent and child) that would take care of the problem. The goal is repair, whereas the goal of consequences is to teach the child a lesson, which is punitive.

- Consequences are almost always designed to hurt a child - either financially (pay for a broken item), socially (grounding or taking away cell phone), emotionally (time-out) or physically (hard physical labor). Problem-solving is designed to be pain-neutral. The goal is not to hurt the child, but help the situation. The goal is to fix the problem. Sometimes that is financial or physical, but the payoff is that the child feels good that they are now owning the solution and not just the problem. Children are very fair and more likely to dive into helping fix the problem when they know they caused it, because the focus is no longer on what they did, but what they can do to make it right. When they can put effort into fixing the problem, they feel better about themselves, learn real-world solutions and will make better decisions in the future.

- Parents argue, "Yes, but it works! Consequences changed my child's behaviour!" That may be correct, but the price is impaired communication. Parents wonder why they don't enjoy the open, caring, free communication that they once had with their child. They wonder why they are receiving attitude and silence. Push-back of imposed consequences comes in many forms. Ditch the consequences and use the adult method of problem-solving.

School-Ager Discipline - Defiant

"My 10 year-old son is very defiant. When I ask him to do something, he ignores me or say's he will do it and then doesn't. Worse, sometimes he does the opposite just to get my anger going."

Brain development stage: Although most children can think manipulatively at this age, most children do not set out to be mean to you. Most children are just acting to get their needs met, and don't really think about you getting your needs met.

Suggestions:

- Allow yourself to feel angry and annoyed, but watch what you say.
- Go for a walk together and ask your son why he does that. Listen carefully and stay calm.
- Talk to him about problem-solving and assure him that he will get his needs met (his way) if he negotiates with you in collaborative problem-solving.
- Don't take his resistance personally.
- Watch what friend group he is hanging out with. Substitute activities so he spends less time with them and more time with family.
- Pick your battles. Let a lot go, but stay with the few that really matter to you.
- Allow many choices so he doesn't feel boxed in.
- Teach compromises; "I will do this for you, if you can do this for me."
- Be a broken record. "I hear that you hate taking bottles in, but this needs to be done. How can we get it done? Any ideas?" (Then seriously consider his ideas.)

- Diffuse him with humor.
- Have a few family rules that he gives input on. Recite them when he doesn't want to follow them.

....

School-Ager Discipline - Drinking, Drugs, Sex, and Vandalism

"My 12 year-old is out of control. He is experimenting with alcohol, pot, and vandalism. How do I stop this now?"

Brain development stage: Children will experiment with behaviors as they head into the teen years, but with intervention from caregivers, they should stop.

Suggestions:

- Open up the conversation and listen to why he is doing what he does. Discuss the possible outcomes of each behavior and ask about his plan for dealing with the risks.
- Get a one-time consultation scheduled where you lay out all your information on the risks and ask him to stop.
- Active listen to his feelings without judgment, to keep him talking and to build communication.
- Model a healthy lifestyle.
- Help him to feel grown-up in other ways.
- Have a conversation about trust.
- Have conversations about how the media distorts the coolness factor.
- Avoid rescue from natural consequences such as police involvement. Let him face the music, but support him emotionally by listening to him.
- You, as the parent, are the cushion to soften his landing. But let him land and own his part. Your job is to provide emotional support while he fixes his own situation. Your job is not to fix it for him.
- Find him other peer groups that are more responsible. Role play how to say "No" to peers.
- Give him more privileges but tie it in with responsibilities.
- Keep listening more than talking, to build communication. Validate his feelings.
- Problem-solve broken rules.
- Get professional help if nothing changes.

School-Ager Discipline - Steals

"My 12 year-old daughter has been taking things from a nearby store. She has new CDs and shirts that I know she doesn't have money to pay for. How do I confront her?"

Brain development stage: Children at this age steal for many reasons: peer pressure, fun, power, or a real need to have an item. Most of it is experimental, but sometimes it is ongoing.

Suggestions:

- Acknowledge feelings. Say, "I can see that you feel desperate to fit in. But stealing is wrong."

- Express your sadness and disappointment. Children with a good connection to you will feel bad about you feeling bad.

- Don't let it go or ignore it. This is one instance that you do need to address it or it can snowball.

- Coach her through the process of returning the item, apologizing, and making amends. She could return it in person or write a letter. She could donate or work for a community service to feel better about it.

- Be sure to give her information. Age 12 to 13 is an age that a child can be charged with a crime, depending on jurisdiction. Talk to her about the seriousness of it. Avoid rescue from police involvement. Help her with the consequences and carrying out. (If she needs to do community service, be sure she keeps her commitment.)

- Discuss movies and books about theft.

- Model honesty. When you get an item by accident (the clerk makes a mistake), or a server forgets to include an item on a bill, be sure to point it out and pay for it, in front of your child. Explain that it is morally right and that you do it to feel better for yourself. Establish that connection between doing what is right and how one feels about themselves. Teach about integrity.

- Role play how to handle peer pressure. Give her some phrases to decline stealing next time.

- Find a way to help her get what she needs, (acceptance, power, fame) legally and honestly. Problem-solve ways she can earn the money for what she desperately needs.

- Don't lecture, don't over-react, but do address it, every time.

School-Ager Discipline - Destroys Property

"My daughter is very hard on toys, furniture, and other people's belongings. She loses things and handles them hard enough to break them."

Brain development stage: Children will need reminding until the age of 8, or they will forget items behind. They often don't understand how property can get broken.

Suggestions:

- If children are angry, redirect them while reciting the family rule, "When we are irate, we take a break!"
- If they break a toy on purpose, don't replace it. If they want it fixed, they have to purchase parts and help.
- Warn her of what you see. Say, "I'm worried that if you lean back in that chair, the legs might get broken off." She will correct her behavior accordingly. If not, directly ask her to "keep the chair legs on the ground please."

School-Ager Discipline - Ignores Advice and Won't Listen

"My 11 year-old daughter often ignores my advice. She is very persistent and adamant that she is right all the time, even when we both know that she isn't."

Brain development stage: Children can be very independent and want to do what they want to do. They don't like to admit error, because they have been socialized to view errors as a bad thing.

Suggestions:

- If it is safe, don't rescue her from natural consequences (those events that happen and are not pre-arranged). Sometimes children just need to learn things the hard, painful way when they ignore our labor saving advice.
- If you have said, "No", then stay with your "No" as best as you can. Change what you can do.
- Model your good advice.
- If she has said, "No" to you, give her a minute for reconsideration. Ask her if she is sure that is what she wants to say.

- Don't say, "I told you so." Don't rub it in or gloat when things go bad for her. Give her a hug and offer feeling validation and support.

School-Ager Discipline - Dresses Inappropriately

"Kids these days wear the most inappropriate things. How do I convey proper dress to my 12 year-old son?"

Brain development stage: Children need power and appearance is one method of exploring that power and competency and individualism. They also are keenly aware of fitting in and that also dictates choices.

Suggestions:

- Gently suggest. Say, "It looks like rain. Do you think a coat might be a good idea?" If he doesn't wear a coat, leave it be. He is making an informed decision and teens needs to make a lot of decisions to feel confident in them and learn from them.
- Accept that he may have different standards. Remember when you were young!
- Compliment him on his individuality and choices.
- Give a one-time consultation. Agree that he hears you out for a few minutes while you outline your concerns and then leave the decision up to him. Don't nag.
- If he is accepting, offer a coat or pair of socks for his backpack.
- Dress like he does. He might stop!

School-Ager Discipline - Surfs Forbidden Websites

"I don't have a net-nanny, but I have declared certain websites off limits. Now I found out that my 12 year-old daughter is exploring them. Now what?"

Brain development stage: Children are curious. Always. They seek to meet their needs.

Suggestions:

- Problem-solve your concerns about the sites and her curiosity. Decide on mutual rules that would help both your intentions.

- It may be peer pressure. Help her navigate it by role-playing how to deflect peer requests.

- Take a web-building, or networking course together.

- Trust her and tell her that if she encounters anything scary, or someone wanting to meet her in person, that she should tell you. Make sure you promise not to take away her computer, cell-phone or tablet and in return, you will help her if she needs it.

- Open parent-child communication lines keeps kids safe.

- Give her information on your concerns about pornography, body image, relationships etc. Ask for and listen to her opinions.

- Make your home welcoming to her friends so that your house becomes the hangout and you can somewhat monitor activity. What kind of games, music and food would her friends like? When they are at your house, provide "invisible supervision" by occasionally dropping in to their social area by serving snacks. Notice things.

- Set up an internet contract that meets your needs and her needs. Here is a sample one:

NON-PUNITIVE MOBILE-PHONE CONTRACT FOR DIGITAL CITIZENSHIP

A Contract for Digital Health and Safety between Parent and Child

Date:_____

CHILD

- I agree to always ask you for help, explanation, advice and information regarding anything I can't handle myself on the mobile-phone, Internet and computer/video gaming platform.
- I agree to abide by safety and health precautions as outlined between you and myself.
- I agree to never meet strangers in person without your knowledge.
- I agree to discuss and solve any problems that arise from meeting your needs and mine.

Child's Signature_____

PARENT

- I agree to discuss and solve any problems that arise from meeting your needs and mine.
- I agree to never confiscate your mobile-phone, TV, computer, tablet, music player or video game console.

Parent's Signature_____

MUTUAL HEALTH AND SAFETY AGREEMENTS

- Tech-free zones will be meal-times, church, socializing with relatives, and when visitors drop by.
- All electronics will be turned off 1 hour before bedtime.
- Everyone does 30 minutes of physical exercise every day.
- Giving attention to people takes precedence over attention to electronics.
- (More here depending on your family)

Child and Parent's Signatures_____

School-Ager Discipline - Ignores Pet Care

"We got my 8 year-old son a dog because he begged us and promised to do all the pet care. This worked for about a week and now he doesn't anymore. What should we do?"

Brain development stage: Children ages 6-12 need reminding about pet care and often need help with cleaning litter boxes, cages and picking up dog presents outside. Teenagers can take on pet care by themselves.

Suggestions:

- Come up with a plan so the child can help you take care of the pet.
- Draw up an agreement with dates and duties needed to be done.
- Think twice before getting another pet.
- Keep reminding the child about the job that needs to be done.

School-Ager Discipline - Borrows or Lends Items

"My daughter borrows my clothes without asking. We are the same size. She also lends out our family things like books, movies, and video games without telling me."

Brain development stage: Children are naturally generous and want to give things away to others. They are also forgetful about asking permission.

Suggestions:

- When she does ask to borrow, say mostly "Yes" so it will encourage her to keep asking.
- Confront her with an I-statement. "I am frustrated when I go to wear something and it's not clean. I have to take time and money to get it cleaned."
- Always ask permission when using something of theirs.
- When children loan items, have a rule that it gets marked down on the "borrowed" list. Put a date down. That way, when the child forgets where the item is four months from now, you will know who it was loaned to.
- Encourage the child to ask for the items back. If they don't come back, problem-solve with the child on how to replace the item.

School-Ager Discipline - Won't Pick Up Dishes and Clothes

"My 11 year-old son leaves towels in the bathroom, socks all over the floor and jackets and games in common areas. How do I get him to clean up?"

Brain development stage: Children are still learning to think about others.

Suggestions:

- Use humor. Have a sign that says, "Your clothes hamper is hungry. Please feed it."
- Pick it up for him if he agrees to pay you or does a favour for you. Relationships are reciprocal.
- Problem-solve it so he can help come up with solutions.

....

School-Ager Discipline - Won't Clean Room

"My daughter's room is a disaster. She throws clothes, papers, toys, and food in there. I'm tired of nagging her."

Brain development stage: This is a time that children's preference for organization emerges. Some children with a laid-back personality prefer what looks like a mess to everyone else as they can find things when they need them. Other children that have a more compartmentalized personality like to organize, sort and have clutter-free environments. They will continue these habits long after they move out, so your challenge is how to live with your child's habits until they are "under new management" in someone else's house or their own.

Suggestions:

- Minimize clutter. Pack most of the clothes, toys and items away until needed.
- Set up organization drawers and shelving so that everything does have a space to "live in."
- Close the door. It's their room. Insist on common areas of the house being livable and organized though.
- Ban food. Show them what carpet beetles and weevils look like and they most likely will keep food out of their rooms.

- Use storage under the bed to tuck away items.

- Insist on a one-in, one-out rule. When a new toy comes in, something has to be donated.

- Help them clean up once in a while. Promise them a sleepover or a bouquet of flowers when done.

- Make a bingo board and put chores on it. First line of chores that gets done, gets that family member a special treat.

- See more under "chores."

School-Ager Discipline - Refuses Cooperation

"How do I get my daughter to cooperate?"

Brain development stage: Children often do not see the point in what you want them to do. You have to teach, teach, teach. Rather than work on making them do things, change what you will and will not do.

Suggestions:

- Child won't carry backpack - don't do it yourself.

- Child won't eat - give her fresh air and exercise. Make one meal and don't make special treats for her.

- Child won't sleep - give her quiet activities in her room. Wake her up at a normal time every morning.

- Child won't come to the table for dinner - insist on table social time even if she doesn't eat. Have meals and snacks at the same time every day.

School-Ager Discipline - Reneges on Problem-Solving Agreements

"We problem-solve with my 7 year-old and draw up agreements that he reneges on. What do I do then?"

Brain development stage: Children love to problem-solve but only if it meets their needs too. When they renege on agreements, it is very likely the proposed agreement didn't meet their needs.

Suggestions:

- Maintain eye contact, stand by his side, and point to your watch.
- Supervise closely. If a child doesn't do an action they promised, stay with them until it is done.
- Say, "I need a hug." Kids like to be helpful. Then say what else you need done.
- Go back to the drawing board. The agreement probably didn't work for his needs, so he has to provide input into what would work for him.

School-Ager Discipline - Dawdling

"How can I get my 6 year-old out of the house on time? He wakes up okay, but is cranky and snarky."

Brain development stage: Children don't have much of a concept of how long something takes until at least age 7. Their world is still very much play and no deadlines and they tend to be in vacation mode even if their parents are not.

Suggestions:

- Try putting him to bed earlier so he gets more sleep.
- Turn the clocks ahead so he gets to bed earlier. Turn them back when he is in bed.
- Go to bed earlier yourself so you get more sleep and then you will be better able to tolerate his bad mood in the morning.
- Give him responsibility for lunch or dressing and let him figure out what he misses or needs. Warn the teacher beforehand that you are going to do this.
- Dress him in the next day's clean clothes for bed, so you don't have to argue about dressing the next day.
- Pack a breakfast for the car if he is not a breakfast eater.
- Avoid too many demands on him during his most cranky time of day which is early morning.
- Have a breakfast that he can drink fast. Children are often more cooperative when their tummy is full.
- Do more prep tasks the night before when he is in a more cooperative mood.

School-Ager Discipline - Friend's Bad Manners

"Should I correct my children's friend's manners when they are school-aged? I have to drive my daughter and her friend for the next 6 months to a weekly activity, and the friend doesn't ever say "Thanks"."

Brain development stage: Children are forgetful at this age.

Suggestions:

- When I was a child and adults were annoyed at me, I would have preferred to know why.
- Perhaps have a quiet word with the friend and a gentle reminder of manners. It takes a village to raise a child.
- If you are not feeling appreciated, say it to her in an "I-statement" like you would anyone else.
- Perhaps get your daughter to mention it to her friend, that she should say an occasional, "Thank you, Mrs. Smith, for the ride."
- Say "You are welcome for the ride!" the next time you car pool.

School-Ager Discipline - Undesirable Friends

"My 12 year-old son has bad friends. How can I discourage their friendship?"

Brain development stage: As children move into the teen years, they base their friendships on shared interests, values, beliefs and opinions.

Suggestions:

- Examine why those friends are desirable for your son and find other ways for him to get what he is looking for; power, control, attention, competency.
- Accept them. The more you reject them, the more their appeal may be.
- Don't rescue him when those friends get him into trouble.
- Allow socializing at your house within the family rules.

School-Ager Discipline - Hitting

"My 8 year-old son punched another child in the face. This is not a typical behavior for him. I'm not sure how to deal with this."

Brain development stage: School-agers are still perfecting the art of self-control and sometimes make mistakes. Be sure to let him know that it is not okay and you expect alternative ways to express his anger.

Suggestions:

- Ask him, "What do you think a good solution is?" See what they come up with for problem-solving.
- Talk to him about it. Focus on positives. Every time he handles issues without hitting is a good reason to celebrate.
- Try to understand his feelings. What can he do when he is frustrated? Give him a lot of actions to do instead of hitting. Role play and practice those with him.
- Remind him about acceptable behavior. Remind him that hitting is absolutely unacceptable and that at 12, the law and society expects him to have enough self-control to not hit people.
- Work on empathy skills. Ask him how he might think the other child felt?
- Be vigilant on the playground if possible.
- Role-play and practice his reaction when kids are mean to him.
- Don't protect him from the outcomes of his actions. If he is punished at school for hitting, let him accept the punishment. At home, help him by working on anger management skills.
- If he is still hitting around ages 11 to 12, consider professional help for him.
- See "hitting" under other age categories as well.

School-Ager Discipline - Back-Talk

"My 8 year-old daughter "talks back" to me. How do I encourage compliance when she argues a lot? She does the same with my partner and she is very stubborn."

Brain development stage: Children's compliance becomes better with age, but they are not more than 60% there yet.

Suggestions:

- Let her have as much control over her life as possible. She needs autonomy.

- Be empathetic. Use "I-statements" such as "I don't like being spoken to that way. Please use these words." You could even write out the words for her if she is reading, so she can see what she is supposed to say.

- Ignore her unless she speaks to you in a respectful tone. Just like whining, you could say, "I can't hear what you are saying when you use disrespectful words. Try it again, please."

- Point out to her what voice tone is respectful and when, who and where to use it.

- Give praise when you hear her politeness and respectful voice.

- Speak respectfully to other people in your lives such as; the cleaning person, the guy who serves you coffee, etc.

- Model respect even when you are fighting with your partner. Children need to see that adults argue issues with "I-statements" and not attack the person.

- Don't stay and be a target. Protect yourself first.

- Don't be surly back to her. Model how you want her to be.

- Don't tell friends that she is in her "terrible teens" or "that stage." Remember that it could become a self-fulfilling prophesy.

- Monitor her friends and the media she is watching. She may be picking it up from there. Enroll her in activities with a more respectful group.

- Listen to the message, and tell her you hear it, but would like it rephrased in a respectful way. Tell her the words to say.

- Avoid "stepping in the power struggle ring." Let mistakes happen.

- Reflect back her feelings to help calm the feeling. It prevents a huge blowout. "You are upset because you can't go to the movie today."

- If you have issued consequences that haven't worked, don't repeat them.

- Insist on getting an apology. If you wait until she cools down, you will get it.

- Look at her persistence as a blessing – she will not be easily influenced by you or by her peers later on.

School-Ager Feeding - Picky Eating

"My 8 year-old son is still a picky eater. What should I do?"

Brain development stage: Children who are still picky eaters during the school years may be a picky eater for life.

Suggestions:

- Teach him how to cook and prepare alternate food that he will accept.
- Put something on the table you know he will eat; like bread, cheese, fruit.
- Don't worry. He will get all the nutrition he needs.

School-Ager Feeding - Bad Table Manners

"My son has really bad table manners."

Brain development stage: Children adapt quickly to a routine if they are taught proper manners.

Suggestions:

- Tolerate some bad manners at home but expect proper manners when eating out.
- Take him out to a formal restaurant and teach formal dining etiquette so you know he can "step up to the plate" when he has to.
- Have one formal dinner per week at home too.
- Have one meal a week that is no-manners dinner. Eat with your fingers, burp and do whatever is funny so that he gets it out of his system.

School-Ager Feeding - Leaves Kitchen Messes

"When my 9 year-old makes a sandwich, he leaves a disaster area. How do I get my budding cooks to clean up the kitchen?"

Brain development stage: Children love to create, but often don't know the steps in cleaning up or the expectations of standards.

Suggestions:

- Stay with them and insist that the kitchen gets cleaned up before anything else gets attended to.
- Give them a time frame to do it in. Say, "I see that you are busy with that computer game. I'd appreciate a kitchen clean-up by 4 pm, please."

- Get eye contact. Have them repeat instructions to you.
- Brainstorm some family rules of clean-up at the next family meeting.

School-Ager Feeding - Self-Serves Treats

"My kids help themselves to food designated for special times. How do I get them to stop this."

Brain development stage: Children are easy to talk to at this age. Explain the rule.

Suggestions:

- Hide cookies and treats in empty broccoli bags in the freezer!
- Label off-limited food with a special sticker.
- Divide the fridge, freezer and cupboards with special drawers or a side that is only available through asking permission.
- Have them replace anything they eat and don't have permission to eat.
- Schedule Junk Runs. Buy no junk food except for special occasions like sleepovers. Then take all the guests to a grocery store on a "junk run" and allow each guest to choose a treat to bring home and share. The next morning, send it all home with them.

School-Ager Health - Getting Children to Exercise

"How do I get my screen zombie moving?"

Brain development stage: Children in the school age years require about 1/2 hour of active physical activity per day.

Suggestions:

- **Set blackout periods.** Have specific times of the day or week that no electricity is on for machines. Well, except for lights of course! The children will find physically active things to do. Even more so if you send them outside to play. They may balk at first, but after a while, they will be having so much fun outside, that they will balk at coming back in.

- **Get children involved in volunteering.** Many family volunteer jobs include physical activity, whether it's at the local food bank, or shoveling the neighbors walk, or cleaning up the city pathways or riverbanks. Many paid jobs for teens also involve lifting, moving and carrying, which is a good way for teens to get exercise.

- **Do it with them.** Most children will get involved if Mom or Dad is also involved. Invite your child for a bike ride, rollerblade excursion, or time at the basketball net. Driving them to the swimming pool and then texting on your Blackberry in the viewing area sends them the wrong message. Get in the pool too! Besides, most adults could use a little more activity in their life. It's good for everyone.

- **Refuse to drive.** When children need to get somewhere, encourage them to bike, rollerblade, scooter, skate board, walk with their gang or take the bus. Even when children access the bus system, they still expand energy walking (or running if they are late) to and from the bus stop.

- **Plan friend and family activity dates.** Rather than meeting friends or family members at a restaurant, plan a sport or physical activity for a "play date".

- **Play active games.** Be open to providing funds for active games such as video game dance mats or the new get-fit video sports games on the market. Also offer to pay for outside or indoor sports equipment, but not for sedentary video games. Put your money where your values are and children will see that physical activity is important.

- **Picnic, camp, or hike.** Get outdoors and the physical activity will happen. Bring Frisbees, balls, bikes and other sports equipment for a day at a local or distant park.

- **Swim.** Most children love to swim if you drop them off at the local pool for the afternoon along with some buddies.

- **Start a "walking school bus."** Offer to walk the neighborhood children to school if you are already walking yours. Parents could rotate turns.

- **Start a "playground swap."** Parents who work during the day could reciprocate the favour of the walking school bus parents, by offering to be the parent supervisor at the neighborhood playground after supper. Designate a place and time for all the participating children to meet and one or two adults will walk all the kids to the playground and return back to the meeting spot at a designated time. Parents could rotate turns.

- **Small bits add up.** Staying physically fit doesn't have to be a big effort. Ten minutes here and fifteen minutes there all add up. Build small amounts of activity in every day and your whole family will notice the difference both in physical health and emotional closeness.

School-Ager Health - Public Bathrooms

"How do I get my child to stay with me while I am using a public bathroom stall?"

Brain development stage: Children over age 7 should use their own gender's bathroom in public.

Suggestions:

- Ask them to wait outside the stall and recite the alphabet while showing you their foot under the stall. They can shift to the to other foot every other letter.
- Give kids a rubber bracelet when out in public with your cell number written on the inside if they get lost.
- Keep your eye on them as much as you can.

School-Ager Parenting Partner - Different Parenting

"My son notices that my partner and I handle things differently - especially discipline. His father spanks and I problem-solve with him. Is this going to harm him?"

Brain development stage: Children over the age of 18 months can understand different parenting styles and expectations and act accordingly. Although both parents should provide nurturing and structure, children can handle day-to-day differences. In fact, it stimulates different parts of the brain.

Suggestions:

- Model the parenting you would like your partner to pick up. If he sees that it works, he may start adopting your techniques.
- Encourage him to sign up for a class with or without you.
- Spanking is only one ACE (Adverse Childhood Experience). By itself, it is unlikely to have long term effects on your son.

- Have a quiet word with your partner in private about how much spanking riles you. Use your I-statement.

- Agree that you both are different. Don't expect him to do things your way and he doesn't expect you to do things his way.

- Agree that what one parent starts, the other parent finishes. If he puts the kids in time-out, he should be the one to enforce and monitor it and not expect you to do it. He should be the one to end the time-out.

- You are each building a relationship with your son and you each own it and care for it. Do what works for both of you. He may notice your communication is better because you don't spank and may reconsider his parenting tools on his own.

- Don't disagree with your partner in front of your son, but don't support the spanking either. You can talk privately with your son, about the reasons you don't support spanking, and encourage him to chat with his Dad about it too.

- If you and your partner live in separate homes, it's okay to parent differently.

- Show him research that a warm and nurturing parenting style has better outcomes for your son. Check out the National Longitudinal Survey on Children and Youth in Canada for a valid study.

School-Ager Parenting Partner - Bonding with Step-Child

"I'm a step-parent. How do I attach with my new children?"

Brain development stage: Children under age 5 easily form attachments with anyone. Children older than age 5 take about two years to form and trust a relationship.

Suggestions:

- Take an active part in comforting the child when he is hurt, sick or upset. This forms attachment.

- Don't do the discipline for the first three years. Work on building respect and the relationship first.

- Acknowledge the child's feelings whenever he is upset. This doesn't mean you disagree with him, but that you are validating where he is at emotionally. This also builds attachment.

- Attend the child's activities and cheer him on! Be his supporter.

- Disagree with the other parent in private and work on solutions together. The child's parent should be the person to hand down new rules during the first two years.

....

School-Ager Play - Family Game Night

"How do we make family game night smoother?"

Brain development stage: Children this age love games but hate losing.

Suggestions:

Have a simple dinner. Order in pizza so that there are not many dishes to clean up and cooking is not necessary. If pizza is too expensive, plan to have a "snack" tray instead. Get a set of muffin tins or any compartmentalized tray and serve cheese cubes, fruit cubes, vegetable sticks, a few dips, meat roll-ups, raisins, nuts (not for under 4 year-olds though), crackers, pita pieces, hummus, and various finger foods. This takes hardly any dishes, and Mom is not always getting up between game turns to cook, serve and clean-up dinner.

Maintain a "Missing Pieces" bucket. Have a catch-all bucket for wayward game pieces, puzzle pieces, dice, and cards that get stuck under the sofa, behind tables and dropped into the carpet. That way, when a certain game is pulled out, the bucket can be checked for "lost" pieces before play begins.

Use plastic bags for pieces. When game boxes get wrecked from overuse, use clear locking plastic bags to contain cards and all pieces. Remember to hole-punch the bag if you have young children present so it is not a suffocation hazard. Bags are also handy for travelling because they keep out dirt and are less bulky to pack than board game boxes.

Roll dice in containers. Save those big plastic clear pill or dip containers for dice containers. Clean them out really well, and put two dice in them and then snap on the lid. It's great for little hands to shake the dice and not spill them all over the table and floor. The clear sides allow everyone to see the dice roll.

Paint backs of puzzles. Put a dab of paint or nail polish on the back of every puzzle piece and clean up will be easy.

Make a shield. Prop big hard cover books up in front of small children, so little ones can spread out their game cards on the table in front of them. One problem with family game night is that little hands have trouble holding the cards. You could also buy a child's card holder.

Play cooperative games. The ages of 6-8 years are the hardest times for children to accept losing. After eight years of age, it becomes easier for children to deal with the disappointment of not winning. Have a rule that the winner cleans up the game pieces and it might make losing a bit more palatable.

Partner up. Assign a non-reading child to an adult partner to help him read his game pieces and or write his answers, and they will play as a team.

With summer coming, consider games that go beyond the kitchen table. Head to the park and play tag, red rover, duck-duck-goose, Fox and rabbit, and various skipping games. Google the individual games to find instructions and rules of play, on the internet. Buy a big bucket of sidewalk chalk and use your driveway as a huge game board. You could play X's and 0's on the driveway as well as hopscotch, Snakes and Ladders and other simple games.

School-Ager Play - Drops Friendships

"My 12 year-old daughter is losing her best friend. They have been best buddies since they were 2. How can I help her cope?"

Brain development stage: Many children lose their friendships during the teen years transition because they have diverging interests, values, and attitudes.

Suggestions:

- Spend more time with her doing parent-teen activities.
- Get her involved in group activities outside of school where she can make new friends according to what her interests are.
- Assure her that friends tend to float in and out of our lives when we enter a new life stage and that it is normal to keep and lose friends.

School-Ager and Siblings - Car Fights

"How do I handle fighting children when we travel by car?"

Brain development stage: When children are feeling bored, they can become irritable and pick fights.

Suggestions:

- Get a travel bag of games/activities/stickers/paint-with-water books.
- Anything that distracts them is good. Teach that distracting you is dangerous.
- Give them a craft to do on a baking sheet. Baking sheets contain all the mess and work great for laps.
- Load all the luggage between them so they can't see each other.
- Bring earplugs for you while driving.
- Tell them what behavior is expected.
- Pull the vehicle over and get yourself calm. Resume journey only when the kids have come to some agreement on the problem.
- Keep them on a schedule even on vacation.
- Go to restaurants that are quick such as buffets.
- Count motorcycles, green signs or wildlife.
- Play "I Spy" or "License Plate Bingo"
- Use your "I-statements." "I'm upset when you scream while we are driving because it can be dangerous."
- String a ribbon up across the roof. Make a little car cut-out and every hour, move the car along the ribbon. Children can actually "see" how far they came and how long to go.

School-Ager Sleep - Night Anxiety

"My 7 year-old son wakes often through the night. He has worries and displays anxiety about all kinds of things."

Brain development stage: Children often have anxiety and worry that keeps them up through the school-age years, more so than separation anxiety in the preschooler years.

Suggestions:

- Institute some rituals to get rid of monsters. Talk about them and assure him that they don't exist.
- Teach him some self-soothing methods – deep breathing, write down anxieties and crumple up the paper to go into a worry box.
- Designate worrying to one chair or one room, preferably not in the bedroom
- Use a dimmer switch.
- Help him to get more exercise and fresh air.
- Have structured bedtime routines – homework, play, books, door closed.
- His rising time will set his sleeping time at this age.
- Be sure to power down electronics at least an hour before bedtime.
- Allow him to read as late as he wishes until he is sleepy.

School-Ager Sleep - Stays Up Too Late

"My 12 year-old daughter is beginning to stay up way too late. She needs sleep. Then she can't get out of bed in the morning. How can I stop this?"

Brain development stage: Children have different sleep needs.

Suggestions:

- You can facilitate sleep but can't force it.
- Ensure that the next day commitments are still attended to, even if she is tired.
- Let her face the day late and don't rescue her from consequences of others.
- Look at her sleep needs. Perhaps she doesn't need a lot of sleep.
- Discuss how your child's late bedtime, and late morning affects you and problem-solve what to do about it.

School-Ager Toileting - Bed Wetting

"My 6 year-old daughter still wets the bed at night. Is this normal?"

Brain development stage: Children who wet the bed past age six could have enuresis. See a doctor for diagnoses and action.

Suggestions:

- Use night-time diapers to protect the bed.
- Wake her up before you go to bed and steer her to the bathroom even though she may be half asleep. She will still go.

Teenagers 13-19 Years

The stage of "I don't need you - I need you."

....

What Can Teenagers Do?

Younger Teenagers 13 to 15 Years: Formal-Operational Stage

Physical

- Can do all chores physically and intellectually that adults do

- Sleeps nine to ten hours but circadian rhythm pushes bedtime to later in the evening; may be tired from not enough rest

- Can clean the entire house

- Can cook and bake with the oven and stove, and prepare dinner for the family

- Appetite increases

- Puberty changes: menstruation begins, breast growth, curves appear, penis grows, muscles grow, shoulders and hips widen, body hair grows, voice changes, and height dramatically increases

- Girls grow most from eleven to sixteen years of age; boys from thirteen to seventeen years of age

- Hormones in full production; acne appears

- Can be clumsy because bodies are growing inconsistently

- Both sexes eat more

- Permanent teeth are in by age thirteen

Cognitive

- Starting to take full control of homework, school registration, and course choice

- Attention span is the same as adults; good time for visiting museums, theatres, plays, and lectures

- Abstract learners: can understand intangible concepts such as algebra, religion, politics, theories and death

- Can analyse and think critically

- Makes mistakes, decisions and learns from them

- Can make own phone calls and appointments

- Can get around the city on public transit

- Able to understand the rights and responsibilities of owning a smart-phone.

- Understands values and morals of sexual behavior

- Needs independence and control over decisions

- Executive Function skills of self-control, planning, focus and working memory increase to age 25 where they plateau

Social and Emotional

- Developing own philosophy, values, and belief systems

- Takes responsibility for her own needs, feelings and behaviors

- Interested in adult conversations

- Physically separates from family to find out who she is but is still emotionally connected; family still matters more than peers

- Can address store and business personnel directly

- Craves independence rather than control by others

- Experimenting with behaviors and substances to handle stress: exercise, alcohol, drugs, internet, social relationships

- Moody

- Impulsive

- Interested in sexuality

- Craves and very protective of privacy

- Lack of confidence saying "No" to others, especially peers

- Very self-conscious

- Peer pressure peaks

- Bullying peaks

- Stops hitting when angry

- Expresses individuality in dress, music, art, and decor that reflects her own values, tastes, beliefs, and preferences

- Explores new identities and roles

- Can babysit younger children

*Compliance is 80% successful.

Older Teenagers 16 to 18 Years: Pre-Frontal Cortex Maturation Stage

Physical

- Has mostly reached adult height, weight, and size

- Brain still changing especially pre-frontal cortex

- Getting wisdom teeth

Cognitive

- Becomes more academically serious

- Can obtain his first job and drivers licence

- Can stay home alone overnight

- Critical thinking blooms; interested in world social, political, economic news

- Can understand mutual funds, Registered Retirement Savings Plans (RRSP), and other financial products and do taxes, and banking

- Sense of omnipotence and grandiosity; believes nothing will hurt them

- Can take full responsibility for school, homework and future planning

- Healthy decision-making, planning and self-control increasing

Social and Emotional

- Anxiety, stress, depression and mental health issues may erupt

- Searching for identity

- Solidifying own values, beliefs, and viewpoints

- Preparing to live in the adult world of work or post-secondary education and living away from home

- Still needs practice in assertiveness skills with teachers, bosses, friends, and service venues

- Needs to prove he is grown up to himself and peers

- Becoming more confident in honouring own values and decisions

- Can stay home alone overnight

- Honing conversation skills

*Compliance is 90% successful.

Teenager Behavior - Any Issue Not Covered Previously

"I have a problem with my teenager's behavior? What can I do?"

Brain development stage: Teenagers are in the final third of parenting - the home run stretch to adulthood. They can think critically, understand consequences, and creatively come up with brainstormed solutions. Work with them as a "parent-child team against the problem."

Suggestions:

- Problem-solve every issue with them, not at them.
- Check out more teen solutions in the General AP Parenting Tips Section.
- Decide what you will do, not what you will make them do.
- Be firm and kind, but open to negotiation as to what you will do.
- Model who you would like them to be.
- Model consent and ask for theirs.
- Listen more than talk. Acknowledge their feelings. Validate them.
- Be their advisor, mentor, consultant, coach, and sounding board, but ask permission first if they want your advice.
- Create rules and routines together to ensure everyone's safety and fun.
- Avoid rescuing them from natural consequences or other people's logical consequences if safe. Don't impose logical consequences yourself if they are punitive. Help them come up with adult solutions that will fix things to everyone's satisfaction.
- Grow your influence by eliminating all punishments and consequences. You are building a relationship that the rest of the world is not. Problem-solve instead.
- Continue to unobtrusively monitor their whereabouts and state your concerns when you have them.
- Offer help if you can help.
- Take a genuine interest in their world. Keep spending time with them.
- Love them unconditionally.

The Problem-Solving Method:

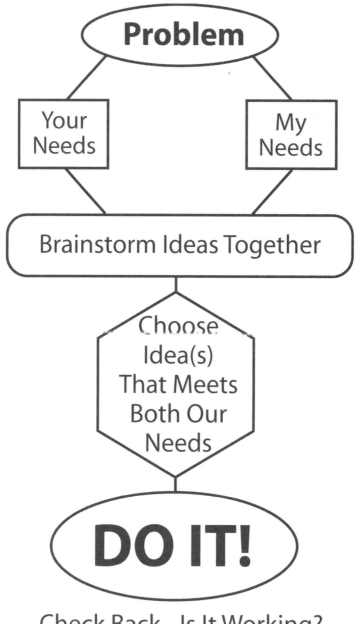

Check Back - Is It Working?

Emerging Adults 19-25 Years

The stage of lifelong friendship and mutual mentorship.

....

What Can Emerging Adults Do?

Emerging Adults 19 to 25 years: Final Changes of Mature Brain Development and Executive Function

Physical

- Same as later teenager

Cognitive

- Prefrontal cortex finishes development, which controls adult ability to plan, make decisions, and think critically

- Gaining more common sense

Social and Emotional

- Adult stability. Critical thinking over-rides desire for immediate gratification.

* Compliance means that children comply with a directive from a parent in a totally non-punitive parent-child relationship. A non-punitive relationship is one in which no punishments are ever used; instead, active listening, I-statements and problem-solving are used to resolve every discipline issue within an environment of mutual respect and open communication.

General Parenting Tips For All Ages

3 Essential Communication Skills for Every Parent

1. Active listening/acknowledging feelings. Used when the child has the problem.

Tell the child what you think she is feeling and with the surrounding context or reason. Say, "I can see that you are feeling angry because I asked you to walk the dog and you are busy playing computer."

2. I-statements. Used when the parent has the problem.

Use an I-statement with 3 parts including 1)how you feel, about 2)the specific behavior and 3)the effect on you. Say, "I am feeling angry because I asked you to walk the dog and you aren't. This means I have to walk her, when I want to start supper."

3. Problem-solving: see chart on P.272. Used to solve every conflict between parent and child.

General Tips for Easier Parenting

- Keep socks in a basket by the door. Have door stations for everyone to put outerwear and items on for going out.

- Buy only one color (and one size) socks for the whole family so there is no need to waste time sorting. All white or all black is easiest.

- Wash clothes by child rather than colors. Separate darks and lights though.

- Laundry every day or once per week, whatever works best. Make sure everyone has enough underwear to last two weeks.

- Put toddler socks in a mesh bag to wash.

- Speed up drying time by putting a dry towel in the dryer to absorb water from wet clothes.

- Put white chalk on oily food stains and then launder.

- Use socks instead of mitts – kids can't take them off.

- Resign yourself to mess – give up trying to maintain clean at least for a few years.

- Don't fold. Put things back into drawers as they come out.

- Have the kids sleep in their next day clean clothes. Give up pajamas.

- Get clothes laid out the night before, for you and your kids.

- Give up bedtime battles, and sleep with the kids.

- Trim nails, put on sunscreen, brush teeth and clip bangs while the kids are in a deep sleep. Put a towel over the pillowcase and under their heads to catch clippings.

- Shower or bath with the kids to save time supervising.

- If you are not sure of clothes on the floor being clean or dirty, assume they are clean (unless they have food stains).

- Bring an activity bag of things to do and make use of filler moments – read, draw, color, play games. Get into a "busy bag exchange" to keep activities fresh.

- Spend $1 on a roll of cello tape. Kids love to play and make things with it while you are in line-ups.

- Always keep food and drink in the car when hunger hits – granola bars and juice boxes.

- Pick your battles. In a tense moment, use music: break out in song with music from the phone, or have an instant dance party to diffuse anger from children or you.

- Be okay with the kids helping – they will get more practiced.

- Keep spare underwear, clothes, towels and swimsuits in the car, just in case you drive by a pool, park or need a clothing change.
- Have hooks everywhere and especially around the door so kids can hang things up.
- Put a clear shower curtain rod inside your regular one. That way, you can contain your child splashing but still watch her and you can pull your decorative one over when she is done.
- Hooks in bathrooms are easier for kids to hang towels on instead of towel bars.
- Clear plastic bins are great for helping kids sort their toys.
- Join a babysitting co-op in your neighborhood.
- Cook with a group of friends and divvy up the results.
- Plan menus for a week and shop once.
- Buy vegetables already washed and bagged or sign up for the "Good Food Box".
- Buy day old bread at a bread discounter store and freeze it.
- Cook double batches and freeze one.
- Make dinner at naptime or even breakfast while children are still in a good mood. Get to know your slow-cooker and instant-pot.
- Have a spare fridge, especially for milk, drinks and entertaining platters.
- Grocery shop at night, or online, without children – you save much more money.
- Do all your errands on Saturday and plan a loop – it's faster.
- Have planned "home days" that are relaxed and have built in play times.
- Have a day for planning with your partner. Sunday evening is a good time. Plan meals, appointments and activities for the week and communicate it to everyone in the family.
- Set a time limit for doing online work - otherwise, you could be on the laptop/phone all day.

Motivating an Uncooperative Family

- You have three avenues: Surrender (accept and let it go), Leave (walk away), or Negotiate (problem-solving).

How to Handle Negative Parenting Judgement

- Remember to trust yourself.
- With random strangers, brush if off with a "Thanks."
- Hang out with people you feel good about.
- With relatives, say, "My doctor said..." Older people tend to defer to doctors' advice.
- Say, "Thanks, this is what works for us." The all-round standard answer.
- Say, "Excuse me, what did you say?" People might think twice about what they just commented.
- Grow a thick skin. People that are unhappy with their life the most, tend to judge others the most.

....

Handling Meddling Visitors and Unwelcome Advice

- Tell the visitors, "Thank you," and then do whatever you want.
- Ask your partner to take time off to ferry the visitors around if they are his relatives.
- Pre-organize someone else to vent to when you feel like you are going to blow up.
- Tell them that "This works for our family. Thank you for your good intent and concern though. We know you love your grandchildren."
- Book into a hotel or spa or retreat centre for you to take some time off while they are visiting.

....

Visiting Fairs Tips

How to take children to a fair without going broke or losing them?

- Best day to attend is usually the Kid's Day after 3 p.m. Most kids have gone home to nap and the older kids are not present due to day-camps and part-time jobs.
- Pack a backpack full of healthy foods and empty water bottles to fill up when you arrive at the grounds. Give each child $10 to choose a treat.
- Standing room tickets are often available each day for the evening shows at reduced prices.

- Dress all the children in one color like neon orange. It's easier to do a quick count.

- Give them those rubber bracelets with your cell phone number written on the inside with permanent marker so if they get lost, someone can phone you.

- If you are attending the a parade, bring diversions so they can be entertained while waiting. Games of "rock, paper, scissors" or small bottles of bubbles, balloons, or cards can be played while waiting. Tablet apps and hand-held gaming consoles come in handy too.

- Don't forget sunscreen, hats, and bug spray! Kids older than 5 can carry their own backpack with an empty water bottle, jacket and room for all the things you are going to buy.

Managing Sibling Conflict-All Ages

Not helpful

- Taking sides based on age, maturity, gender, etc.
- Yelling.
- Comparisons and labeling.
- Talking negatively about one to the other.
- Taking away the disputed toy.
- Jail-like time-outs.
- Constant refereeing.
- Punishing both for fighting. They need to learn HOW to get along.

Helpful

- Have planned separations.
- Ignoring sometimes helps. Put in earplugs, music player or go into the bathroom.
- Anticipate what could happen and plan ahead.
- Introverts need space. Give your children their time and a quiet place.
- If the two kids made a deal and they are both happy, even though you think it is unfair, let it be.
- Hold the fought-over toy until they can come up with a plan then give it back.
- When they tattle, empathize with them. Acknowledge their feelings, but don't admonish the other child. There are three sides to every story - two versions and the truth.

- Encourage them to tell their tattles to the family pet.

- Model ways to not grab from each other.

- Give them new things to do.

- Distract with circle time, movie, etc.

- Change of scenery. Go out somewhere.

- Give them the power. If they fight over who gets the special seat or anything "first", draw up a calendar and ask them to pick which days each child gets to be first or gets the special seat. Block off a few "flex" days that can be designated for the child who gets a missed day (such as getting home late and they don't get the first.)

- Have a "favorite kid" day and he gets to pick everything. Alternate days.

- Give them some physical energy burners - trampoline, walk, etc.

- Invite other kids over for a play date to diffuse the dynamics.

- Have some one-on-one time with each one.

- Acknowledge that they will have better days and some not so good ones.

- Encourage 'time sharing' the toys. Allot a certain amount of time for each child to play with the toy before passing it over. Use a timer.

- Read books on sharing.

- Be consistent and always encourage sharing, while also allowing the children their own "alone time."

- Allow each child the right to not share and say, "No." They soon discover the law of reciprocity and will be more willing to share if they are denied by their siblings. As well, they learn that having control doesn't mean you have to use it.

- Active Listen to each person in front of the other person. "You felt____ (insert feeling word here) because ___(insert their situation)." And Jason, you felt____ (insert feeling word here) because ____(insert their situation.)"

- Have them repeat their feeling/annoyance in an "I-statement." "Hey, I feel annoyed when I wait here forever and you won't give up the game." "Well, I feel pressured when you want the game and I haven't gone up the level I am aiming for."

- Ask: "What are your options?" Surrender, Leave, or Negotiate?

Surrender is accepting it, letting it go and not letting it bother you anymore.

Leaving is leaving the situation either physically, emotionally or both.

Negotiating is problem-solving: determining what everyone needs, brainstorming solutions, then evaluating them, and choosing a few to try out. Evaluating the solutions after a period will help determine if you need to rework a few.

What are some other ways to work it out?

- Generate class/family/group "rules" from the affected family members. If they generate the rules, they "own" them.
- "Rock, paper, scissors" game
- Pick a number from one to ten
- Put names/ideas in a hat and draw one
- Flip a coin with heads or tails
- "Reserved" or name cards
- "Bigger person" button. Give a special button or trophy to the person who concedes the argument.
- Have a "Chooser" button. Swap out days, but the wearer gets to pick everything that day.
- Use time schedules, sign-up sheets, contracts, and tokens.
- Suggest/reject volley - one person suggests. If the other person rejects the idea, then they have to come up with something. If the other person rejects, they have to come up with a new idea. So on and so on until both parties scream with anguish!
- Offer a more desired alternative to get what you want.
- Make a rule that the person who goes first gets a shorter turn.

Sex Education by Age

Toddlers:

- Give them proper words for body parts – penis, vagina, vulva, testicles, urine, stool, menstruation, etc.
- Acknowledge that although touching themselves in their genitals (penis, and vagina area) feels good, it should be done when they are in a private area.
- Teach public behavior and private behavior. Butt-scratching, masturbation, nail clipping, tooth flossing, nose-picking and swearing are all private behaviors and best done in the bathroom or alone in the bedroom.

Preschoolers:

- Begin teaching your values about sex and sexuality. For example, you might say, "I believe that marriage is only for two people who love each other." As your child enters adolescence, they will develop their own values, but as a parent, you have a heavy influence, beginning when they can understand language.

- Answer any questions children have with simple, accurate language. For example, a child might ask, "How does a baby get made?" Your answer might be, "A baby begins as a tiny cluster of cells when a man and a woman love each other. The man and woman lie close together on a bed and the man puts his penis into a woman's vagina. Sperm comes out of his penis and swims up the woman's vagina and finds an egg. When the sperm goes into the egg, a baby begins to grow." This explanation may even spur more questions such as "How long does it take?" Does it hurt?" "Do you have to do that to get a baby?" "Do you have to have a man and a woman?" Again, give accurate, simple answers.

- Don't worry about getting too detailed or giving too much information. Children will only take as much information as they can understand. It's better to give too much information than too little.

- We often give too little information and not enough. Children are always taking in information about sex from friends, TV, Internet, movies and even children's media. They need your values and accurate information most.

- The most important benefit of answering questions is that you give your child the message that you are approachable and willing to talk about his questions. He knows that he can ask you anything.

- Teach your child that it's "Her body, Her rules!" This is the beginning of teaching consent. Whenever she is uncomfortable with anything regarding her body and another person, she has the right to say, "No!," and that must be respected. If she doesn't want to kiss Grandma good-bye, she is saying "No," and Grandma has to accept that. If she doesn't want to take her pants off for the doctor, she must be respected. Perhaps she needs more explanation and preparation for the next visit.

- This is a good age for children to begin asking questions as they often see their mothers or mother's friends breastfeeding children. They often follow you into the toilet and see first-hand how things work.

- Continue to talk about "private" versus "public" behavior in terms of masturbation, nose-picking, farting, and other behaviors.

- Exploratory behavior between similar aged children is very normal at this stage. Looking and touching sibling or friend's private parts are common. However, children should be taught to not touch other children or adults. It becomes a problem and possibly criminal behavior when a child is over age 12 and/or there is 5 years age difference between the children.

- This is a good time to begin discussions about consent. Talk about what family, friends, doctors and others can do with the child's body. Basically, if the child says "No," their wishes must be respected and it is up to you as the parent to enforce that. Say, "Whoever says "No!", rules! Model consent by example. Ask your partner if he wants a hug. Ask your child's permission to brush their hair.

School-agers:

- Continue putting comments out there such as, "When you begin menstruating, we will purchase some pads for you." This invites your child to ask questions as they know you are willing to talk.
- Recognise that there will not be one talk; there will be many little talks.
- Give information on puberty changes, the mechanics of sexual intercourse, how babies are born, sexual transmitted infections, birth control and anything else they want to know.
- If they don't ask questions, respect that
- Use media as a talking point; Say, "What do you know about abortion? Would you like me to explain it to you?" after watching a movie such as "Dirty Dancing."
- Do more listening to your child rather than lecturing.
- Most children around this age become very modest. Respect their choice by covering up yourself and closing your bathroom door.
- Don't use your child as a confidante. They are embarrassed easily. Let them set the pace for questions, but you can throw comments out there to let them know it is okay to ask you.
- If your child agrees, celebrate first occasions by going for lunch when your daughter gets her period, or going for coffee when your son learns how to shave.
- Be sure to share your values when listening to their music, movies and videos.
- Children at this age are developing their gender identity as a male or female.
- If your child accidentally walks in your bedroom and see you dressing, just cover up. If she walks in and sees you and your partner making love, just call it "Parent-couple private time," and ask for privacy. Get a lock for your door next time.

Teenagers:

- Attend your city's gay pride parade with or without them. Show your support and let your child know that he will be supported if he comes out as a person who is LGBTQ2S (Lesbian, Gay, Bi-sexual, Transgendered, Queer, Two Spirit.)

- Provide information and websites about contraception and body changes.

- Leave books in the bathroom so they can pick them up and read them.

- Discuss healthy dating, intimacy, relationships and consent from talking points such as movies etc.

- Have conversations and practice refusal skills and well as initiation skills. How to ask for a date and how to refuse unwanted attention.

- Discuss what is appropriate to put online. Photos of body parts, drinking and drugs, and relationship status, as well as personal information is a no-no on social media.

Travel Tips

Packing Essentials

My husband and I enjoy holidays away from home. We have traveled overseas 12 times and even took our babies camping from the time they were 3 weeks old.

We have traveled by airplane, car, ship and train. We have stayed with relatives, with friends, at hotels, at rental houses, at beach cabins, and in trailers and tents. We have learned the hard way about the challenges of travelling with children, including jet-lagged babies wide-awake at midnight, toddler tantrums on crowded airplanes, car-sick and home-sick children, and bored teens enduring an endless torment of art galleries and museums. From our experience, I have developed the following list of essentials for travelling with children.

Small stuffed toys: Youngsters (and older ones too, though they won't admit it) appreciate a stuffy each, as a reminder of home, and as a pillow. Makes a strange bed more welcoming. Just make sure it's not a special one because it could get lost.

Entertainment technology: A hand-held game console, music player, or tablet can be a lifesaver in the middle of the night for an exhausted parent trying to settle a wide-awake child. Or to distract bored children from fighting or climbing the drapes while you are chatting with relatives in their homes containing glass-sided cabinets of crystal and china. Or to make long flights shorter. Or to provide familiar music for homesick teens. Or even to sooth parents whose patience is ragged from endless "How much longer; are we there yet?"

Batteries and chargers: You can never have too many batteries.

Cheap and useful activity toys: Flashlight, roll of tape, pair of scissors, deck of cards, Rubik's cube, tape measure, markers, pads of paper, fake wallet with inactivated gift cards, dice, dictionary, ball of string and lump of play-dough. Very versatile for keeping kids busy. Flashlights can be used to play ceiling tag at bedtime. The roll of tape is great for toddlers to pull off pieces and stick them anywhere. Toddlers also love tape measures, play-dough and balls of string. Markers and pads of paper can be used by school-aged children, to draw paper dolls, animals and various scenes to play dolls with. Drawing, coloring and cutting out are all part of the fun of playing dolls.

Plastic shovels and pails: Some of our best moments have been on a park or beach bench with a glass of wine, while the children dig holes, make sand-castles, and nature soup, and collect rocks, shells, twigs, beetles and frogs.

Digital camera and binoculars: For teens and school-aged children.

Plastic rubbery charity wristbands: Write your cell number in permanent marker inside the wristband in case you and your child gets separated.

Laptop computer: Laptop computers typically contain basic software games such as Paint and solitaire, and most can play DVD or online movies. Useful for teens to make a journal, make a photo scrapbook of the trip, and catch up on social media with their friends back home. Many libraries and visitor centers have cheap Internet access.

DVD: Leave the cases at home and just bring the discs in a portable disc case. Ask for a vacation extension to cover the time you have them.

Bring a current converter and a outlet converter for different countries so you can recharge devices even though they are a different power voltage.

Pillowcases: The most versatile item for a trip. We try to find inexpensive accommodation, and often find ourselves short of pillows. A pillowcase can be stuffed with coats to make a huge pillow for the plane or for the hotel. They are easy to pack, lightweight, foldable and cheap. Here are some other uses for pillowcases.

- **Hotel comfort item** – something from home that you can put over their pillows. Helps children deal with their homesickness when they see a familiar pillow.
- **Extra beach bag -** for wet towels, garbage, food containers, toys, and clothes.
- **Bib -** you need a safety pin or clothes pin to fasten.
- **Cape -** for little boys and girls to pretend they are superheroes.
- **Spare pillow** - stuff with coats, jackets, hats and mitts for a nice BIG pillow on the plane or in the car. Keeps everything together in winter.

- **Picnic placemat** – a clean cloth to put plates and cups on at the beach or picnic area.
- **Spare diaper change mat** – be sure to wash after!
- **Spare shopping bag** – handy for drippy items because it's easy to wash.
- **Laundry bag** – for clean or dirty clothes.
- **Instant gift wrap** – for a hostess gift.
- **Spare towel** – for the beach or pool.

Cheap lightweight sleeping bags: You only need inexpensive little summer-weight sleeping bags (under 2lbs). About the size of a rolled-up beach towel, it can be spread to make an instant bed on a sofa, or carpet, and can be used as a pillow in an airplane or a car.

Lighter: You'd be surprised how much you'll need a lighter when travelling. Try lighting a camping gas stove without one.

Snacks: Always travel with a bag of non-spoiling snacks such as crackers, granola bars, and boxed juice. Travel food is often expensive, and not always available.

Wipes: and a roll of kitchen paper towels and hand sanitizer if car traveling.

Spare shirt for you and your child: Someone will always gets sick. Pack in your carry-on.

Large clear zip-up kitchen food bags: Perfect as wet swimsuit and dirty wash bags, as food bags, and perfect containment for potentially messy things like toothpaste. You would be horrified how far shampoo can spread within your suitcase during depressurization.

Hand sanitizer: Public washrooms usually do not provide soap.

One water bottle per person.

Medications: Acetaminophen, Ibuprophen, thermometer, multivitamins, oral rehydration solution, sunscreen, bug spray (<10% Deet) bandages, tweezers.

Finally, always pack light. Don't bring more than three outfits per child, two pairs of shoes and bring extra empty pack-flat travel bags for the souvenirs and clothes that you will inevitably accumulate as you travel.

More Tips for the Journey

- Bring your own snacks, diapers, wipes, etc.

- Don't rely on the plane's entertainment system. Bring your own – tablet, phone or computer will play DVD's or online movies for your older children. Bring ear-buds as the airlines don't like your big headphones.

- Buy knick knack toys from the dollar store and wrap them in many layers to keep the little ones busy – felt, stickers, tape, picture books, little animals, magna doodle boards, play-dough, foil, etc.

- Ask for help from the flight attendant.

- If it's a charter flight, prepare for having baby on your lap and get a carrier to give your arms a rest.

- Take your time going through security. You have yourself and your little ones to get through and don't worry about hurrying. Other people need to have patience while you have your hands full.

- Pack the backpack for your things. Get each child a carry-on with wheels for their things. Don't get the kiddie ones for school-aged kids, but a full-size adult one, to maximize space.

- Get your partner to board first with all the gear and you wait in the waiting area with the little ones. You want to be the last on the plane and the first off, not the other way around! Kids need as little time as possible in the plane's cramped quarters.

- Take empty water bottles in your carry-on and fill them up after going through security.

- Book the aisle and the window seat in a row and leave the middle seat empty. Chances are good that no one will take them and if they do, they will be more than happy to switch after boarding.

- Bring an empty spray bottle and spray and hang your clothes at the hotel. No wrinkles.

- Bring your own ear-buds for you and your children from previous flights.

- Bring a pillowcase for each child to stuff their coats and items in. This makes a great pillow.

- As soon as the pilot says, "Flight crew, prepare for take-off," look around and grab whatever empty seats remain as there probably won't be any more passengers boarding.

- Bring a deck of playing cards and a deck of UNO cards. Great for all those waiting times.

- Relax about baby crying. No one past the first three rows can hear anything anyways.

- Get Nexus for you and your partner. Kids are free.

- Use a leash in crowded places like airports and bus terminals. Don't worry what other people think.

- Bring your car seat on a plane. It's comforting to children as it is familiar and it protects them better in a plane, taxi or bus.

- Beg, borrow or buy a pop-up frame which adds a stroller frame to a car seat. Easy, lightweight and collapsible, plus children feel secure in their car seat.

- Always bring a lot of snacks and drinks.

- Buy an item in a store when you are settled in, and get the store logo bag. Use it to carry camera, maps and items so you don't look like a tourist. Leave the backpack at home.

- Carry your child's toothbrush and underwear and a change of clothes in your carry-on in case baggage gets lost.

- Beg, borrow or buy a 3x3 foot children's tent. It is a little tent that keeps the noise and light blocked in hotel rooms and tents. With a white noise machine, children will sleep easier away from home knowing they have their comfort surroundings.

- Have one activity kit for the journey there and one new kit for the way back.

- If you are driving, hang a ribbon over the dash of the car and put a little car on it. Move the car as you travel so children have a visual sense of how far you have come and how much travel is left.

- Keep a potty seat in the car to use for the side of the road, etc.

- Buy an over-the-door shoe caddy to use in the car and hang it over the back of the seat. Fill the pockets with games, snacks, stickers, books, and pencils so your child can help themselves.

- If you are camping, have one parent set up and the other parent watch the kids.

- Bring cookie sheet trays for activities. Bring post-it notes, markers, tape, stickers, and paint with water books.

- Bring a recently emptied dish soap bottle and fill it with water. That and a small hand towel is so handy.

- Bring extra T-shirts for you and the kids.

- Bring extra garbage bags for laundry etc.

- Bring a cooler and books hotels with kitchenettes. If your hotel only has a small fridge, buy a set of paper bowls and spoons, milk and cereal for snacks, breakfasts, and lunch. Supplement with fruit and vegetables.

Travel Visiting and Hosting Etiquette

A few simple rules of courtesy can help smooth the way for a fun and pleasant visit for everyone.

Rules for Guests

- Parenting styles can clash. Learn the rules of the house, and explain to your kids why things are different here.

- Your children might be picky about unfamiliar food. Don't insist that they eat up, but teach them to be polite in their refusal, and buy lots of bread and cheese and apples.

- Teach your children to pick up after themselves promptly.

- Communicate kitchen expectations: is this a help-yourself kitchen, or should permission be sought?

- Offer to make some of the meals, and take out your hosts, and definitely supplement the groceries and the wine.

- Your family should do more than their share of table setting, dish clearing, and dishwashing!

- If the home has hazards for children, seek permission to childproof. Older people forget what children can get into. They will appreciate that you care about their home as well as the safety of your children.

- Be willing to go to events to which your host invites you, even though you would rather sprawl in front of your hosts' television.

- Don't hog the house! Plan some independent activities, so the host family has some quiet time at their home.

- Bite your tongue when your host disciplines your child. Just let it go without comment (except for abuse of course). If they make a wrong call, talk to your child later in private about different personalities and parenting styles and how to handle issues in the future.

- When visiting local points of interest and restaurants, be prepared to pay for your host too.

- Be generous guests. And don't forget to leave a gift.

- Before leaving, return all things borrowed, including house keys. Strip beds, and put towels and sheets in the laundry room. Clean up your bags and garbage.

Rules for Hosts

- Show your guests where to find the phone, emergency numbers, laundry facilities, dishes, food, sleep areas etc.

- Turn off your security system unless you really need it. Wandering guests can inadvertently awake the entire street at 3:00 a.m.

- Recognize that the noise, mess, and work level may increase, and find ways to increase your tolerance for it or schedule breaks from it.

- If you have special requirements, such as a quiet house at 10 p.m., communicate your house rules.

- If your guests include young children, they might be picky eaters, so obtain a variety of foods.

- If you publicly offer something to your own child, then offer the same to the visiting children.

- Bite your tongue. Some things will annoy you, but try to be diplomatic. The visit will end, but hurt feelings from words said in anger will not.

- Include guests in outings and family events.

- Don't discipline guest's children. Speak up to the parent instead.

- Be flexible about sleeping arrangements. Sometimes visiting children get homesick and prefer to pile on the floor with their parents instead of their assigned room.

- Respect your guest's room. It's their territory for the visit, and hence, is private.

- Childproof your house for babies, toddlers and pre-schoolers.

- Offer age-appropriate entertainment for your guest's children.

Sometimes the hosts and the guests each need to bend over backwards, but by following these simple rules of courtesy, communication and respect, the visit will be enjoyable and memorable for all!

Grocery Shopping With Children: Tips by Age

Babies

- Before going, feed, change and play with them. You want a tired, napping baby during the trip.

- Carry in backpack or carrier if possible.

Toddlers

- Shop when it's quiet and there are no line-ups.

- If they want to "help" let them put the odd item in the cart. Separate and cull at the till.

- If a tantrum occurs, let it ride. Wait it out in the car and see if it is possible to come back. You may have to wait until later to get groceries when you have childcare.
- Avoid the cookie and candy aisles.
- Point out items while saying words. This builds literacy skills.
- Bring a snack or promise one treat when at the store. Don't worry; this is only a stage and won't last forever.

Preschoolers

- Before going, set expectations. They are better able to understand limits but will still ask! Say, "We are getting groceries, and you are allowed one treat. Just one!" Stick to it!
- Have pictures of items on a checklist for them to check off.
- Name items by letter sounds: M is for meat.

School-agers

- Before going, go over the list that they are going to shop for. Get separate carts.
- Set a meeting place.
- Get them to empty the cart on the belt.

Teens

- Get them to carry the bags, and help load the car as well as bring the items into the house. Show them where the items go in the cupboards and fridge.
- When they drive, give them the list, the cash and keep your fingers crossed they have learned the shopping skills all those years!

Easy Foods That Kids Love

- Anything with dip - yogurt, hummus, ketchup, tzatziki, or cottage cheese
- Separate food items into muffin cups or partitioned plates
- Sticklike food is popular, such as carrots or pretzels
- Cut up cubes of cheese, ham, tofu, etc.
- Fruit kebabs, dried fruit and finger foods
- Peanut butter and jam anything
- Eggs: cooked any way, but especially hard boiled
- Kids will drink milk if they can blow bubbles

- Have a "common" plate that they add foods they don't want and can take donated foods from.
- Put on a movie and slide a plate of vegetables and dip under their noses so they aren't aware of what they are eating.
- Cheese cut in various shapes
- Sweet potatoes, peas, carrots, broccoli, cauliflower, corn and tomatoes, frozen or fresh
- Green vegetables pureed in blender
- Smoothies and yogurt
- Plain food – no salt, butter, sauce etc
- Roasted chickpeas, greek yogurt, and quinoa provide a good source of protein. Vegetable patties are good too and can be warmed in the toaster.
- Noodles of any kind but sauce on the side
- Fruit such as apples, bananas, pears
- Toast, pancakes, muffins, and French toast – can make sweet or savory and put pretty well anything in or on them.
- Shrimp rings, fish sticks and sushi
- Rice with grated cheese on top or left plain. Some kids like butter or soy sauce on it.
- Cottage cheese (Can make pancakes with ½ cup cottage cheese, ¼ cup flour, 2 eggs, 1 tsp vanilla, 1 tsp baking power)
- Peanut, sesame, and almond butter.

Tips for Hosting a Home Birthday Party

- Ask for help. You can always use an extra pair of adult hands. Round up the older children to write invitations, shop for supplies, prepare food and decorations and treat bags. They can also serve refreshments and help with games.
- Keep a bucket of warm soapy water and a cloth handy for spills, throw up, and potty accidents.
- Serve tiny portions of food and slivers of cake. Children are often too excited to eat.
- Serve lots of drinks, but in small portions. Children are always more thirsty than hungry.

- Parties for children ages one to three are really for the parents, who love to chat while keeping careful eyes open for their little sweeties, so have some adult refreshments on hand too.

- Parties for children ages four and up, begin to learn social graces – how to accept unwanted presents, how to share, take turns at games. As a hostess, you have to gently help them with the skills if parents are not staying.

- It's the certainty of treat bags that counts, not the quality. One toy and one candy treat is adequate.

- Time: 1 hour for under 2 years of age, 2 hours for under 5 years and 3 hours for under 10 years.

- Don't clean BEFORE the party! No one will notice.

- Pack away all breakables, and provide unstructured group toys for children under four. Also, you could set up stations such as paper and markers, paint, or play dough, and have little groups of children work at one station for 15 minutes and then switch as a group. Have an adult sit at each station so one of the guests doesn't color your bathroom while you are serving cake.

- Save your baby gates to partition off bedrooms, halls and other off-limits places.

- Encourage kids to watch the cake and gift opening but don't force them to. A great way to decide whose gift to open first is to use the months of guest's birthdays. January birthday guests go first, then February, etc. For cake serving, start with December birthday guests and go backwards.

7 Commandments for Party Guests

1. Don't bring extra siblings or children unless permission is granted before hand.

2. Warn your child that a treat bag may or may not appear.

3. RSVP on the deadline or before. Nothing is more frustrating to an organizer than having to phone people who don't RSVP. If you say that you are coming, please show up! If you say that you're not coming, don't show up unannounced at the last minute!

4. Be cheerful and participate in all the activities in the spirit of the party.

5. If you are an adult staying with your child, be helpful. This is not the time for a heart to heart chat with the party hostess. Save that for after the party.

6. Teach your child discretion in sparing other children's feelings. Teach them to not talk about the party before it occurs and after.

7. Encourage your child to write thank you notes for the parents who were not present. It's good practice and a nice touch.

7 Commandments for Party Host/Hostesses

1. Don't ask for the gift receipt so you can return the gift. Say a sincere thank you, and if it's not suitable, give it to a sibling, a charity, or try to return it without a receipt, or even re-gift it.

2. Disclose full information about the party – If the party is half at home and half somewhere else, the parents need to know where the children are going, who is supervising, who is driving, how many seatbelts are available, and what the guest is required to bring.

3. Don't state preferred presents or money. It's okay to mention desirables if specifically asked.

4. Try to avoid competitive games. Cooperative games are more fun for all the guests and build friendships. Piñatas often encourage aggressive behavior.

5. Don't distribute invitations at the school/preschool unless everyone is invited. Use email, social media, or send a note to parents to contact you. Children tend to use invitation distribution at school as social currency and it is hurtful to those children who are not invited. Teach your child to not talk about the party plans before it occurs or rehash the event after it occurs.

6. Don't feel you have to include treat bags but if you do, one treat and one toy should suffice.

7. Feel free to put parents staying to work in helping you with serving, clean-up and crowd control. They are a valuable resource!

Enjoy the festivities!

Cold Weather Holiday Play Ideas

Connect with Each Other:

- Have one-on-one time with each child. Go to a movie, restaurant, or coffee date with one and just enjoy that time together.

- Get to a job that is on your to-do list and invite a child to help. Promise a goody after! Kids open up when doing activities with a parent.

- Volunteer for an organization. Grab a group and go caroling at a hospice, serve dinner at a drop-in centre, or make beds at a homeless shelter.

Create Traditions:

- A weekly board game night could be a Christmas holiday tradition that can include several board game nights over the holidays with different family friends. Our family (the gift is addressed to the family as a whole so that no one child gets ownership of the games) gets two new board games for Christmas, and we invite another family over to play (preferably with kids the same age). Everyone brings snacks to contribute. My five kids have loved this tradition.

- Skate, ski, snowboard, or toboggan day where the whole family goes and participates.

- Watch the same traditional family movie every Christmas holiday. Ours is *The Sound of Music.*

- Baking. Not during the frenzy before holidays but during or even after is better. Get some new cookbooks from the library and have a pie or cookie baking session with jobs doled out to the whole family. Wrap the presents up and deliver them to people over the holidays – the lady at the post office, the garbage collectors, the hairstylist, your favorite cashier at the grocery store. People, who don't expect a gift from you, but know you, and would be delighted. Kids can really feel the joy of the season when they do something that is fun, yummy, not rushed and done together with parents.

- Home movie, or photo night. Review the year on the big screen TV by hooking up videos and photos taken throughout the year for the whole family to enjoy.

- Christmas craft kits and gingerbread house kits are on sale after the 25th and it's a tradition to buy them then and make them when time is more relaxed. Not everything has to be done BEFORE Christmas. Save old Halloween candy to add to the houses.

- Learn a new card game. Say, "This Christmas, we are going to learn how to play poker as a family." Some of our favorite times were playing blackjack with wrapped caramels, chocolates, and candies as betting items!

- Go to second hand shops (which really not busy this time of year) and pick up new games and kits.

- Fill empty plastic soap/spray containers with colored water to squirt/paint the snow.

- Give a toddler a clean dustpan for a snow shovel. (Put rubber gloves over a child's gloves so they won't get wet when they play outside with wet snow days.)

- The most important point is that kids remember the "doing" part of Christmas the most rather than the "getting." They don't remember what they got for gifts the last year or previous years. But they do remember the family times spent doing activities that are fun, relaxed and stress-free.

Rainy Day Play Ideas

- Get them dressed in rain gear and go out to splash in the puddles.
- Bake together.
- Go to Ikea and Mcdonalds play centres.
- Get a magnetic fishing kit and fish in the bathtub.
- If the basement floor is concrete, get a mini-trampoline, ride on toys, bouncy balls, scooters or small bikes, and let the kids bounce, and ride. Make stoplights out of milk cartons.
- Go to the Zoo. It won't be crowded.
- Make an indoor sandbox with a baby sized swimming pool or big rubber bin, and install rice, puffed wheat or lentils as the sand. Add mixing and pouring containers, cars and trucks, measuring cups and spoons.
- Make "Goop" or "Play-dough" or "GAK" and spend the time at the kitchen table. Google for recipes.
- Get out old sheets, chairs and sofa cushions and make indoor forts. Use "masking tape" to secure the sheets.
- Have an indoor picnic on play dishes and a sheet on the floor.
- Go to the library and load up on books.
- Arrange a play date swap with another parent.
- Cover your kitchen table with brown kitchen paper and let the kids at it with markers, paper, glitter, glue, play-dough, paint etc.
- Hire a sitter. They often have fresh ideas and you get a break.
- Get out the craft, building and science kits that didn't get opened at holidays or birthdays.
- Put on some music you love and have a half-hour dance party.
- Shout out, "It's '5 pt-harness-time'!" and load the van with the kids and get out of the house.
- Go for a drive and be sure to stop at a drive-through.
- Have a tickle or pillow fight with the kids and make it fun.
- Put a movie on for the kids and make yourself a cup of tea and read a magazine.
- Spend one night away in a hotel in the city, preferably one with a pool.

Summer Break Play Ideas

Toddlers 1-2 Years

- Drape sheets and sofa cushions over chairs and tables on the deck for an outdoor fort.
- Spread paint out on a piece of paper on a cookie sheet and let them drive cars and marbles in the paint. Use anything with texture for interesting pictures.
- Buy a case of individually wrapped rolls of toilet paper and use them as blocks.
- Stock up on empty boxes and let them play with them.
- Pull the kids around the floor while they sit on old sheets. (Doesn't work on carpet!)
- Set aside one day per week to just play – no housework.
- Make GAK which is a goopy play material. Take oversized Rubbermaid containers and put in cornstarch and water.
- Get canvasses from dollar stores that they can paint on.
- Give them bath tub crayons.
- Color eggs for Spring celebrations.
- Get a zip-lock bag and put in blue gelatin – add some gummy fish and seal it and let them play before eating it.
- Google "crafts for 2 year-olds" or for whatever age you need.
- Have an easy to reach craft box or dresser drawer filled with odds and ends: ribbons, cards, paper, markers, scissors, glue or glue sticks, glitter, paint, rulers, cardboard pieces, etc so the kids can help themselves and create a craft that is unstructured and entirely of their own imagination.
- Assemble a box of dress up clothes and items for props. Check out finds from the dollar store and thrift shop for castoffs.
- Have a dirt pile in the backyard and run a hose through it. The neighbors will not like it, but the kids will have a blast. Send them home if they have to use your bathroom, though!
- Make homemade play-dough and let the kids press in different shapes and items such as rings, straws, beads, etc.
- Fill the baby bathtub or bowl of soapy water in the bathtub and let them play. Add food colored ice cubes, spoons, and cups for pouring. Be sure to supervise all water play.
- Use a small stool (with bottom grippers) as a play table in the bathtub and give them cups to pour from and in.

- Get a small rebounder or personal trampoline to jump on. Or designate certain sofa cushions for jumping on and fort building.

- Use jumping balls in the house to work off excess energy.

- In the bathtub with no water, put your child in the tub dressed only with old underwear, and add a bowl of chocolate pudding. Allow finger painting on the walls, tub and themselves. A wonderful, sensuous feeling and much easier clean-up than finger- painting. Just hose down the walls and the child with a little soap and the showerhead afterwards.

- For children past the tasting stage, put small amounts of shaving cream in a muffin tin and tint with food color. Allow finger painting on the tub walls.

- Play "I spy" or "Rock, paper, scissors," when you are stuck waiting somewhere.

- Get a basic car track that you put together in a line. Then use pillows to make hills and valleys. See how far the cars will go.

- Place white paper over any etched surface, or coins if they have stopped putting things in their mouths, and rub with crayons.

- Put a plastic swimming pool under a slide.

- Make white play-dough and roll it out. Give the children markers to draw on the play-dough and watch the colors squish into patterns.

- Paint the house outside with water filled pails and paintbrushes or sponges. Let children wash the car, bikes, or bike trailer.

- Blow bubbles from bubble solution on the kitchen floor. Use the excess soap to mop the floor after.

- Use a shaker filled with cornstarch that they can sprinkle it outdoors.

- Buy a couple of cheap wallets from garage sales and collect old used gift cards to put in them. Add some play money. Toddlers love to pull the cards out of the slots.

- Have a decoy drawer of real, unused, broken items that are old cell phones and keyboards that they can play with.

Preschoolers 3-5 Years

- Darken the room and hang a sheet with tape across a corner from one wall to the other wall. Shine a flashlight over the sheet. Make shadow puppets out of hands or objects from behind the sheet.

- Drape old sheets over the bunk-bed top for a puppet or stuffy theatre show.

- Get big boxes from appliance shops for fort making. Let them paint and decorate it.

- Collect empty food boxes from the pantry and play "store".

- Let the kids have the kitchen to play "potion store" and put together unusual ingredients and condiments that they can mix and match and "sell" as potions.

- Have a "treat picnic" and take them to the store. Each child gets to pick one treat. Go to a park and sit on a blanket and share each child's pick. Let them burn off the energy at the playground after.

- Throw an old mattress on the basement floor and let the children jump. Old couch cushions work great for forts and old sheets for roofs, walls, and draping.

- Tables and chairs would also hold sheets for fort play.

- Throw a small piece of cloth (thumb size) in the bath water so they can play catch.

- Save junk mail, envelopes and stickers and let the children play post office.

- Buy an old turntable at a garage sale. Put paper on the spindle and give markers and crayons for children to draw on while it is spinning.

- Use a portable carpenter's tray to carry markers, scissors, and rulers. Makes for easy cleanup and moving around the house.

- Have a dedicated craft table if you have room. Sometimes building projects take more than a few days and will be out of the way.

- Melt broken crayons into foil lined muffin cups for mosaic crayons.

- Pre-hammer some nails into wood scraps and let preschoolers hammer the rest in. They love real tools.

- Make goop (cornstarch and water), play-dough and gak. If it falls on the floor, let it dry and crust and then just vacuum later.

- Get new batches of stickers. Be prepared to remove them off the dog, and furniture later.

- Put Lego blocks in a fitted sheet on the floor and have the children play by it. Makes it easy to clean-up.

- Buy cheap boxes of bandages from the dollar store. Children love to put them all over dolls and stuffies and it builds their fine motor skills.

- Use technology when you need to rest. Go to the library and stock up on videos. Get out the tablet, computer or whatever.

- Rotate toys and bring out a fresh bucket of things when you really need a couch snooze.

- Give children a spray bottle of water and a cloth to "clean" smooth surfaces around the house.

- Use some drop-in daycares. Keep a pillow in the car and snooze in the car.

- Draw on an old shower curtain a number of roads, buildings and city features so they can customize a car play mat.
- Kids still love playing with blankets, sheets and sofa cushions even into the school-age years. Keep a supply for building forts.

School-Agers 6-12 Years

- Have a good old-fashioned lemonade or iced tea stand.
- Give them a low-supervision job that can easily be fixed such as sanding decks, weeding the garden, or painting fences. You may have to pay them for those!
- Help them set up a neighborhood lawn-mowing business with a hand mower.
- Teach them how to cook, bake or assemble food.
- Together, embark on the annual Halloween or Comic-con costume sewing project early and teach them to sew.
- Bring out saved new toys and kits that were put away after birthday parties.
- Consider drop-in day camps for just the day.
- Allow the children to use your video camera or phone to make Lego™ movies after you've given a care lesson and are supervising.
- Have a video game swap among friends.
- Host a mid-summer toy swap among the neighbors.
- Go Geo-caching.
- Paper Dolls are still fun. Give them white paper and markers and challenge them to make a house, zoo, store, pool, school, library out of each sheet of paper. They can also draw and cut out people, pets and items. Before long, children will be acting out roles and scenarios!
- Egg drop test. Hard boil a dozen eggs and cool. Assemble lots of materials and packaging and challenge the kids to wrap the egg so that it won't crack when dropped from six feet above the floor. Great for problem-solving and learning science.
- Have a "Christmas in July" day – decorate a backyard tree with popcorn, and with pinecones dipped in peanut butter (for the birds to eat) and rolled in birdseed. Using newspaper, wrap "used, but loved" gifts taken from around the house and finish it off with a turkey dinner.
- Have a board game day.
- Teach a new card game.
- Drop your tweens and teens off at the local library to try new programs on the computers.

- Any small gadget or appliance that is broken is wonderful to take apart and unscrew with parent supervision. Check out second-hand shops and garage sales for free stuff.

- Have a history theme day. For example, declare a "prehistoric" day and make cave paintings, eat with your hands, camp out in a tent in the back yard and wear draped sheets. Try to talk via writing instead of talking.

- Have a backwards day where you have a bedtime story, bath, dinner, then lunch and breakfast last.

- Play potions. Experiment in the kitchen by making different combos of liquids that are edible and see what tastes, properties and observations can be made from combining different mixtures.

- Go for a walk in nature reserves or the zoo

- Play "Hide and Seek, or Capture the Flag" outdoors in a new park

- Give Easter treats that are different than chocolate - sidewalk chalk, bubbles, skipping ropes, remote control cars, balls, badminton sets

- Send them outside with a small task to do. Once they are outside, kids find interesting things to do on their own. It's just getting them out that is hard.

- Dig out those Christmas puzzles, craft kits, paint by number kits and building kits that never got opened or didn't get finished at Christmas

- Go to a second hand children's store and pick up some treasures. We just got a kit of Snap Circuits that kept the kids busy for a week building the circuit boards.

- Dig out the Nerf guns and bullets – let them go wild in the house. Even better, someone could host a couple of kids and a Nerf party in their house or a nearby park.

- Have a theme movie week or movie binge day such as The Harry Potter movie fest. Watch one movie per day in a week, or watch all of them in one day!

- Camp inside the family room, or set up a tent in the backyard or drag out the sleeping bags on the trampoline.

- Go on a "junk-run," for a treat picnic or sleepover.

- Watch movies in the cool basement.

- Play computer games on the back deck.

- Garden with the kids

- Go to spray parks

- Re-learn how to skip and teach the children how.

- Go on walks and throw rocks into the river.

- Visit the zoo and spend time with a specific animal for the day or go to museum park to see a specific building. Get a pass so you don't have to feel like you have to see it all to get your money's worth.
- Go on bike rides and use the bikes for all neighborhood errands.
- Take in the various festivals going on.

Teenagers 13–19 Years

- Drop them off at the library for a day to immerse in reading books, trying out the computer terminals and use new software applications that libraries offer, but you may not have at home.
- Teens love grown-up board games and especially old favorite card games.
- Summer is a great time to volunteer at many worthwhile places.
- Teach your teen how to drive.
- Show them how to set up a few yard sales so they can earn cash to buy new play items.
- Most teens would be interested in the school-aged play ideas also.
- Organize a regular teen lunch at the mall or movie night and have all friends bus to the meeting place at a regular time each week.
- Start a project such as cleaning out the basement or painting a room. Get the teens to help.
- Pay the teens to do a big job such as categorize, digitize and print all those photos on your computer.

Tips for Smoother Weekday Mornings and After-Work Pick-Ups

- Lack of time and organization causes stress. Items get lost and valuable time is spent looking for them. have a specific place for these items to be kept. (keys, papers, money etc)
- Power struggles over clothes, lunches etc. Give the kids the control of what to wear and eat. Hide the junk food and let them choose from healthy food choices from the four food groups. Parents still have control over what is bought and brought into the house.
- Teens that take too long in the bathroom. Sit down and problem-solve with them. Do they need a clock in the bathroom?

- Kids that don't "listen" to directives. Get eye contact with them. Realize that small children under age five, only comply about 40% of the time and that is normal behavior. Get more organized or streamline the absolute necessities that have to be done, at least until they are older and more capable to follow directions.

- Get yourself ready first so you look pulled together and presentable. The kids can go in whatever state they end up in. (Remind yourself that you are not responsible for how they look.)

- Kids can get caught up in their game/TV show and don't want to leave. Warn them before that they only have a certain time to watch and get their agreement before the show/computer goes on.

Tips for getting out of the door alive!

- Let the kids sleep in their next day clean clothes so you don't have to nag them to get dressed. Sweatpants and T-shirts work great for this.

- Have snack bags in the car with juice boxes, fruit, and granola/nutrition bars for the children who hate breakfast.

- Have a "door" centre in the form of a desk, box, or sorting cabinet that holds keys, backpacks, paper sorters and everything one needs to bring out the door for the next day. Thus, when school field trip forms are signed, they go to the "door" centre or in someone's backpack. When a project is done, it goes to the "door" centre to be sure that it is taken out the next day.

- Buy socks in all one size and solid color as much as possible. Have a clean sock/mitt/hat bucket that all the kids can draw from and then it's much easier to do laundry without the necessary sorting.

- Buy 20 or 30 little re-sealable, spill proof lunch boxes and store chopped vegetables, nuts, crackers, cheese and meat cubes in for after-school driving, lunches, and snacks for siblings at practices, etc. Spend one night a week assembling the boxes, for fridge storage, and you have "grab and go" snacks all week.

- Limit clothing choices by removing most of the clothes in the child's drawers and keep only what they love to wear.

- Have spare bags at the "door centre" so you can grab one and fill with the hats, mitts and coats that the children refuse to wear, but need as soon as they get chilled in the car.

- Buy duvets and covers so even little children can make a bed presentable by shaking and smoothing. Hospital corners are so hard!

- Take photos of the morning routine and upload them to photo processing sites to make a picture book. Cuddle up at night and go through the book of what kids should be expected to do in the morning. Read and talk about it like a picture book.

Tips for smoother homecomings

- Don't stop to shop at all costs! Do without or borrow from the neighbors. Cranky, hungry, and tired children dragged out shopping are a sure-fire recipe for tantrums after pick-up from daycare or school.

- Spend twenty minutes of quality time with your child after you have hung up your coat and changed clothes. Read a book or play Lego together. It's a quiet moment to reconnect after a long day of separation. This time will fill up your child's need for you, and they will be more willing to play on their own and let you start dinner, laundry etc. After reconnection time, ask them to help put away lunch boxes and prep for the next day.

- If you don't have time to reconnect, then involve your child in your tasks as much as possible. Get your child to shred lettuce for salad, or coat the chicken in batter. They can help put things away. Children love to help as long as they are beside you. It teaches them valuable skills and gives you time together.

Boundaries With Families

How do we navigate others' expectations of us during our maternity leave? I'm taking one so I can spend time with my kids. My family members (one is a mom herself) expect me to return their texts, emails, calls and visits yet, I feel that I am stretched already.

- Say "No!" Tell your relatives that you are sorry it upsets them, but this is what you need to do for your new family.

- Young children naturally want and need attention, but adults are able to regulate their needs.

- We can't change others, but we can change our reaction to others, and what we do in response.

- Define your boundaries in what works for you and stick to them.

- Give a certain amount of time and then abide by it. Cut them off. Don't respond to texts or phone calls.

- Have a plan of activities for each day.

- You are not responsible for their feelings - they own them.

- Imagine what you want your child to do in that situation. Model taking care of yourself.
- Every parent is a working parent. You do a valuable job and even though it is unpaid, it is very important.

Public Etiquette of Parenting Practices

Babies 0-1 years

- If your baby is crying for more than five minutes in a restaurant, party, or public venue, leave the room and try to calm the baby somewhere privately, so others can still enjoy their activity in the room.
- You can breastfeed your baby anywhere you wish and do not need to wear a cover-up.
- If the invite says "adult only" please don't bring your children. Decline with thanks or find a sitter. It's rude to the hosts and unfair to the other guests who have paid for a sitter to bring along children to their child-free event.
- Never change your child's diaper in any room other than a bathroom. You need to wash surfaces that come into contact with your child's diaper and you need to wash your hands after with soap and water and that can only be done in a bathroom.

If you are not a parent, you should know that babies are developmentally programmed to cry when they are little. Older babies can shriek, which makes your ears hurt, but parents can't stop either response. They are normal behaviors and help the child grow and thrive. Wear earplugs and smile.

If you don't want children at your social event, be very clear about expectations. Say, "Dinner is at eight. Do you need help finding a sitter?"

Be aware that parenting is an endeavor close to the heart and soul of people. Friendships and relationships can be severed over parenting-related issues. When friends become parents, changes have to occur, and you must decide if the friendship is worth continuing. They can still blossom with patience, flexibility, and humor from both parties.

Toddlers 1-3 years

- If your child is making a fuss in an adult venue, leave after the 2nd Shhhhhh or take them to a quieter place to change the situation. This is not a misbehavior issue, because adult venues are not appropriate for the needs of children. Children get bored, tired and don't understand content. This is about development - the venue is not set up for children's enjoyment. You will have plenty of time to enrich their lives with theatre, concerts, dining, and travel later on when they are school-aged and have more patience and attention.

- Your child makes a mess in a store or public place. You should clean it up. You are modeling to your child problem-solving and responsibility.

- When your child is misbehaving, intervene immediately. Apologize to any affected children or their parents and offer to fix things. Deal with your own child later in private. Onlookers expect you to address the situation and the worst thing you can do is ignore it. If your child doesn't volunteer an apology, you do it for him. It teaches him the necessary social skills required for the situation, by watching you model it.

- Don't discipline your own child in public. Take them to a private area to talk to them and help them calm down. This is essential in the case of temper tantrums. Never spank, hit or time-out your child in public. (You shouldn't do it in private either! Teach and repeat.)

- Talk to your child during meals and waiting times. You are teaching them rudeness when you are on your screens and they are bored. Talking to them builds their brain and language skills. If you want discussions with your later teens, start the conversation habit now with your toddler.

If you are not a parent, you should know that toddlerhood is one of the most challenging stages for their parents. Toddlers are fast, ego-centric, emotional and have very little self-control and knowledge of manners or safety. Caregivers need to act fast, and scoop them out of danger, rather than speak commands and hope the child "listens." Toddler tantrums are a normal developmental behavior and is a good sign of the emotional development of the brain. It is not a sign of bad parenting.

Offer help and empathy for the struggling parent, not judgment. It can be as simple as offering to help steer their grocery cart to their car while they carry their child. Remember that our society is not set up to be child friendly. Children are expected to wait quietly long before they are developmentally ready. We wouldn't punish a person in a wheelchair for not climbing stairs, so why would we punish a two- year-old for exploding while in an endlessly long line-up?

Preschoolers 3-5 years

- Your child accidentally breaks something in a store or makes it unsalable. Offer to pay for it.

- Your child is rude to someone. Offer apologies from you or your child if he is ready.

- Teach your child to not explore other people's fridge, cupboards, closets, or any other rooms than the bathroom, living-room, playroom or other rooms designated by the host parent. Teach your child not to take anything either.
- Teach your child not to open packages in stores or use the store's display models inappropriately.
- Don't threaten to leave your child there if they don't listen to your commands to come. It destroys trust and security. Scoop them up and carry them with you.
- Teach your children to be responsible for their own garbage. Teach them to clean up their fast food garbage in restaurants, to pick up their wrappings in other people's cars and clean up their lunch leftovers at school.

If you are not the parent, and the child is doing something that wrecks your property, your house, your child, or is going to hurt themselves, speak directly to the child, if the parent is ignoring the situation. Be polite, respectful, kind and firm. Use your I-statement by saying, "I'm worried that my white leather sofa might be damaged by your bag of cheese puffs. Let's eat them at the table." If the child still doesn't listen, address their parent. If the parent doesn't listen, rethink future invites.

Never criticize the parent if they are addressing their child in a parenting style that you think is inappropriate. Only offer the parent help and empathy, not advice. Offer the child a hug, smile or kind word.

Power struggles, constant questions, interruptions and whining are normal developmental behaviors for this stage. All kids do it to some degree.

School-Agers 6-13

- Teach your child not to let their friends jump the queue in front of others in line-ups. "Holding the place for a friend," is budging in and not polite.
- Don't take "parent" parking spots unless you are expecting or have a child seat in your car.
- Teach your child that if they eat treats in public, to offer one around the group or share the lot. Otherwise, eat in private.
- Children aged six and over should not run around naked on public beaches, streets, or other venues.
- Children this age should also be using gender assigned change rooms and bathrooms. If you or they are not comfortable, use the family rooms.
- Teach your child to say "Please" and "Thank you" at other peoples' houses and venues, especially during the car pool run, play-dates, sleepovers and birthday parties.

- Teach your child not to boast about what they can do, what they own and where they are going. Teach them to ask questions about the friend and really listen to the answers.

- It's okay to ask if the play-date could be at the other person's house as long as the hosting is reciprocated shortly.

- Teach your child that it's okay to say that they are hungry, sick or need to use the bathroom or phone at play-dates. Introduce them to the adult in charge so they know who to access for help.

- Parents are responsible for both the drop-off and pick-up at the host play-date's house.

- Parents are responsible for damage caused by their child, wherever it may be: school, play-dates, and public venues.

- Teach your child to be respectful of rules in public places. Obey them yourself when you are out with children.

- Teach your child about expectations of their behavior in public without parents – no swearing, bullying, stealing, or vandalism is allowed.

- Teach your child not to talk, eat or use their cell-phones in theatres, and other quiet places of public performances. Your children are watching you so model this.

- Teach your child to be respectful and polite to adults, but to assert their needs with "I-statements." EG "I need to use your phone please."

- Make logistic arrangements with your child's friend's parent, as well as your child. Cell-phones allow you to hammer out details with your child, but the hosting parent is clueless to what has been arranged. Let the kids work out the original arrangements but because the social plans still involve an adult to drive and supervise, adults need to be consulted. Teens who can drive can arrange their own plans without parent consultation.

- Bring your own bedding for sleepovers unless the parent says not to.

- Children should not be left home alone until age 10

- Children should not babysit other children, including siblings, until age 12.

- Teach your children to cancel activities and relationships over the phone, not in a text or email. Sure, it is a tough thing to do, but future employers will value it.

- Teach your children to be responsible by modeling commitment. If you say that you are going to be somewhere, do your very best to be there. Insist on them keeping agreements also.

If you are not the parent, by all means, step in and speak up to the child if something is bothering you. Say, "I'm thinking that swear words might offend people. Could you please tone it down while my young son is here?" Be respectful, kind and aware that children and their parents have feelings, but may simply not know the expectations. Children this age can handle and understand different ways of doing things.

Teenagers 13-20

By now you should be done teaching and teenagers should have a pretty good idea of the norms of society and what is expected of adult behavior. However, they may need reminding every now and then by parents and everyone else. It takes a village to raise a child.

Best Advice for New Parents

- Happy parents equal happy babies. Make sure your needs are met too.

- Remember that children are new to the world – teach them – don't get angry.

- Kids have so little control – look for opportunities to give them choice.

- Don't listen to all the parent peer pressure. If you don't want to send them to preschool, stay with your resolve and don't do it.

- There is no one right way to parent. There are many, many goods ways to parent and a few not-so-good ways. We all make mistakes. You are the best person in the world for your child.

- Everything is a stage. Children change in a few weeks or months.

- There is no such thing as creating bad habits. If children change so fast, habits can to. Habits can be changed in 3 days for children and 21 days for parents.

- You will sleep a full 10 hours a night again.

- Everyone turns out okay.

- Be flexible in getting things done. They will be done eventually.

- Ask for help. Use your I-statements. Be specific about date and time.

- Children grow so fast – enjoy their childhood as much as you can.

- Give a lot of love and attention and take care of yourself.

- Read the parent books, see what fits for you, and then ignore the rest – instead of always second guessing yourself.

- Accept all offers of food. Try and make some ahead of time.

- Bank sleep before the baby comes.

- It took 9 months to put on the baby weight and will be another 9 months before it starts to come off.

- Parenting is the best. You are growing friends for life.

....

Keeping Kids Busy During Wait Times Without Electronics

- **Pipe-cleaners**: These versatile little wires can be molded into cars, people and many other items for make-believe play.

- **Play-dough**: Keep moist in a plastic Ziploc bag. Kids can make 3D sculptures for toys. With a phone camera, teens can make animated figure movies.

- **Masking tape or cello-tape**

- **Scissors**

- **Small whiteboard** and dry-erase markers, with a cloth for erasing. Endless opportunities to make signs, keep game scores, or play picture games.

- **Coloring markers**: My kids used to color the doctor's waiting room bed-covering paper!

- **Pens and Pencils**: Play hangman or other words games. Write in a journal or just draw!

- **Plain paper**: for drawing houses and scenes, or constructing cars, buildings, items and people, to be colored, cut out and assembled with tape and scissors.

- **Deck of cards**: Great for teens to play Cheat, Snap, Spoons, Blackjack, Uno and many other games.

- **Dice**: for playing addition, multiplication, and chance challenges. Dice also work with homemade board games created from above items.

- **Flashlight**

- **Binoculars**

- **Square sheet of foil**

....

Keeping Cool

How to chill in the moment when we are really angry? Try these tips:

- Say to yourself, "Stop. Breathe. What do I need?"

- Say, "I'm really angry!" Research shows that expressing feelings verbally reduces Cortisol levels (the stress hormone).

- Tell your child, "Mommy is angry and needs to defuse." This lets you express your feelings but tells the child that you "own" how you feel and how you are going to deal with it – an emotionally intelligent response.

- If you need to release your anger physically, stomp your feet, pound your fists to the ground, or take a plastic bat to a well-padded pillow. (Many children and adults need to release their anger physically and if you demonstrate to your child a way to do it without hitting anyone or wrecking anything, then they will copy what you do.)

- Say, "Mommy needs a time-out. I'm going into the bathroom to handle my anger." Turn on the shower and cry, scream, vent or whatever you need to do. Scream into the toilet and flush away your anger. Make sure the children are safe. This is a great way to show children that time-outs are a great tool, not a punishment

- Anger is very personal and universal. Teach your child how to handle anger by demonstrating it. Make sure it doesn't hurt anyone or anything and you are probably on safe ground. Talk about handling anger and a new calm-down tool when everyone is calm. Try out different expressions and see which are satisfying and which don't work for you and your children.

- Grit your teeth.

- Stomp your feet.

- Drink water.

- Breathe.

- Scrub the sink.

- Play some music.

- Put a movie on and cry.

- Phone a friend and vent.

- Yell into the toilet and then flush.

- Hammer a stake in the garden.

- Pound some red play-dough.

- Declare your feelings, "I'm feeling really angry. I'm frustrated that you are fighting."

- Don't talk at all. Just do what you need to do.

- Use self-talk. Think, "She is just doing, what children her age are supposed to do."

- Take a mommy time-out. Make sure the kids are safe.

- Have a coffee/tea break.

- Turn on the TV/tablet to diffuse situation.

- Keep repeating what you need to say – "Just one more minute."

- Run around, go outside, get a change of scenery.

- Ask for a hug.

- Take vitamins (especially D).

- Go to a book store or coffee shop and get some alone time.

- Lock yourself into the bathroom for some quiet time.

- Have your partner take the kids out (preventative).

- Walk away – go to a room with glass doors so kids can see you and can feel assured, but leave you alone.

- Tell the kids you feel angry and it has nothing to do with them. You own it and will deal with it.

- Apologize after yelling – try again.

- Ask kids to give you a sign that you are losing it.

- Have a white board with the message, "Deep breathe. Say what you are feeling. Count to ten." It helps with pent-up anger for both parents and kids.

Developing Patience (and Our Executive Function)

- Set aside a time limit. Say, "For the next half hour, I will be patient." Extend your time limit as you get better at it.

- If you do nothing else, say nothing. Zipping it means that you won't say anything you will regret later. Act, don't rant. Do something, and don't swear, threat, or berate.

- See the good intent of others. They are not trying to bug you. It's not about you. It's all about them. Children are born egocentric and learn about others as they grow. Read more about children's executive function and how they acquire it with age.

- Wear earplugs. When noise gets out of hand, remember that children are naturally noisy, messy and forgetful. They are not being bad; they are just in that stage of childhood.

- Prepare for delay. Carry around a good book or something to do when waiting for others.

- Live in the present. Forget about the future and all that needs to be done. Relish what is happening now. When you are distressed and more patient, things get done more efficiently, even if it's later.

- Keep perspective. Has anyone died because of this roadblock? Will it really matter a year from now?

- Be grateful. When you are delayed, think of all the people you are grateful for. Carry around a notebook in your purse and write a short note to tell them what you appreciate about them. This helps put you in a way better mood.

- Have quiet time every day – ten minutes on the front step admiring nature, or five minutes in the shower. Even for school aged children, remove yourself for a half-hour and savor the quietness. Be sure younger children are engaged in an activity and safe. You can have a few minutes alone. Hooray for the tablet.

- Take 1 day each month to check into a hotel. Sleep, eat from room service, swim and relax.

- Have a time-out room for you! Make it inviting, soothing, calming. A bedroom with crystals, a water feature, stereo with spa or massage music, candles, calming artwork, plants, books, and cozy pillows. A welcoming, relaxing room to have a peaceful moment. If you have a TV or computer in your bedroom, cover it with a white sheet, so it doesn't remind you of work to be done.

- Avoid multi-tasking. Living a more peaceful, patient life means taking one thing at a time. Doing multiple things causes stress and hurriedness, which feeds itself in the frenzy.

- Take the "level of acceptance" to the ground. Accept all and everything! Say "yes" to the children as much as possible, to entertain themselves and you can have some time to do what you want to do.

- Take a course so you have to get out regularly.

- Have a standing order to go to the movies. My friend goes to a first run movie, every Friday night, by herself.

- Go to bed at the same time as the kids and get up before they do, so you have your "me time" in the early morning and don't have to fight for it at night when you are tired and less patient.

- Take a shower and lock the door.

- Go to a bookstore, or a coffee shop, or for a quick walk, as soon as your parenting partner gets home.

- Take your time-out - get calm for a few minutes.

- Find regular time for you. Take breaks in the day. What can you do in 5 minutes; check social media, read the paper, have a cup of tea, sit and relax, phone a friend. What can you do in 20 minutes? Have a quick nap, read a bit of a book, color your hair. What can you do during a two hour window at naptime? Take a nap yourself, watch a movie, organize photos.

Managing Stress Levels

- Meditate.
- Talk it through with an empathetic and good listener friend.
- Distract yourself with socializing, video games, movies.
- Get out and socialize to get your mind off the issue.
- Reframe it - will it matter in 10 days, 10 months or 10 years?
- Be sure to get healthy eating, sleep, and exercise.
- Treat yourself to a spa, massage, bath, or swim.
- Indulge in a favorite hobby such as Lego, painting, boxing, or gardening.
- Find the humor in stress. Laugh, share it with someone and take a photo.
- Have a good cry.
- Get outside in nature and go for a walk.
- Gaze at an aquarium or the moon.
- Listen to music or play virtual reality technology.
- Sing, dance, do Yoga.
- Bake and cook if that relaxes you.
- Look at photo albums or read.
- Have some chocolate or wine.
- Sort out messes in your living space to clear your head. Clean.
- Have some quiet time.
- Have boundaries. Turn off the email and phone after supper, and weekends.
- Deep breathe.
- Pray or go to church.

Taking a Calm-Down Parent Time-out With Little Ones Underfoot

- Use a music player filled with your favorite songs to distract you. Dance.

- Have earplugs everywhere. In the car, kitchen, purse, and bathroom. They take the edge off a child's screaming that can damage your ears.

- Lock yourself in the bathroom. Tell the children that you love them, and Mommy/Daddy is feeling angry, and needs to take a time-out for herself or himself. Turn on the fan or shower so you can't hear the children, and breathe slowly. Visualize yourself in a calm place.

- Do the Hokey-Pokey, and shake it out! Smile and make a funny noise and you will all be laughing.

- Phone a friend to have a brief conversation. Tell her how you feel. Call from the closet or a bathroom if you have to.

- Distract yourself with a magazine.

- Drop everything, dress your children and yourself for the weather, and put them in the stroller. Go for a brief walk outside. Exercise, fresh air, peace and quiet! Children will be distracted by the sights and sounds and you can think out your anger in peace.

- Turn on the television. It will either distract you or your child, and will give both of you time to calm down.

- If you are in the car, pull over to a parking lot or some other safe place. Get out of the car, leave the children in there, and walk around the car 20 times. Cry, deep breathe, vent or stomp. Get back in the car when you have calmed down.

- Imagine a soundproof, gentle, clear shell around yourself to protect you from screaming children.

- Sit on the porch, find a closet, basement, or somewhere you can be alone. Make sure the children are in a safe place.

- Tell your child that you both need a group hug. It can be very hard to hug someone that you feel angry with, but the touch is soothing and helps to heal the anger. It works well for some people.

- Use "Self-Talk" Say over and over to yourself, "My child is not trying to bug me right now. She is only coping with her strong feelings in the only way she knows how. "But me first."

- Remember the phrase: "Get myself calm, Get my child calm, and then solve the problem."

Turning Negative Commands into Positive Ones

- Instead of saying, "Don't hit!" ... Say, "Hitting hurts people. We talk with our voices, not our hands."

- Instead of, "Don't run!" ...Say, "Walk please. Use your walking feet. Slow down."
- Instead of, "I don't want to..." ... Say, "Thanks anyways."
- Instead of, "Be careful!" ...Say, "Watch out for..."
- Instead of "Settle down!" ...Say, "Calm down. Breathe. Hum."
- Instead of, "Smarten up!" ...Say, "I don't want you to get hurt – do this..."
- Instead of, "Don't splash!" ...Say, "Keep the water with the water."
- Instead of, "Don't touch!" ...Say, "Hands on your belly please. We look with our hands. Leave the toy. Wave goodbye to the toy."

Making Holidays Memorable

My friend's suggestion is to write these activities on to a piece of paper and put them into a Holiday Jar. Let the kids take turns picking out of the jar and you all do the activity as a family that day. You could do the same for Lent, Advent, or Hanukkah by writing a service project down on each piece of paper and using the same jar. Children won't remember stuff they got for seasonal holidays, but they will remember activities you did with them.

- Make and decorate a gingerbread house.
- Go to a farm and cut down a tree to decorate.
- Decorate the house (in and out) and tree
- Go to a community holiday party.
- Make cards for friends.
- Bake and decorate cookies.
- Deliver baked goods to friends and family.
- Make snow globes.
- Have a special lunch at a restaurant.
- Attend a special holiday play or concert.
- Go sledding or skating.
- Have friends over for a pajama holiday movie party or go to the theatre in pyjamas.
- Drive around the city and look at lights while drinking hot chocolate and singing holiday songs.
- Set up luminaries, candles or ice lanterns outside on a snowy wintery evening.
- Have a family holiday photo viewing night at home.

- Pick a special treat (book or small toy).

- Make a snowman, snow woman, or snow children and animals.

- Go to a Holiday build-it workshop at a home renovation store.

- Go grocery shopping and donate to the local food bank.

- Winter solstice celebrations (we did two days of this, one was a solstice craft day at a friends and another was on the solstice at a park with a fire).

- Attend a school holiday party or play (many are open to the public).

- Have a holiday craft day (we made wreaths for kids bedroom doors and paper trees).

- Paint ornaments for the tree or house decor.

Getting Kids Off Electronics

Yes, there are some non-punitive ways to get kids off of video games, cell phones and computers without tears and tantrums! The key is to involve them.

- Redirect to other stimulation. Have board games set up, sports equipment ready to go, or recipe ingredients laid out ready for a baking session.

- Be involved and knowledgeable of where they travel on the Internet and whom they play games with. Spend time building the parent-child relationship by taking an interest in their on-line gaming and chatting pursuits. It's easier to direct them to your activities after you connect for a while in their playground.

- Don't punish – problem solve! It's not a battle of you against them. It's you and your child working against the problem. You are both on the same team! Work the problem out together to everyone's satisfaction and enjoy the new rules and increased connection. Tell your child about your concerns with her health, and then invite brainstorming solutions.

- Model a balanced life that includes seven keys to health and happiness. Invite your child to participate with you in your pursuit of the seven keys of a balanced life. Many children will get active if the parents or the whole family is involved:

- Negotiate! Make good use of Family Conferences, "parent concern" consulting, and negotiation sessions to discuss time limits that meet everyone's needs.

- Issue time tokens. Each hour of physical activity will garner a child an hour of screen time.

- Get it in writing. Draw up a daily schedule and discuss where screen time fits in with the day's already scheduled activities. Children can sign into time slots.

- Contract. Draw up a weekly or monthly agreement that has limits decided by both the parent and child together. Display in a prominent place. Point to it when the complaining occurs. Discuss when the contract is up for renewal and be open to changes at renewal time.

- Change the environment. Sometimes, it's easier to move around the setting than to change the other person. Seriously consider whether adding more equipment and hardware will add to the screen time and decide to not bring it into the house. Move the computer and gaming systems into the main family area. Having one unit for the children to share means more fighting over screen time, but can also mean more time spent in learning the valuable skill of negotiating and less individual screen time.

- Teach your child the fine art of Haggling! "Hey, Eric, Wow, you made another level! Good for you! Now, I need you to do the dishes. What time would you like to get at them?" Insist they give you a time and haggle when they give you an outrageous one. Choice from your child makes it easier for them to abide by it.

- Remember that you have the most power to negotiate rules and limits before the power button goes on! Go for it!

7 Keys to a Balanced Life:

1. Social time - time spent with friends
2. Physical activity time - exercise, sports, active play
3. Mental exercise time - educational activities, games, puzzles, homework, reading
4. Spiritual time – volunteering, meditating, solitude, unstructured play, church
5. Family time – doing projects
6. Financial time – job
7. Hobby time – leisure pursuits and projects

....

Teaching Internet Safety

Mobile Phone Safety

- Hotels, cafes, airports and anywhere there is free public wifi access are the worst places for hackers to see what you are getting on your phone. Try to wait until you are in a password protected area before using the internet. At the very least, don't make any financial transactions or input any passwords to get to your favorite sites. Do not access your bank, paypal, or credit cards websites.

- Change your passwords every month. An easy way to change passwords often is to use a single word that has a Capital letter and is more than 6 letters long such as - Summer4. Add a number at the end and each month "change" the password by increasing or decreasing the number.

- If you can, use the "forget password" link most often and then you generate a new password each time you log in, which adds a safety measure to your sites.

- Companies have policies on phone use and photo taking. Many companies state that if they sense you are on the phone while driving and speaking with them, regardless of having a hands-free model, they will automatically hang up for distracted driving and safety reasons. As well, many stores, leisure centers and venues are banning photographs and video taking. Be sure you know the organization's policies.

- If someone asks to borrow your phone because their battery is dead, do not hand over your phone. Direct them to a store or offer to make the call for them. Don't let your phone leave your hands.

- Ladies should never hang their handbags over the backs of their chairs. Keep it on your body.

- Give your child an unlimited texting plan. Average use is 2200 texts a month.

- Get teens to pay for their phones. Have a discussion of roaming charges, and data. Discuss the "fine print" which states which harmless diversions such as "voting" and downloading ringtones or calling/texting any 900 number can incur charges. Discuss how much is a gigabyte versus a megabyte.

- Model boundaries. Be unavailable at times, so kids can learn to solve their own problems.

- Establish phone contracts with kids – usage, knowledge of laws, payment, etc. Have both kids and parents sign and post the contract where everyone can see it.

Computer/Internet Safety

- Never leave your laptop on a restaurant table or in the care of others. Take it with you to the restroom.

- Children under 18 should have aliases on all social media accounts.

- Parents, friends and relatives should be made aware not to tag children's names on photographs. Set up social media settings that give alerts when photos are tags.

- Teach that true friends respect one's wishes, including asking permission to post photos.

- Warn kids not give friends their gaming passwords. Their friends can now give their other friends the passwords to play with them and before they know it, they have been locked out of their games for bad behavior.

- Teach kids how to manage their gaming passwords. Keep a little book they can write email address the account is billed to, the username and the password.

- When discussing sensitive issues by email, pick up the phone instead. Email can be used as evidence in court and can easily be copied.

- Parents, have one rule to never meet anyone from the internet without parent's supervision. Talk about grooming (gaining trust, praising, active listening by perpetrator), luring and what constitutes friendship. Don't lecture. Listen more than talk. Watch the movie, "Trust" (2010, Directed by David Swimmer, Rated R) to learn about how luring works. Consider watching it together with your teen and have a discussion after.

- Know the risk factors of luring: age range of 10-14, fear of parents, fear of losing cell-phone or computer, peer dependency, few friends, and no activities outside of school.

- Teach kids how to avoid cyber-bullying: Prevention is the best defense. Don't be in a position where alcohol or nudity photographs are being taken. Take action when offensive postings are up.

- Discuss "friend" settings. On social media, "friends" of "friends" settings is really public.

- Put Google alerts on kids and elderly parent's names. Anywhere the name is mentioned on the internet will show up in your email inbox.

- Children should be made aware of local laws regarding texting/emailing of photographs. They need to know what constitutes pornography. Sending photos of naked body parts to anyone under age 18 is illegal.

- Review social media settings every month. They change and default to lower standards without users knowing.

- Watch identifying details on photographs and in postings – school names, person's name, sports team names, birth year, birthday, addresses, house numbers, home town, etc.

- "Permission" is the golden word of netiquette – Ensure children know copyright rules and laws. Insist they don't post anything not belonging to them such as friend's photos, school work, songs, videos, without asking the owner's permission first.

- Discuss spam. People who send an email to more than a group of 25 to 50 recipients may find themselves blacklisted. They need to clear off their account with their internet provider and be on a blacklist probation period for a few weeks until they have been cleared. This means that no email may go out.

- Show kids and seniors what spam and phishing emails look like. Ask them to point out clues: misspellings, bad grammar, generic addresses, threatening language, no contacts other than links (that capture your email address as "live" if you investigate the link).

- If anyone calls about your credit card being compromised in any way and want to know information from you including the number, tell them you will call them back. Then call the number on the back of the card and if they don't know anything, it was not a legitimate query.

- Help children make a purchase online. Show what information is important and what is not. Many online marketers want demographic information that goes beyond what is necessary to make the purchase. Show kids that only the red stars are the ones they need and many of those fields can be filled out with fake information. (If the store is not delivering product, they don't need your physical address.)

- Look for sites that have the "s" in the URL address which means it is a financially secure site. Sites must have credit card encryption if they are going to accept credit cards.

- Be sure your home network is password protected to ward off drive-by hackers. Change it after your company and guests leave.

- Teach kids and seniors that all reputable sites have easy contact information that must include names, phone numbers, emails, and physical addresses.

- Every adult should have a junk email address (hotmail) and an important one that they check every day.

- Teach how photographs can go viral. Show how to copy a photograph and save it and also how to copy website text into a word file and save it on hard drives.

- Show how to capture a screen. Push "PrntScr" button in the left hand corner of the keyboard. Then "control" and "c" together. Then open up "paint" and push "control" and "v" together. Save it as a new file. You now have a copy of anything on the internet and can put it on Facebook, in an email, in a power-point or anywhere.

- Teach virus management. Download free virus protection such as adware, malware bytes, cc cleaner, McAfee, and show how to use it at least monthly.

- Don't open emails from friends that have one word generic subject lines such as "Amazing!" or seem like an out of characteristic tone for the sender such as "Look at this!" or "Brittany's Naked Video!" They are often a sign that your friend's computer has been attacked by a virus and is now sending out baiting emails under their name. Don't bite by clicking it open or clicking on the links. Delete it and ask your friend if they sent it.

- Always ask organizations about posting and privacy policies. Many school council minutes are being posted on the internet because no one has questioned its privacy level.

- Use portable hard drives to back up at least monthly. Keep one off-site. An easy way to back up is to use a web-based cloud email service such as gmail and email yourself attachments or documents.

- Watch email names – hotsexychick@hotmail.com is not one of the best.

- Think of your child as a future teenager. Will they want your posting available to their peers? Could their peers use it to bully your child?

- Google yourself and your children's names often and see what comes up. Contact organizations if you see postings that you do not wish to see and want them removed.

Managing Parent's Online Time

How to manage your online time to make it more efficient.

- Never check social networks in the morning – you can easily lose track of time catching up on what your friends had for breakfast.

- Do breastfeed and cuddle your infant in front of the computer. It's a great way to get some snuggle time in as well as some adult company on the screen.

- Don't ignore your toddler while you are in front of the computer or cell-phone. Toddlers are fast, unable to comprehend safety and need constant supervision. As toddlers need zero screen time, and constant five sense stimulation, take your toddler on playgroups and experiential field trips. Let them explore their environment, and make it focused, attentive time. Save your screen time for their naps and bedtimes.

- Check email twice a day: once in the morning (after breakfast and with coffee), and once at suppertime. 70% of adults now check email before breakfast – is that what we want to model to our kids? Most businesses expect a response within a day or two, so you still have four times to check and catch items in those 48 hours.

- Don't read email late at night. Upsetting news can keep your mind going at night before and while you are in bed, until you finally get up at 4 am with a perfectly crafted email response and then have to face the next day on three hours of sleep. Not worth it. Problem emails look much easier to respond to at 8 am with a full night's sleep.

- Limit the number of websites that you need to log into. I am forced to check several websites per day (like libraries, workplace, schools etc.), but I will not sign on to any that are not essential, or don't give me a link direct to my email inbox. Websites have to make it easy for me to access or I just won't visit them.

- Avoid getting on newsletter contact sheets. Don't fill out draws at trade shows or give your email to businesses. If you have to, omit a letter of your email address. Otherwise, you will have to spend your valuable time unsubscribing to unwanted inbox clutter.

- Get in the habit of cleaning (yes, another item in the house to clean!) out your recycle bin and email boxes at least twice a month. Even twice a year if you are not up to the task monthly.

- Buy an external hard drive and be sure to save precious video and photographs every month or upload to a cloud service.

- Set a timer to alert yourself to the end of a gaming session. Establish good habits for yourself and your children will follow.

- Write everything online as if your mother will read it. It it's not appropriate for her to read, think twice about posting. Better yet, write it for the world to see it. Consider yourself and your reputation – emails can be entered as evidence in court. Even if you delete it immediately, it could have been easily copied by someone else. Consider your young child as a teenager, who will be very sensitive to what you write about them. Consider the photos you post now. Will your 17 year-old son be happy to have his buddies see photos of himself breastfeeding at three years old?

- Once in a while, you absolutely need a whole day to get cyber-chores done. Enlist the help of a babysitting co-op, or a partner to take the kids out, or if you have older children, invite kids over for a play date. Surprisingly, having a houseful of kids keeps them busy and provides you with time to get things done, in between serving snacks and mediating fights. If you nix their access to the computer, it can leave you with a few hours to get your internet chores done. Use a slow cooker to throw some meat and vegetables in for supper and you are set. If no one is around, take the kids out for a walk to the library and load up on materials, and let them vegetate for a few hours in front of a book or movie so you can catch up on cyber chores and feel halfway accomplished. Don't use that time for social media!

- Get to know your privacy settings and use them.

- Don't multitask during family time. If you are watching a movie with the kids, resist the temptation to check social media or email. Remember that laps are for children, not cell-phones. Be truly present for them.

- On the same note, keep your laptop/cell-phone out of the bedroom. Electronics should not be in a space dedicated to rest, relaxation and love.

- Think twice before wading into hot topics on discussion groups. Often, after two days of intense flurry of emails, time is wasted arguing a point that eventually everyone will agree to disagree about. Meanwhile, it can be easy to snap at a needy child while in the middle of writing the stellar post, and it won't matter in 20 years what you said in the group, but your child will still remember those tense, anxiety filled moments that you lost it with her because you needed to respond to a flaming posting. Put the energy into positive venues and take your child to the park, meet another mom in person to vent, or channel your anger over someone's post into exercise or housecleaning. This is much more productive than posting a possible flame, or even mildly heated response that you will regret later. In time, you can develop the self control to let others respond. It's not your battle. Life is too short!

- If you really need to email a response to a heated issue, assume people's best intentions, and pick up the phone to talk in person. You both will feel much better and you can still attend to children while on the phone (sort of) much more than trying to concentrate on creating an email response.

- If you are a WAHM, get your computer work done, then check email and respond, and then treat yourself to social media. If it's the other way around, you will lose the day in the social media black hole.

- Use "message rules" for emails. It will sort your inbox into critical items and not so critical folders. Helps prioritize before you even start the day.

- Remember that real life touch, smiles, stories, laughter and hugs are better than digital communication! Online communication supplements your life; it isn't your life. Be sure you virtually live, not live virtually.

....

Chore Capability by Age

2-3 years of age (with adult)

- Empty small wastebaskets
- Put on pyjamas
- Pick up trash in yard
- Wash face
- Brush teeth
- Comb hair
- Help set table

- Clear table
- Help load dishwasher
- Help put laundry in dryer or on drying rack
- Pick up toys
- Put dirty clothes in hamper

4-5 years of age (with adult)

- Get dressed
- Make Bed with Duvet
- Pick up room
- Dust their room
- Hang wet laundry on clothes rack
- Clean TV screen
- Help in the yard
- Get ready for bed (brush teeth, put on pj's, etc)
- Lay out clothes for next day

6-7 years of age (with adult)

- Brush teeth (still with adult)
- Set breakfast table
- Help with dishes
- Change sheets (help from parent)
- Feed dog or cat
- Vacuum room
- Take out trash
- Dust room
- Sweep porch
- Clean inside of car
- Help with dinner
- Sweep porches and walks
- Help with dinner clean up
- Dust baseboards
- Fold laundry
- Carry in groceries

- Empty backpack lunch containers by the sink
- Make sure backpack and school papers are by the door and ready to go
- Carry their own backpack to and from school as well as lessons

8-9 years of age (with reminders)

- Start ironing easy items
- Clean sliding door and window glass
- Clean fingerprints from doors
- Dust other rooms
- Wash car

10 years old and up (with reminders)

- They can do all that the other ages do plus:
- Change their sheets by themselves
- Clean the bathroom
- Clean up kitchen
- Help with cooking meals and baking
- Scrub floors
- Water plants
- Straighten bookcases
- Wipe down washer and dryer
- Sew and mend
- Put away groceries

12 years old and up (no reminders)

- Clean entire bathroom
- Clean kitchen alone
- Vacuum entire house
- Do grocery shopping
- Sew and mend
- Repair jobs
- Clean range
- Help with heavy spring cleaning
- Paint

- Straighten closets and drawers
- Get groceries
- Do almost everything an adult can.

....

Social Skills by Age

Children are socialized by four agents in society: parents, school, communities, and media. What skills should children have by what age?

A person with good social skills...

- Greets people with a "Hello," and a handshake. Asks how people are and listens to the response.
- Can start a conversation by noticing a detail.
- Maintains eye contact.
- Smiles and nods while listening.
- Respects other people's personal space. In North America, it's a peripheral of about 18 inches around a person.
- Ask questions, listens and responds after listening.
- Gives opinions that are generally positive and upbeat. Doesn't criticize excessively and never criticizes other people.
- Doesn't talk about other people negatively. Discusses ideas, opinions and own anecdotes rather than other people.
- Talks for 15 seconds and then listens while the other person takes a turn to talk for about 15 seconds.
- Doesn't talk too much about themselves. Doesn't share too little about themselves so the other person in the conversation has nothing to ask them about. Visibly shows an interest in the other person by maintaining eye contact.
- Is not distracted from a conversation by cell-phone, or electronic devices or other people walking by.
- Doesn't interrupt conversations. Can wait and determine the proper moment to interject into the conversation with own insights.
- Can interpret visual and auditory clues to people's moods, such as expressions, voice tone, and gestures. If exceptionally skilled, can articulate the other's people's feelings with empathy to encourage the other person to share.
- Gives encouragement and empathy when others talk about their woes. Doesn't try to best them with own examples.

- Can exit a conversation by saying "Thank-you, it was nice to speak with you," and "Goodbye."

- Uses "Please, May I, and Thank-you as well as "I'm very sorry."

- Asks permission to use other's belongings. Articulates when not sure about a situation to seek other people's guidance.

- Knows what constitutes private behavior and public behavior such as swearing, picking noses, and letting out gas.

- Knows when it is appropriate not to speak.

- Politely and respectfully uses I-statements beginning with "I think.., I feel..., I would like..., I am disappointed...," to assert ones' needs.

- Initiates and co-operates with problem-solving for win-win solutions when there is a difference of opinion or plans.

- Knows their own limitations and is comfortable saying "No, thank-you," to requests.

- Shares, take turns, and offers help to people in need.

- Knows the different levels of conversation and which is appropriate for different audiences and situations. For example, level one is making small talk for strangers, level two is sharing facts with acquaintances, level three is sharing beliefs and opinions with friends and lastly, level four, is sharing feelings with family and intimate friends.

- Is not feeling lonely in solitude. Knows when they want to be alone and when they want to be with other people.

- Queues in public line-ups and does not let joining friends into their space in line.

- Can find common ground for conversation with people of different ages, cultures, religions, uniforms, genders and social status (bosses, police, etc).

It's important to remember that most of these skills are learned in the school-aged, teen and emerging adult years. It takes a lot of practice but will come with time. Children don't need a whole plethora of friends to learn socialization. All a child needs for healthy development is at least one good friend and a lot of supportive adults in their lives.

Teaching Empathy by Age

Babies

- Consistently respond with nurturing especially when crying, upset, hurt or sick. Give all children (even teens!), all ages, hugs, holding, and soft words.

Toddler

- Show how to care for pets.
- Talk to strangers and help when possible.
- Model how you would want to be treated...listen, and speak respectfully.

Preschooler

- Share what we can.
- Volunteer by helping out after disasters. Assist neighbors.
- Give food gift cards or certificates to homeless.
- Model caring and politeness to service people.

School-Age

- Pick up garbage and care for parks and the environment.
- Invite people for dinner from different cultures, religion and sexual orientation.
- Point out things in the newspaper and have discussions.
- Say "I-statements" – how you feel about things.
- Talk about how other people feel when you can't see them online.
- Watch movies and read books and talk about how people feel and what motivates them.
- Encourage sharing – money, toys, clothes, and time.
- Travel – not tours in tourist destinations, but real places with real people. Share food, customs and be respectful of their surroundings.
- Buy or make little gifts for people.
- Volunteer informally – make shoeboxes, shovel walks, bake cookies, carol at centers.

Teens

- Introduce news articles on suffering in the world and have discussions – what do you think? What could we do?
- Travel – research politics, environment, culture before you go.
- Volunteer formally - food banks, soup kitchens, and many other projects.

Best Tips for Harmony in Stepfamilies

Examine your expectations and myths:

- Everyone will adjust quickly? No. A family who blends take anywhere from 3 to 8 years to function effectively. Issues that come up are very normal.

- Parents will love the stepchildren and stepchildren will love the parents from the start? No. Love takes time to grow. However, everyone needs to feel safe, cared for and respected. Love will grow from that.

- No one will argue? No. Parenting styles, money, and chores are complex issues. There is no one correct way to handle things for every family.

Listen to each other:

- Be empathetic to another's feelings. They have a right to them, no matter how irrational. Acknowledge their feelings. Listening is loving.

- Learn about each other when spending time together for dinners, breakfasts, activities and other events.

- Have regular family meetings to iron out problems and conflicts. Allow everyone to speak without interruption. Brainstorm ideas and then evaluate ideas. Choose the most win-win idea.

Include everyone:

- Put your marriage first. Make his or her status in the family clear to the children.

- Have one-on-one time alone with each of your children.

- Have one-on-one time alone with each of your stepchildren without their biological parent there. It gives you both time to build your own unique relationship.

- Encourage children to join the family without renouncing their former family. Don't force the use of the titles of Mom, Dad, family etc.

- Each child should have their own space in the home, a place at the table and chores, even if they only stay part-time.

- It might be valuable to move to a new family home or renovate the existing home so that no one feels they are intruders on someone else's space.

Parenting styles:

- Each parent is their own agent and can't control what the other parent does. Each parent builds their own unique relationship with each child.

- Iron out serious parenting disagreements in private but give each other a full license to parent their way and style when they are on duty.

- Have a family meeting to iron out house rules in which everyone creates.

- What Mom does in her house and what Dad does in his house can be totally different. Children older than 3 can adapt to different values, rules and expectations.

8 Quick Steps to Managing Angry Children at Any Age

1. Put away your irreplaceable treasures.

2. Stay calm yourself

3. Stick with your "No" if you said "No."

4. Redirect him or her to somewhere they can anger safely. See #6

5. Don't punish her anger. She is learning how to manage it and she is still a child. She has until age 12 to get it right, and it takes many practices.

6. After she is calm, validate her feelings. "You were really mad at me for not letting you have a cookie. It's okay to be angry. It's not okay to hit your brother. Next time you are angry, lets kick this bean bag chair."

7. When she is not angry, talk about what she can do next time when she is angry: hit a bean bag chair, stomp her feet, deep breathe, yell into the toilet, etc. (See the book, *Parenting With Patience*, for over 88 ideas). I used to put the kids in their carseats if out in public. They are safe, contained, and we just wait out the meltdown. At home, I would re-direct to the trampoline or a bean bag chair or a pillow. If she destroys things while angry, leave the mess until she is calm and get her to help you clean up. Every time. She owns it.

8. Keep at this over and over and over again. She will have more self-control as her brain develops, and she will eventually learn to handle anger as an adult in ways that don't hurt anybody or anything.

Teaching Money Management by Age

A common question I get from parents is when and how should kids start learning about money. Here is an age-by-age primer of what your child needs to know at each age group, from babies to university students.

Young children (Ages 0-5) - Age to model money transactions but you keep control of it

Small children before the age of 5, are not reliable with money. They are naturally forgetful, lose money, and don't understand the exchange of a symbol (coins, paper or plastic) for "ownership" of items. This is a good age to begin chores, but not to pay for them. (In fact, don't ever pay for them!) You can model how to purchase items, but don't give any money to the child.

Early school-age (Ages 5-8) – Age to start allowances

Children should have a coin purse with real money (coins and bills) at around age five when they start to understand the exchange of money for goods. Parents must still keep a close eye on it though, if the child brings it to the store, because children are still forgetful until about age 10 and might lose it. Many parents begin allowances with the 4 compartment bank which has a separate section for spending, saving, investing and sharing. Let's look at these 4 uses of money.

Children should have an allowance for spending. A good rule of thumb is one dollar per week for each of their year of age. For example, a 5 year-old would receive $5 per week. For parents that gasp at this statement, I ask them to add up everything they spend on their child in a week such as treats, movies, dollar store toys, games, candy, etc. Then they realize that they spend much more than that on their child. I tell them that they are still outlaying the same amount, but now they are just handing over the control of the money to the child, allowing him or her the opportunity to budget, spend and make decisions about allotments for what they desire.

When parents only give a child a dollar or two per week, the child doesn't have much choice to purchase anything other than candy or cheap dollar store toys, both of which is not good for the child. It takes forever to save up for something decent like a book or video game, and the child doesn't learn that reasonable saving will get them what they want – a life lesson that we need to teach kids. As children get older, parents can require the child to buy more and more of their needs – clothes, shampoo, birthday gifts, cell phone plan, etc., and hand over more control of the money they will need.

Part of the allowance should be for short term savings and also for long term savings or investing, including university. It can be deposited in an "at-home bank" where parents can just keep track of totals on a chart or in a little passbook. Interest rates are so low, it makes no sense to keep it at a real bank, because trips to the bank are not worth the gas money.

Should parents have restrictions on what kids can spend the money on? Absolutely not. It's very difficult for parents to do this, but necessary. By allowing a child total freedom over their "spending" money, (not the saving portion,) they allow the child to make choices and mistakes while they are still young. Children learn that they pay good money for cheap toys that break, or they lose the toys, and it's a very valuable lesson. Parents can talk about how cheap things are made, but children need to make those mistakes themselves to learn from them. Children also learn that what is promised in advertising on the box, TV, or the Internet is not always the reality. The kids in the picture on the box may look like they are having fun, but your child may not feel the toy is fun and may question the truth of the advertising, which is another good lesson.

Allowance should never be tied to chores. When you do tie chores to allowance, you are giving your child the opportunity to say "No thanks, to the allowance and the chores." Then you are stuck doing the chores yourself. You want your child to learn all about money management and if they opt of chores, they don't get the opportunity to have money to use. Chores (I prefer to call them duties) should start at age 3 and continue as long as the child is living at home. Chores should not be optional as they teach children a valuable set of skills such as commitment, empathy, and self-discipline.

The last part of the allowance is for sharing. It can be saved for charities or bringing happiness in any manner a child chooses. Buying a coveted toy for a friend is very kind too, as well as donating it to a charity that a child wishes to support.

Bring your child with you when shopping, getting money out of an ATM, buying online and show them what you are doing. Model good money habits and recordkeeping.

Tweens (Ages 9-12) – Age to start a debit card, learn gift card redemption practices, online shopping and password management.

There is no benefit to a child having a bank account until they need and can use a debit card. Again, a debit account can start when a child is about 10 (or beyond the age of losing their items). That is around the time girls start to carry purses and boys can carry a wallet. They often go to the store with buddies on their own and can make a few of their own purchases with a debit card, rather than carrying around cash.

Most banks don't charge children fees when they are under 18 years old. Parents can help them open savings account but the fees and the interest rate right now are not worth the hassle of running to the bank to deposit money for the child. Parents are better off to use the actual money to pay down their own debts and keep a tangible record of the child's "bank account" like a sheet on the wall that the child can track ins and outs. When it is time for the child to get a debit card, then the parents can hand over the "real" money from the "bank account" record sheet.

Again, don't put restrictions on what they purchase. Remember, that children this age are more than halfway to adulthood, so they have limited time to make mistakes. It's much cheaper to make mistakes at this age, than later at university, when they are away from parental guidance.

This is also a good age to teach about the various charities and where the child might wish to donate some of the sharing funds. The tween years are also a good age to guide and help children research reviews about purchasing their own gifts, some clothes, and electronics online. Teach them how to spot scams and how to start a method of managing passwords.

Teens (Ages 13-18) – Age to start buying stocks, spot online scams, and learn money saving shopping skills, receipt management, bank statements, job forms, employment rights, cell phone contracts and tax returns.

Now is a good time to teach about stocks, mutual funds, and company investments. Together with your teen, use some of their birthday money to buy some stocks in their favorite companies that they shop from, so they can learn how the economic system works. You can even read annual reports together.

Offload more and more expenses such as clothes, books, gifts, and entertainment to your teens as they get jobs outside the home. Continue the allowance, as you don't want to penalize them for getting jobs, and also continue the chores as you don't want to be stuck doing all the work!

Continue teaching about money and all aspects of financing in this last third of parenting. Somewhere between now and when children turn 18, parents can teach about receipt management, online purchase management, store returns, cell phone payment management, gift card management, online refunds, and rebates.

Emerging adults (Ages 18-25) - Age to obtain credit cards, TSFA's, student loans, insurance, RRSPs, tax returns, finances for travel, landlord and tenant deposits and everything else

Help your emerging adult obtain a credit card with a limit, perhaps with their savings tied to it, in order to establish a credit history, and make online purchases with parents supervision. Remind them to pay the bill monthly for the first six months, (yes, they still need help with organizational skills) and then let them remember on their own. You may need to help them set up a system for remembering such as paying the bill online as soon as it comes due, in order to not forget to pay it. Go over the rules of credit cards. Be sure your child knows how interest is calculated and that they have to pay the minimum every month by the due date to keep a good credit history.

Be sure to remind your daughters and sons to never give up their own credit card in their own name, if they become stay at home parents, or entrepreneurs, as it will be harder to establish a credit history in their own name if they don't have income coming in.

Help them understand bank fees and how to reduce them. Help them open up a line of credit for starting their own business or show them how to fill out student loan forms.

Explain how insurance works and what is covered for cars and residence.

Help them navigate landlord and tenant agreements with deposits, interest and contracts. Show them how to take photos of damage before they move in. If kids are still living at home, many parents charge them rent and secretly save it for them for a house down payment later.

Help them establish a TFSA (Tax Free Savings Account). Show them how to open up an RRSP (Registered Retirement Savings Account) if they are working and earning more than about $40,000 per year. Show them how to fill out their own tax forms. The online software now makes it easy for them to do.

After age 18, FOIP and privacy laws kick in and the bank will glare at you if you accompany your child to get money. If you feel that your child is not able to handle finances on his own, get him to write a generic letter authorizing you to help him with his financial affairs on his behalf. Even universities and medical professionals require this type of consent and may have their own form letter. You may hand over a cheque to the university paying your child's account, but you can't make inquiries at the fees office without your child's written authorization. Your child may need help to check that his fees are being correctly assessed.

Money Smarts for College-Bound Kids

Parents, should you pay for post-secondary?

If a child is living at home and going to university full time (that's at least a three course load) then that is their "job." I wouldn't expect regular contribution for rent and groceries. However, it wouldn't hurt for them to pick up the gas or a grocery order once in awhile. If they have a part time job, that money should be going to their future school costs and discretionary expenses.

They no longer are entitled to be supported by law. Thus, they should put some funds into the cost of their post-secondary education. If they work hard in high school and get scholarships, that may be their contribution. If they have part time jobs, they should put some of that amount into their total university costs. If they don't have either, they should apply for student loans. This is only my personal opinion, but the more "investment" children personally have put to their education, the more they will buckle down and study. The harder they work for that money (such as with a minimum-wage job) they less they will covet the latest $200 jeans.

Even if parents decide to pay the bare minimum such as tuition, books, rent, groceries, utilities, and bus pass, (and no child ever needs a car for school), then kids should be paying for their own clothes, parking tickets, beer money, cell phone (yes, a smart phone is a nice to have, but not needs to have), restaurants and all other extra expenses out of their own savings.

....

8 Persistent Parenting Myths Not Backed By Research

There are always some common parenting myths that seem to pop up as questions in my classes of teaching parenting over the last twenty years. I am constantly amazed at how wide-spread they are across North America and Europe. There is no research that supports the myths, but they tend to persist as advice gets passed down from the generations.

1. Bad Habits last a lifetime.

I'm sure you have heard at least one relative or friend say, "You don't want to bring your baby into bed with you, because then you are starting a bad habit and he will never leave!"

If that was the case, we would never start our babies off in diapers for fear that they will get too cozy in them and never learn to use the toilet. I often ask parents, "Should I start hitting my child over the head with a fry pan now so he gets used to the pain when he begins having childhood headaches later? No!"

It's the same with other lessons in life. Preparation is good, but it doesn't take years. It takes days. Children change and learn new things when they need to learn them. They even learn faster when their brains are more developed. Bad habits take 3 days for children to break and 21 days for adults. (We are a little more set in our ways as we age!) So do what works now. When the time comes to make changes, such as when the situation no longer works for anyone, then make the change. This applies to everything in parenting, from sleep hygiene, to bribing kids to use the toilet, to instilling good study habits.

2. Children should have impulse control by age 3 and should therefore "Listen" to the adults.

No, they don't have impulse control by age 3. Young toddlers and preschoolers are ego-centric, meaning that their needs matter more than your needs. As it should - this is normal development. As they get into the school-age years, they grow aware of and begin to care about other's needs. They will have better executive function (self-control, listening, focusing, planning, paying attention) by age 5 and 6, which is why they don't start mandatory school until that age. Even through the school years, they don't have maximum executive function. They begin to have a good dose of it in puberty.

Educators have long known that preschool children's brain development is not there yet, to hold off on their self-desires for the needs of someone else. Parents have to learn this too. Even though young children know that "No!" is a sharp word that means something scary, they still don't have the self-control to restrain their wants when it is said.

3. You must correct things in the moment or young children will immediately forget.

Again, there is no research that supports this. Yes, children forget the place in time when events occur, but they do remember something from earlier in the day. If you are angry, take your ten minute time-out to calm down and then come back to address the situation - calmly and wisely. Or, address it at bedtime when everyone is feeling good and the teaching might stick. Young children will still remember! Lots of repetition will help them develop routine choices.

4. Children remember things forever, so pack in lots of learning, activities, lessons, experiences and travel while they are young and before they resist as teenagers.

I wish! For all the world-wide travelling we did carting 5 children across the globe, they remember nothing before age 12. For all those lessons we stuffed into their heads, they remember nothing now, years after they dropped them. Well, maybe one or two memories stick out, like three wheeled cars in England, and sinking boats in the bathtub as a science experiment, or the one cool snack someone brought to the soccer game when they were six, but nothing else brought back memories, when I showed them photographs of when they were young. I'm sure those experiences built their brains unconsciously, but they don't even remember their childhood best friends. On the flip side, when I asked my university-aged kids if they remember how much yelling I did when they were young, they replied, "None!" Good thing too!

5. Toddlers need harsh discipline to nip bad deeds in the bud, or their deeds will snowball and they will turn into raging, rebellious teenagers at age 16.

Children develop and grow their brain in stages. Caregivers should learn about physical, emotional, brain, and social development and what to expect at each stage. A child at 13 is a different child than age three. He has a much more developed brain to understand needs and adjust his behavior. He has much more self-control to hold off on hitting and using his words instead.

Don't project ahead. You have many years in the school-age years to teach and explain, and it will stick because then they will get it. Parents feel they have to teach the most important lessons, hard, at a time when young children's brains are least equipped to understand them. That doesn't mean you just let little Nathan hit his friends. Address the behavior with teaching words -over and over again. "No, we don't hit our friends. Here, stomp your feet when you are mad!" By 13, Nathan will have the self-control to do it on his own. Aggression is like water coming from a tap - none in the baby stage, full gush at age 2, flow at age 4, trickle at age 6, dribble at age 8 and occasional drip at age 10. By age 12, most children use their words instead of their hands, simply because of brain development and self-control, and certainly less, because of harsh discipline.

6. If I don't enforce consequences on my child, how will she learn how the world works? She needs to be punished to learn.

All the other "parents" in your child's world, including teachers, friend's parents, coaches, etc., will be happy to issue consequences to your child, along with jail time-outs, taking away privileges, and a host of other punishments. Let them.

You, on the other hand, have the vested interest in your child of teaching a real life, handy skill, called problem-solving. It takes time but pays off in increased communication, mutual respect and love. When you problem-solve with your child, aiming for a win-win solution that works for her and you, you are teaching her a great employment and relationship skill that is valued much more and has greater long term use than punishments. There is no research that supports that punishment enhances parent-child respect, communication and close relationships. There are plenty of studies that show how detrimental it is.

7. Children want limits to feel secure.

No they don't! In fact, children want their way just like adults do. We hate it when we really want something and someone says "No" to us and children feel the very same way. What makes children and adults feel secure is maintaining their autonomy while being informed of expectations. For example, if we are attending a ball, we want to know some idea of what to wear. We don't want to be dictated to, or demanded that we wear a certain item. We want the choice, but also want to know what is expected so we can make an appropriate choice. Children are the same way. They want information and the ability to choose. That is why offering children choices, along with a little background information, helps them with decision making and gives them empowerment.

8. Teens don't want to hang around with parents.

Wrong. Most studies done on teens who rebel, act out and engage in delinquent behavior, do not have warm, caring parents who have structure in the home. Teens want privacy, but they want involved parents who respect them, care about where they are, worry about them, and help them navigate the world. Teen's don't want or need parents that punish, belittle or dismiss them. Be close to your children but let them set the pace for contact. If you are their trusted coach, non-judgmental information source, and problem-solving mentor, as well as a fun person they can beat in video gaming, they will love you forever!

5 Best Tips for a Solid Parenting Partner Relationship

1. Really listen to each other. Listening is loving.

2. Be flexible.

3. Spend time together and apart.

4. Prioritize each other's needs.

5. Compromise when solving problems.

How to Change Your Parenting Style

Do you come from a "dysfunctional family?" Is your ACE (Adverse Childhood Experiences) score so high that you worry about doing the same to your kids? Can parenting habits change in one generation? Yes, you can change your child's destiny! Many parents with ACE scores as high as 7 has raised children with 1 or less. You can too!

If you were raised by less-than-stellar parents, here are some changes you can make to become the parent you wished you had, for the next generation that you are raising. You do not have to repeat negative parenting habits with your own children. You can change your parenting style from over permissive or authoritarian, to a collaborative/democratic positive parenting style.

- Fake it until you make it. Act like the parents you admire. Copy what they do.

- Start with yourself. Learn to love you. Change self-talk into positive, loving thoughts about how you look, and what you do, and who you are.

- Learn the language of respectful communication. Take a course through colleges, universities, churches, parent centers or community centers. Learn how to use I-statements, active listening and problem-solving.

- Learn child development through courses, or books, to help you know what to expect from children at different ages. Only 23% of parents know child development past the infant stage, and it's essential for parenting.

- If you were excessively criticized as a child, consciously make the effort to encourage your own children and hold back the negative.

- If you were not hugged or touched as a child, make a concerted effort to hug, cuddle and hold your own children, even if it feels alien to you.

- If you were hurt, upset or sick and were told to "buck up, suck it up, or shut up", give your child comfort by saying "It's okay to feel what you do." And hug, caress and pat your child with non-sexual touch.

- If you were ignored as a child, respond right away to your own children. Give focused attention when they need it and even when they don't. It's ok to have fun with your children.

- If your parents never played with you as a child, read, talk with and play with your own children.

- When you are angry, take a time out. Your time-out. Not your child's. What need of yours is not getting met? How can you meet it? Work on your anger first and you will make better parenting decisions when you are calm.

- Forgive your parents. They probably did the best they knew how at the time, with the resources they had.

- Know what your triggers and hot buttons are. We all have sensitive areas in parenting, no matter what our background was, and our awareness of them helps us to come up with alternative behaviors and coping strategies.

- Start looking at your life through the lens of gratitude. Being grateful enriches life.

Parenting, for the most part, is a learned pattern. We can change parenting patterns and develop new ones. When we become aware of our shortfalls and make a conscious effort to change how we behave, we become really good at parenting after lots of practice.

Don't worry if you make mistakes. Rome was not built in a day. Even with new learned behaviors, in times of stress, we tend to fall back on our old habits. Apologize and vow to do better next time. With renewed commitment, we get better at changing old habits with time, practice, information and continuance. You can change family dynamics in one generation and give your child the healthy gift of less ACES in their childhood. It all starts with you!

Best Parenting Advice From Fellow AP Parents

Sleep cures all: Half of all discipline issues could be prevented if parents could secure a full eight hours of sleep in a 24 hour day. Make sleep a priority. The meals, laundry, and clutter will always be there, but a rested, contented parent is the biggest asset for patience, calmness and joy in parenting.

"I'm not their mom": When your children are out in public with you and misbehaving badly, pretend that you are the aunt taking the kids for the day. Say loudly, "Just wait until your mother hears about this!" and go about your usual routine.

Bad days: In the midst of chaos, centre yourself first, before you calm down any screaming, or crying children. Make sure everyone is safe. Don't focus on teaching lessons; focus on damage control and getting through the day while loving. Lie in the middle of the living room floor, put on your music player, close your eyes and deep breathe. Get calm and centered. Then get up and decide what everyone needs in order to turn the day around: food, nap, walk, outing, or hugs.

Your relationship, not obedience, is most important: Rather than focus on your child's obedience as a gauge of how well you parent, focus on the quality of your relationship. Is your child still communicating with you, sharing feelings, opinions and values? If so, you are a success.

Stop punishing your children: Respect never includes punishment in a love relationship, no matter what the ages of the people involved. And parenting is a love relationship. Instead of looking at issues of discipline as behavior to be corrected, look at it as conflicts to be resolved.

ABC's of loving parenting: "A" is for Acknowledging the feelings of your child. Feelings have no limits. They are as real and normal as skin. "B" is for Behavior communication. What is your child trying to tell you? Look at their needs and feelings that drive the behavior. "C" is for Calming down. Get yourself calm, then get your child calm, then mutually problem-solve the issue.

Build your parent-child relationship first, and their résumé second: Unconditional love is support, encouragement and help in discovering who your child is and what they are capable of. When you love them unconditionally, they learn to love themselves, unconditionally and will grow into the wonderful people they are meant to be.

Peace in the world begins in the home: The family is the training ground for all future relationships in love, work, politics, religion and friendship. If we treat our babies with love, safety and respect, as we would want to be treated, we will raise the next generation equipped to change the world a child at a time.

Separate your anger from your discipline: When we are angry, we lose our self-control and issue punishments that we have no intention of carrying out when we are calm. Because the purpose of discipline is to teach self-control of behavior and self-regulation of emotions in our children, we need to demonstrate the same in ourselves. When we are calm, we make much better decisions and most always can focus on solving the problem with clarity of thinking. We don't have to hurt children to teach them. In fact, they learn much better when not under stress.

It takes a village, to cherish a parent, to nurture a child: Parents are the very first relationship builders. We can't control our children, but we have tremendous influence. Parents need support, encouragement and practical help, not judgment. Hug, smile at, high five, give an A-OK, a kind word, encouragement, or give a pat on the back, to a parent you know who needs support. Sometimes they don't need a problem-solver ; sometimes they just need a listening ear, and re-assurance that they are an awesome parent.

Hugs: the best discipline tool ever! The child that needs our attention the most, is usually the one that "deserves" it the least. If you ever are in the position of not knowing what to do in any parenting situation (as most parents routinely are), then default to a hug. If learning follows, you will be coming from a place of acceptance and caring and the message will stick much more with your child.

Use your kindest words at home with those you love the most: Too often, we are the nicest, politest, kindest people to strangers. The store clerk, the plumber and the teacher all get our best behavior, when we should be giving it to those we love – our family.

Time-outs are for parents, time-in is for the child: Parents need to take a minute to get themselves calmed-down. They teach children how time-out works, not by forcing the child into time-out, but by taking a time-out themselves.

My fear is that we are raising an entire generation adverse to taking a time-out, because they have only experienced it as a punishment. Time-out is a wonderful life skill. Let's demonstrate that by our actions. Giving a child time-in means to stay with him in a calming environment to help him gain self-control again. It's not meant to be isolating and may include items to help him calm down in his learning style.

Expressions of all feelings is absolutely necessary for health:
Feelings are as common to our body as our big toe. The most respectful way to express feelings is to talk about them. Saying "I feel..." can be very therapeutic for children trying to sort out their feelings.

We need to help our children deal with their frustrations, not to help your children avoid them:
Our job as parents is to help our children sort out their unhappy feelings, by acknowledging that they exist and validating them. It doesn't mean that we agree with them or understand them. It just means that we accept them.

Children learn better by discovery than by being told:
There are many lessons in parenting that parents cannot teach. Life will teach them if we let it unfold.

Instead of punishment, problem-solve the issue:
It's not you against me. Instead, it's both of us working together against the problem. With two or more brains working in synergy, we can come up with solutions acceptable to both of us.

Modeling is discipline taught 24 hours a day, 365 days a year:
In fact, if we provided no other interference in our children's actions, other than modeling correct behavior, within the context of building a great relationship with our children, we would raise responsible, caring, respectful citizens.

We underestimate our children's ability to solve problems:
Even a baby knows how to alleviate hunger. In childhood, negotiation is treated as an 11 letter swear word, yet, it is very needed in every love relationship. Often, our child's first experience of negotiation is when their employer gives them training courses as adults. It's a life skill that needs practice in a safe environment, such as the home, and with safe people such as parents, who will ensure safe consequences, while children are still young.

Children crave teaching, direction and advice:
Like adults, they want to know how to do the right thing, but not be forced to do it.

The biggest technological advances in the past twenty years have been in communications, yet, our biggest hurdle in our relationships have been in interpersonal communications: Amid cell phones, internet, computers, video games, and consoles, there is one thing that every parent can provide their children that no advancement of technology will replace. Human touch...hugs, pats, snuggles, attention and love.

You are the best person in the world for your child. Pamper yourself and your loved ones. Enjoy your time with them. You are growing friends for life.

Child Development References

- Alberta Family Wellness, and Harvard Centre on the Developing Child, 2017, *Brain Core Story Certification Course*, Palix Foundation, Calgary, AB

- Barker, Leslie, Editor, 2012, *Terrific Toddlers*: *A facilitators manual*, Alberta Health Services, Calgary, AB

- Barker, Leslie, and Terry Bullick, 2012, *Growing Miracles*, 4th Edition, Alberta Health Services, Calgary, AB

- Berk, Laura E., PhD, 2000, *Child Development*, 5th Edition, Pearson Education, Massachusetts, IL

- Bibby, Reginald W. PhD, 2001, *Canada's Teens: Today, yesterday, and tomorrow*, Stoddart Publishing Company Limited, Toronto, ON

- Boyd, Denise, and Paul Johnson, Helen Bee, 2012, *Lifespan Development*, 4th Canadian Edition, Pearson Education Canada Inc., Toronto, ON

- Durrant, Joan E., PhD, 2011, *Positive Discipline for Everyday Parenting,* 2nd Edition, Save the Children Sweden, Stockholm, Sweden

- Gray, Peter, PhD, 1994, *Psychology*, 2nd Edition, Worth Publishers, Boston College, Massachusetts, IL

About the Author

Judy Arnall, BA, DTM, CCFE

Conference Speaker, Trainer and Bestselling Author

Judy is an international award-winning professional speaker and a sought-after Canadian expert in non-punitive education and parenting practices. She regularly appears on television interviews on CBC, CTV, and Global as well as publications including Chatelaine, Today's Parent, Canadian Living, Parents magazine, The Globe and Mail, Metro and Postmedia News.

As a Certified Canadian Family Life Educator (CCFE), Judy teaches family communication and parenting leadership at the University of Calgary, Continuing Education, and has taught for Alberta Health Services for 13 years. Judy founded the non-profit organization, Attachment Parenting Canada Association, which offers public information sessions across North America. Judy is an authorized facilitator of Parent Effectiveness Training (P.E.T.), AHS's Terrific Toddlers program, Positive Discipline In Every Day Life, Attached At The Heart, and The Growing Brain by Zero To Three.

Holding a Distinguished Toastmaster accreditation, Judy is a dynamic conference keynoter that engages audiences in interactive activities. Her keynote, "Play Is The Key To University" is popular with corporations, Teachers Conventions and associations.

As a specialist in child development, Judy is the author of the worldwide print bestseller, *Discipline Without Distress: 135 Tools for raising caring, responsible children without time-out, spanking, punishment or bribery.* As a parent of five children, Judy has a broad understanding of the issues facing families in the digital age and has authored a DVD titled *Plugged-In Parenting: Connecting with the digital generation for health, safety and love.* She is also the author of *Parenting With Patience: Turn frustration into connection with 3 easy steps,* and the parenting journal, *The Last Word on Parenting Advice.* Her latest book is *Unschooling To University: Relationships matter most in a world crammed with content.*

www.professionalparenting.ca

www.judyarnall.com

www.unschoolingtouniversity.com

@parentingexpert

jarnall@shaw.ca

Also by Judy Arnall

Specialist in Non-Punitive Parenting and Education Practices

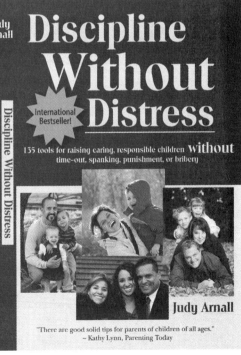

Parenting/Childcare

Discipline that you and your child will feel good about!

At last, a positive discipline book that is chock-full of practical tips, strategies, skills, and ideas for parents of babies through teenagers, and tells you EXACTLY what to do "in the moment" for every type of behavior, from whining to web surfing.

Parents and children today face very different challenges from those faced by the previous generation. Today's children play not only in the sandbox down the street, but also in the World Wide Web, which is too big and complex for parents to control and supervise. As young as age four, your children can contact the world, and the world can contact them. A strong bond between you and your child is critical in order for your child to regard you as their trusted advisor. Traditional discipline methods no longer work with today's children, and they destroy your ability to influence your increasingly vulnerable children who need you as their lifeline! Spanking and time-outs do not work. You need new discipline tools!

Help your child gain:

- Strong communication skills for school, career, and relationship success.
- Healthy self-esteem, confidence, and greater emotional intelligence.
- Assertiveness, empathy, problem-solving, and anger management skills.
- A respectful, loving connection with you!

You will gain:

- An end to resentment, frustration, anger, tears, and defiance in your parent-child relationship.
- Tools to respectfully handle most modern challenging parenting situations, including biting, hitting, tantrums, bedtimes, picky eating, chores, homework, sibling wars, smoking, "attitude," and video/computer games.
- Help for controlling your anger "in the moment" during those trying times.
- A loving, respectful, teaching and fun connection with your child!

"Offers a wealth of ideas and suggestions for raising children without the use of punishment of any kind." ~ Linda Adams, President of Gordon Training International - P.E.T.

BONUS! 50-page quick reference tool guide included

Judy Arnall, BA, is a Parent Educator for several health organizations, a Toastmaster trained speaker, and mother of five children. She has taught thousands of parents respectful, research-based parenting tools that have brought them closer to their children and they will work for your family too.

Professional Parenting
Canada
www.ProfessionalParenting.ca

ISBN-13 978-0-97 805 0-90-0

$24.95 CND $19.95 US

Judy Arnall

Discipline Without Distress

135 tools for raising caring, responsible children without time-out, spanking, punishment, or bribery

Discipline Without Distress

International Bestseller!

135 tools for raising caring, responsible children **without** time-out, spanking, punishment, or bribery

Judy Arnall

"There are good solid tips for parents of children of all ages."
~ Kathy Lynn, Parenting Today

School is one option for education; homeschooling is the second, and unschooling is the third.

Many parents are frustrated by the school system, perhaps because of bullying, crowded classrooms, and outdated, dull, online courses. Disengaged learners that have no say in their coerced curriculum tend to act out, tune out, or drop out. Education must change and unschooling is the fastest-growing alternative method of learning.

Two decades ago, students registered with their local school based on their house address. Now, with the internet, students are borderless. Learning can occur anywhere, anytime, anyway and from anyone—including self-taught.

Self-directing their education, unschoolers learn through:

- Play
- Volunteering
- Mentorship
- Projects
- Video games
- Travel
- Reading
- Sports
- Life

This book explores the path of 30 unschooled children who self-directed all or part of their education and were accepted by universities, colleges, and other postsecondary schools. Most have already graduated.

What children need most are close relationships-parents, teachers, siblings, relatives, coaches, and mentors within a wider community, not just within an institutional school. Educational content is everywhere. Caring relationships are not.

Families that embrace unschooling do not have to choose between a quality education and a relaxed, connected family lifestyle. They can have both.

Judy Arnall, BA, DTM, is a certified child development expert, keynote speaker, and master of non-punitive parenting and education practices. She is the bestselling author of four print books that have been translated into five languages.

#UnschoolingToUniversity
@ParentingExpert
www.professionalparenting.ca

"Savy parenting for successful children"

$24.95 USD Print $9.99 USD Ebook

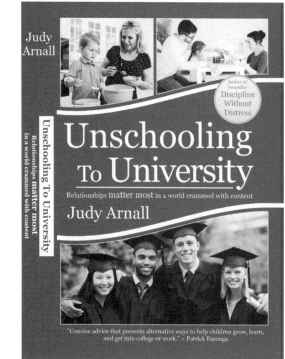

www.YouSpeakProductions.com
Cover design by PeopleWorldz Creative

ISBN 978-0-9780539-1-1

125 minutes $34.95

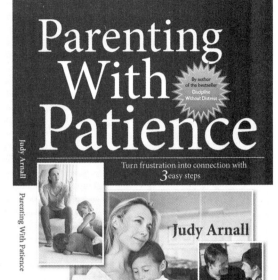
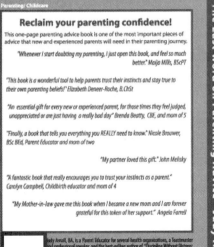